VALUE THEORY AND ECONOMIC PROGRESS: THE INSTITUTIONAL ECONOMICS OF J. FAGG FOSTER

VALUE THEORY AND ECONOMIC PROGRESS: THE INSTITUTIONAL ECONOMICS OF J. FAGG FOSTER

Marc R. Tool
Professor Emeritus of Economics
California State University, Sacramento

KLUWER ACADEMIC PUBLISHERS
Boston / Dordrecht / London

Distributors for North, Central and South America:
Kluwer Academic Publishers
101 Philip Drive
Assinippi Park
Norwell, Massachusetts 02061 USA
Telephone (781) 871-6600
Fax (781) 871-6528
E-Mail <kluwer@wkap.com>

Distributors for all other countries:
Kluwer Academic Publishers Group
Distribution Centre
Post Office Box 322
3300 AH Dordrecht, THE NETHERLANDS
Telephone 31 78 6392 392
Fax 31 78 6546 474
E-Mail <orderdept@wkap.nl>

Electronic Services <http://www.wkap.nl>

Library of Congress Cataloging-in-Publication Data

Tool, Marc R.
Value theory and economic progress : the institutional economics of J. Fagg Foster / Marc R. Tool
p. cm.
Includes bibliographical references and index.
ISBN 0-7923-7830-X
1. Foster, J. Fagg, 1907-1985. 2. Institutional economics. I. Title.

HB99.5 .T675 2000
330--dc21

00-035241

Printed on acid-free paper.

Printed in the United States of America

For

Franklin David Tool

Grandson

and

Emily Rebecca Tool

Granddaughter

TABLE OF CONTENTS

Preface ix

1 Introduction 1

Part I INSTITUTIONAL THEORY

2 The Theory of Scientific Inquiry 7

3 A Critique Of Utility Value 35

4 The Instrumental Theory of Value 63

5 The Theory of Institutional Adjustment 87

Part II APPLICATIONS

6 The American Experience and Contribution 105

7 A Critique of Ism-Ideologies 129

8 Foster and Keynes. 161

9 Instrumental Policy 185

Sources 215

Index 227

PREFACE

J. Fagg Foster (1907-1985) was one of the most significant creators and expounders of institutionalist economic theory in the twentieth century. He wrote and taught in the American intellectual tradition of Thorstein Veblen, John R. Commons, John Dewey and Clarence E. Ayres. This tradition shares purpose and philosophy with the European contributors, Gunnar Myrdal and K. William Kapp.

Because little of Foster's scholarly work was formally published, professional knowledge of his extraordinary contribution, beyond the circle of his students and colleagues, is quite limited. This volume is an attempt to correct in some measure for that deficiency by providing an extended characterization of this missing and crucial component of the development of American heterodox economic thought. Its purpose is to demonstrate the timely relevance and significance of this model of inquiry in political economy.

This volume appears at a time in which flawed and inadequate structure and policies in the world's major economies are forcing perceptive policy makers to move beyond the sterile and stagnant dominion of the received doctrines of orthodox neoclassical theory and policy. A new pluralism of perspectives is gradually emerging. Continuing ideological deference to market phenomena, indifference to global mega-corp consolidation, acquiescence in increasing inequalities of employment access and income, and insensitivity to environmental deterioration, for example, drive those with a sense of public concern and/or responsibility, to explore new modes of analysis and new discretionary options for resolving problems. Among the emergent pluralist options are evolutionary and institutional economic analyses.

Foster's contribution will be developed herein as an extension and refinement of American institutional thought. Foster's major contribution is bringing the "what is" in inquiry analytically into congruity with "what ought." Causal explanation and value theory are, for Foster, a part of the same universe of discourse and inquiry. (Subsequent institutionalist scholarship in the tradition of Dewey, Veblen, Ayres, and Foster, has often been identified as "neoinstitutionalism," but Foster did not refer to his own work with this caption.) The much revered normative-positive dichotomy will be seen here as methodologically and analytically indefensible. It is a purpose of this volume to explain that contemporary problem solving means changing "what is" into "what ought to be" through institutional adjustments. Such a demonstration is at the heart of Foster's contribution to institutional thought.

A selection of Foster's short papers, edited by Dr. T. Baldwin Ranson and including a brief biography, was published in *The Journal of Economic Issues* in December, 1981. Dr. Gladys Foster (his widow) edited a selection of Foster's writings on equational justice that was published in *The Journal of Economic Issues* in December 1991. Dr. Edythe S. Miller provided a substantive biographical sketch on Foster for *The Elgar Companion to Institutional and Evolutionary Economics* (1994). Otherwise, Foster's work is accessible mainly "once removed," in the writing and publications of his students who themselves became professional scholars. Although he sometimes spoke of his interest in writing a definitive volume on the *Fundamental Principles of Economics*, encompassing his creative and comprehensive grasp of the structure, functions and warrant of politico-economic systems, such a volume was not completed. His perfectionist ambition "to write so that it could not be misunderstood" set difficult, especially since self-imposed, standards of clarity and coherence. He was mainly a teacher, not a writer.

Accordingly, Foster created instead a viable and expansive oral tradition. Indeed, he may well have concluded that devoting his career to exemplary teaching and to the intellectual empowerment of his students was, in comparison with his own writing, the more "instrumentally efficient" way (of which more later) of enhancing and extending scholarship in institutional political economy.

Institutional economics began roughly a century ago in the United States with Thorstein B. Veblen's *The Theory of the Leisure Class* (1899) and John R. Commons' essays on "sovereignty" in *The American Journal of Sociology* (1899). Walton Hamilton contributed the caption of "institutional economics" at the end of WWI. Rexford Guy Tugwell and institutional economists at the University of Wisconsin were the initiating source of much of the reconstructive social and economic legislation of the New Deal in the Depression Decade. This tradition of the "original institutional economics" (OIE) urges institutional change that fosters the imaginative creation and equitable distribution of real income through social, political and economic institutional adjustments. It supports a political economy the purposes of which are *(a)* to enhance human capacity and intellect, *(b)* to develop and use warranted knowledge, *(c)* to pursue adequate levels and equitable distribution of real income, *(d)* to utilize participatory democratic policy making, *(e)* to hold achieved power to account, *(f)* to ensure environmental sustainability and *(g)* to forestall/erode/remove the invidious use of distinctions among persons. In this inquiry model, participants are educable, discretionary agents, not rationalizing maximizers.

We note in passing that this institutionalist tradition has little in common with the contemporary so-called "new institutional economics" (NIE) of Oliver Williamson and others. The latter is a neoclassically based model addressed mainly to intra- and interfirm transactions involving optimizers and opportunists as agents. Their granting of significance to institutional structures is a modest gain, but the explanatory capabilities of "new institutionalism" are shallow and narrow in comparison with the OIE over this last century. Foster's contribution extends and refines the tradition of the "original institutional economics" in which discretionary agents modify institutional forms.

In *The Leisure Class* (1899) & *The Place of Science* (1919), Veblen initiates a post-Darwinian and therewith a processual view of political economy. In his words, "an evolutionary economics must be the theory of a process of cultural growth as determined by the economic interest, a theory of a cumulative sequence of economic institutions stated in terms of the process itself" (1919, 77). In contrast with prevailing neoclassical orthodoxy, his inquiry model cannot be characterized in Veblen's own terminology as taxonomic, hedonistic, teleological or tautological. Individuals are products of their culture; they develop habits of mind, tastes, and conventions. They manifest the constructive drives of curiosity, workmanship, and concern for others; they exhibit the destructive drives of emulation and predation. Veblen's pervasive dichotomy distinguishes between, and juxtaposes, acquisition vs. production, pecuniary vs. industrial institutions, ceremonial vs. technological purposes, vested vs. public interests, invidious emulation vs. technological efficiency, et cetera. He launches a fundamentally new theory of inquiry rooted in the then emerging scientific mode. But as Foster explains below, he is blocked by the analytical problem of linking "what is" and "what ought to be" in inquiry.

John Dewey's contribution, particularly in his *Logic: The Theory of Inquiry* (1938), and *Theory of Valuation* (1939), is to develop and extend the instrumentalist method of logical inquiry. He abandons Cartesian dualisms—mind/body, value/fact, et cetera—in the development of a theory of social inquiry exhibiting creative formulation of hypotheses and inductive and deductive modes of drawing inferences and of generating and processing knowledge. He demonstrates the relevance of scientific constructs for social inquiry in explaining causal connections in observed phenomena; he brings value and valuation necessarily within the inquiry process; he explores at length the dependency of a democratic society upon the function and processes of education. Foster's theory of social inquiry, then, is rooted philosophically in the instrumentalism of John Dewey and analytically in the institutional economics of Thorstein Veblen.

A half century ago, Clarence Ayres merges the Veblen and Dewey modes and constructs of social inquiry into an integrated method and analysis that provides the initial substantive core of a normative institutional economics. In his *Theory of Economic Progress* (1944) and *Toward a Reasonable Society* (1961) he brings value theory explicitly, continuously and comprehensively within the universe of social inquiry and discourse. Social inquiry includes both normative and positive elements.

Fagg Foster, a doctoral student of Ayres, reconstructs, refines and extends this encompassing theory of political economy. In the three-decade period from his appointment as Professor of Economics at the University of Denver in 1946 until his retirement in 1976, Fagg Foster was a much revered model of scholarly competence and compelling instruction. The present author studied with Professor Foster from 1947 to 1951.

This volume, then, is an attempt to make major contributions of this imaginative, optimistic and path-breaking scholar more accessible to contemporary students, economic theorists and policy makers. Since, as noted, Foster did not publish major works articulating his views, the primary concern here is to convert a limited written output and a somewhat discursive oral tradition into a cogently ordered summation of his contributions. More particularly, the task is to generate from Foster's papers, and other sources, an encompassing formulation of his general theory of political economy. Included are considerations of the assumptions, constructs, analyses and criteria of which his general theory is comprised, together with its applications to contemporary public policy.

Four former graduate students of Fagg Foster, all of whom studied extensively with him, and who are themselves professional economists and published scholars, graciously agreed to provide assistance in the preparation of this volume by reviewing and appraising draft contents. They are: Dr. Paul D. Bush, Professor of Economics, California State University, Fresno; Dr. Gladys P. Foster, Adjunct Professor Emeritus of Economics, University of Colorado, Denver; Dr. Edythe S. Miller, former Chair, Colorado Public Utilities Commission, Professor Emeritus of Economics, Metropolitan State College, Denver and Adjunct Professor, University College, University of Denver; and Dr. T. Baldwin Ranson, Professor Emeritus of Economics, Western State College, University of Maryland in Asia, and American University of Bulgaria. Their contributions to the preparation of this volume have been substantial. I am deeply indebted to each, and am pleased to express my profound thanks to all, for their invaluable assistance and encouragement. A special additional thanks goes to Gladys Foster for making archival and other source materials available for this project and to our son, Dr. Laurence A. Tool, for his comments on the volume in its final stages. Special thanks go also to Steven Fisher, Curator, University of Denver Library Archives, for his assistance. Remaining errors of omission or commission are obviously mine, not theirs.

I wish also to thank Kluwer Academic Publishers for their editorial assistance in the preparation of this volume. In addition, I gratefully acknowledge the permission granted by the *Journal of Economic Issues* to republish extensive material previously appearing in print therein. Finally, let me again acknowledge with profound gratitude and affection, the loving support and professional encouragement of my wife, Lillian.

Marc R. Tool

1 INTRODUCTION

Economics [is the] rational analysis of the determination of real income. J. Fagg Foster

The compelling reason for a fresh presentation of Fagg Foster's scholarly work is the potentially positive impact it may have on the contemporary reconstruction of theoretical analyses of political economy. Indeed that impact is already partially in view in the professional contributions of Foster's students and others who write articles for contemporary heterodox journals, present papers at professional meetings, and write books augmenting the current institutionalist and evolutionary economics literature.

The discipline of economics is in a most tumultuous state with regard both to analytical adequacy and to policy guidance. Ambitious but tenuous claims to rigor, hegemony, significance and policy relevance continue to be made by contemporary orthodox neoclassical scholars. Yet, in recent decades, heterodox contributors from the inside—new institutionalists (NIE), transaction-cost analysts, neo-Austrian theorists, neo-Schumpeterian economists—provide significant challenges to the mainstream dominion and tradition. Heterodox contributors from the outside—original institutionalists (OIE), neoinstitutionalists, social economists, post Keynesians, feminist economists, neo-Polanyians, among others—also contend vigorously for a hearing. Annual international conferences of the Association for Evolutionary Economics, the Association for Institutional Thought, the European Association for Evolutionary Political Economy, the International Thorstein Veblen Association, the Society for the Advancement of Socio-Economics, the International Association for Feminist Economics, and others, open scholarly windows for heterodox exposure. International journals also reflect emerging heterodoxies in many forms. Examples include *The Journal of Economic Issues*, *The Journal of Post-Keynesian Economics*, *The Review of International Political Economy*, *The Journal of Economic Methodology*, *The Review of Political Economy* and *The Cambridge Journal of Economics*. The discipline is becoming more pluralistic in spite of desires and ambitions of conventionalists to ignore, and at times suppress, such increasing scope (Salanti and Screpanti, 1997).

The continuing presence of scholarly tumult and contention is itself indicative of the fact that major and continuing impairments in the processes of production and distribution of real income remain insufficiently addressed and inadequately understood, if they are indeed addressed at all. Even the popular press continues to address "the decline of economics" (Cassidy 1996, 50-60; Ehrenhalt 1997, E 13; Soros 1997, 45-58; Kuttner 1997; Galbraith 2000).

In recent decades, major foci of orthodox analyses have left effective public economic policy still-born: New classical economics (rational expectations theory), dismisses the need for macro-management. Agents act "rationally"; expectations are fulfilled; markets clear; short term efforts to stabilize the level of income and employment are unproductive (Klein 1994, 91-111). Public choice theory extols the virtues of a Constitutional amendment to compel an annually balanced budget (Aranson 1989, 127-31), therewith denying public options to cope with instability. Articulators of the natural rate of unemployment, (NAIRU, the non-accelerating-inflation rate of unemployment), defer to market dominion over income and employment; they oppose efforts to reduce unemployment to a frictional level (Brockway 1995, 897-910; Eisner 1995, 58-63 & 1997, 1-74; Symposium 1997).

In contrast, the pertinence of Foster's contributions, and of heterodox economic inquiry generally, derives expressly from its ability to identify, explore and resolve such contemporary problems as unemployment, instability, maldistribution, underdevelopment and environmental deterioration. Such resolutions necessarily involve the creation and implementation of credible social policies requiring the modification and adjustment of coordinating institutions. Foster suggests clear and cogent ways of reconstructing inquiry in political economy so that its application contributes to the institutional adjustments that constitute resolutions of contemporary economic problems.

Presenting the substance of Foster's contribution to economic analysis, then, is the main object of this volume. But it is crucial to understand at the outset that his mode of inquiry is not just a modest revision in, or addendum to, the way neoclassical scholars perceive economic reality and inquiry. Foster's contribution will represent a encompassing displacement of orthodox neoclassical theory with heterodox institutional theory. Perhaps characterizing it as a revolutionary transformation, in the sense of comprehensive abandonment, is not an exaggeration. Some examples of the character and magnitude of the needed redirections and reformulations of inquiry follow:

In general, Foster's contribution represents, for those interested in methodology: *(a)* a repudiation of individualistic maximizing rationality in favor of acculturative causal rationality of discretionary agents; *(b)* a rejection of deductivistic narrowness in favor of hypothesis creativity and breadth; *(c)* an abandonment of static equilibrium analysis in favor of processual inquiry; *(d)* a shift from positivistic claims of value-free inquiry to recognition of the necessary incorporation of credible normative tenets; *(e)* a renunciation of the utility theory of value and the price theory of valuation in favor of "instrumental efficiency" as value with multiple theories of valuation.

For those more focused on the policy implications of economic inquiry, Foster's contribution encompasses, for example: *(a)* a displacement of ism models (e.g. capitalism) of economic structure with continuous, normatively guided, institutional adjustments; *(b)* a replacement of neoclassically-based apologias that sanction existing economic power systems with the creation of democratic accountability and control; *(c)* an abandonment of the marginal productivity theory of factor pricing in favor of a theory of institutionally defined and modified income flows; *(d)* a rejection of the quest for an annually balanced federal budget as an economic panacea in favor of public macro-management of income and employment; and *(e)* the giving up of the illusion that "privatization" of public functions is inherently efficient and superior with the recognition that the public-private mix of structure is to be determined and revamped in the context of actual problem solving. The neoclassical dominion over economic inquiry will only erode if more persuasive analytical options become available and are tested in the real world context of inquiry and governance. Foster's contribution encourages that erosion by providing an alternative and credible route to scientific social and economic inquiry and to relevant problem-solving through policy initiatives for institutional adjustments.

This volume consists, after this Introductory Chapter, of two major components: Part I (Chapters 2, 3, 4 & 5) presents Foster's formulation of pivotal elements of institutional theory; Part II (Chapters 6, 7, 8, & 9) explores major areas of experience and explanation reflecting Foster's applications of this theory.

In Chapter Two, Foster's theory of scientific social inquiry, that merges science and philosophy, is introduced. Pragmatic instrumentalism is seen as the philosophic focus; instrumental logic stipulates the inquiry mode. The operative roles in inquiry of the methodological tools of induction, deduction and hypotheses creation are examined. The nature of scientific truth is identified.

In Chapter Three, we confront the value problem in economics and discover why utility value theory is unacceptable and inapplicable. The normative-positive distinction is abandoned. The historical emergence of the utility theory of value and its dominion is appraised.

In Chapter Four, Foster's theory of instrumental value is presented. His explanation of the necessary incorporation of warranted criteria of judgment in inquiry is explored. His identification, explanation and defense of "instrumental efficiency" as the definitive value principle is explained.

In Chapter Five, Foster's analysis of the nature of social change and the conditions under which it can succeed are examined. He offers continuing principles of, and necessary conditions for, institutional adjustments. The three principles are technological determination, recognized interdependence and minimal dislocation. This Chapter concludes with an examination of Foster's theory of democracy and its critical role in generating effective structural change.

In Part II, Chapter Six, Foster's account of the cultural origins of institutional thought is examined, including his reflections on the role, impact and significance of a three-century American frontier experience. The intellectual matrix from which institutionalism develops is explored in his review and appraisal of the character and impact of major instrumentalists and institutionalists—Veblen (1934, 1946), Dewey (1938, 1939), Ayres (1961, 1978), et al.

In Chapter Seven, Foster's major and fundamental critiques of ism-ideologies are provided. He addresses the theoretical underpinnings, presumed institutional structure, invidious criteria employed, and the fundamental inadequacies of feudalism, utopian socialism, Marxism, Fabian socialism, capitalism, and fascism.

In Chapter Eight, Foster's perspective on John Maynard Keynes is developed. Keynes's general theoretical position is perceived as being substantially compatible in major respects with institutional economics. Foster sees, in Keynes's *General Theory* (1936), a recognition of institutional variability and change, an explicit theory of income and employment, an implicit instrumental value theory, the critical components of a debt-creation theory of capital formation, and an abiding concern with economic equity, all of which are substantially at variance with neoclassical orthodoxy, from which Keynes acknowledged a "long struggle of escape." Foster anticipates in part what are now emerging as elements of contemporary post Keynesian analysis.

The volume closes, in Chapter Nine, with applications of Foster's general theoretical perspective to instrumental policy making. Examples are drawn both from Foster's own commentaries on policy and from contemporary applications in the U.S. and abroad.

This presentation and assessment of Foster's work draws on four somewhat different sources of materials: *(a)* Foster's papers, published and unpublished; *(b)* taped lectures and their transcription, *(c)* notes taken by graduate students in Foster's classes; and *(d)* published contributions of his former students. In the back matter of this volume are detailed listings of each of these four Sources of information. Materials cited in the text from these Sources appear as References at the end of each Chapter.

Foster's papers: His unpublished doctoral dissertation is entitled "Theoretical Foundations of Government Ownership in a Capitalist Society." It is now in the archives in the library at the University of Texas, Austin. Two other lengthy papers he wrote were "Wage Movements as Institutional Adjustments" and "The Approach to Land Use Planning in a Changing Technology." In addition he wrote a fair number of relatively short papers (some three dozen are listed in Sources) for use in his classes, for public lectures, and for presentations at professional meetings. As noted, T. Baldwin Ranson edited a selection of these papers that appeared in a special issue of *The Journal of Economic Issues* (December 1981). Others are accessible as unpublished monographs in the Library Archives of the University of Denver.

Taped and transcribed lectures: Foster's course lectures on "Value and Its Determinants," in 1948, were taped by Harry Brown and transcribed by Gladys Foster, his wife. It is book length.

Lecture notes: Extensive notes on his lectures were taken by Gladys Foster, and other graduate students, including the present author, in a number of his undergraduate and graduate courses. In a few instances, some of Foster's own notes were also available. Available lecture notes have been transcribed and are listed by note-taker and course in the Sources.

Publications of Foster's students: Foster's contributions appear, predictably somewhat transformed, in the published work of a number of his students who became professional economists. As beneficiaries of Foster's oral tradition, they have absorbed, employed, and in places extended the analyses first introduced to them by Foster. A substantial listing of these publications also appears in the Sources.

The author's approach is to present Foster's theoretical position, section topic by section topic, drawing on all relevant sources. Liberal use will be made of Foster's own words as quotations in the text. One of our major tasks will be to identify, extract, and order theoretical material from his lectures.

Foster taught and wrote as an institutionalist. He was necessarily and conjointly a creator and articulator of institutional thought and a critic of the dominant, indeed imperial, mainstream neoclassical orthodoxy. As with most heterodox scholars, he operated on the fringe of the prestigious and status-driven communities of orthodox scholars. Critics like Foster are, of course, disturbing to orthodox scholars whose views are challenged. But those holding conventional views tend generally to ignore the challenge rather than confront the issues addressed. They rarely engage in dialogue with their institutionalist critics.

However, the contemporary scene is changing. Even the orthodox must now acknowledge that institutions "matter." The structural fabric can no longer be assumed; it must be explained. Richard Nelson & Sidney Winter (1981) and Geoffrey Hodgson (1989, 1999a, 1999b), as evolutionary theorists, and Oliver Williamson (1986) and Douglass North (1990), as neoclassical institutionalists (NIE), have demonstrated as much in the last two decades.

Institutionalists, in pursuing advanced degrees in economics under the professional dominion of neoclassicists, must become conversant with neoclassical orthodoxy. Foster himself was intimately, perhaps astonishingly, conversant with the particulars and mechanics of historic and contemporary orthodoxy. The reverse is not the case. Mainstream economists typically are unfamiliar with the institutionalist literature. Indeed, in the last couple of decades in the U.S., we're told that economics students in many graduate programs are not introduced even to Veblen's work.

Although Foster relished the role of critic, his main concern was to assist with the construction of a more comprehensive and relevant institutionalist theory of political economy. It is to this contribution that we now turn.

REFERENCES

Aronson, Peter H. 1989. "The Democratic Order and Public Choice." In *Politics and Process: New Essays in Democratic Thought*. Geoffrey Brennen, and Loren Lomasky, eds. Cambridge: Cambridge University Press.

Ayres, Clarence E. (1944) 1978. *Theory of Economic Process*, 3rd ed., Kalamazoo: New Issue Press, Western Michigan University.

———. 1961. *Toward a Reasonable Society*. Austin: University of Texas Press.

Brockway, George P. 1995. The NAIRU delusion. *Journal of Economic Issues;* 7:897-910.

Cassidy, John. 1996. The decline of economics. *The New Yorker*. 72, # 37: 50-60.

Dewey, John. 1938. *Logic: The Theory of Inquiry*. New York: Holt, Rinehard, Winston.

———. 1939. *The Theory of Valuation*. Chicago: University of Chicago Press.

Ehrenhalt, Alan. 1997. Keepers of the dismal faith. *The New York Times*. Feb. 23, 1997, E 13.

Eisner, Robert. 1995. Our NAIRU limit. *The American Prospect*. # 21 (Spring):

Galbraith, James K. 2000. How economists got it wrong. *The American Prospect*. 11, #7:18-20.

Hodgson, Geoffrey M. 1988. *Economics and Institutions*, Cambridge: Polity Press.

———. 1999a. *Evolution and Institutions*. Cheltenham: Edward Elgar.

———. 1999b. *Economics and Utopia*. London & New York: Routledge.

Klein, Philip A. 1994. *Beyond Dissent: Essays in Institutional Economics*. Armonk, NY: M.E.Sharpe.

Kuttner, Robert 1997. *Everything for Sale; The Virtues and Limits of Markets*. New York: Alfred A. Knopf.

Nelson, Richard R. And Sidney G. Winter. 1981. *An Evolutionary Theory of Economic Behavior and Capabilities*. Cambridge: Harvard University Press.

North, Douglass C. 1990. *Institutions, Institutional Change and Economic Performance*. Cambridge: Cambridge University Press.

Salanti, Andrea and Ernesto Screpanti. 1997. eds. *Pluralism in Economics: New Perspectives in History and Methodology*. Cheltenham: Edward Elgar.

Soros, George. 1997. The capitalist threat. *The Atlantic Monthly*. 279, No.2: 45-58.

Symposium. 1997. The natural rate of unemployment. *Journal of Economic Perspectives*; 11:3-108.

Veblen, Thorstein B. (1899) 1934. *The Theory of the Leisure Class*. New York: Modern Library.

———. (1919) 1946. *The Place of Science in Modern Civilization*. New York: Russell and Russell.

Williamson, Oliver E. 1986. *Economic Organization: Firms, Markets and Policy Control*. New York: New York University Press.

2 THE THEORY OF SCIENTIFIC INQUIRY

The most obtrusive distinguishing attribute of man is his rational capacity. J. Fagg Foster

INTRODUCTION

We live in a world in which social problems are at times created, constrained, and/or resolved by persons engaged in scientific inquiry. Such problems are commonly perceived as prevailing conditions that in some demonstrable sense require institutional remedies, i.e. changes in behavioral rules. "What is" is not "what ought to be." Indeed the referential content of a "social problem" cannot be conceived except through recourse to some standard, some criterion, that distinguishes between "is" and "ought." Certainly one of the revolutionary contributions of Foster, and therefore one of the main foci of this volume, is his demonstration that, in the social process, questions of "oughtness," criteria of value, can be *scientifically* explored! A social *science* is both possible and essential. We need not, indeed must not be, dependent on cultural certitudes, utilitarian preferences, nationalistic icons, transcendentalistic axioms, or other non-evidential bases as the source of criteria of judgment if rational comprehension and enhancement of the human condition is to continue and accelerate. The central function of economics as a social science is, in Foster's view, to explain causal relationships and make policy recommendations concerning "the provision of the *means* of human life and experience." He explains,

> The word *means* bespeaks an agency function, and the importance of that function to the quality of life as a whole would be difficult to exaggerate. That is why economics is important. The rate of provision of and the character of the means of human experience determine in a very significant way the quality and level of life itself. The kinds of things man uses and the prevalence of those things influence what he does, including how each person relates his behavior to the behavior of others. Fundamentally, the identity between and the sequential continuity of 'means' and 'ends' are inescapable. Economics—rational analysis of the determination of real income—is important

> to any effort to understand human affairs in general and most facets of the social process in particular [(1969)1981, 858 (emphasis in original)].

The fundamental significance, then, of scientific economic inquiry derives entirely from its application to existing world conditions, circumstances, and policies that do or would impair the creation and disposition of real income, the goods and services that comprise the means of human experience. Economically, politically, and socially we analytically identify and normatively deplore global conditions of increasing income inequality, massive involuntary unemployment, and unaccountable concentrations of corporate and governmental power, among others. We analytically identify, and normatively attempt through institutional adjustments, to constrain such threats as national possession of weapons of mass destruction, AIDS epidemics, and intercontinental environmental pollution. Scientific inquiry is the essential analytical vehicle through which the causal determinants of social problems can be identified and with which creative resolutions, reflecting and incorporating normative constructs, can be sought. Foster well understood the power and significance of moving from nonscientific to scientific social inquiry in both defining and resolving social and economic problems through institutional adjustments.

Accordingly, in every paper Foster wrote, in every class he taught, he argued that economic inquiry, if it is to have any relevant and constructive impact on the social order, must be scientific. For him, the tests of relevance are the ability of economic theory to explain in causal terms what it purports to explain, and the accompanying capability of generating reconstructive policies to enhance the quality and flow of real income. Indeed, for reasons presented at length elsewhere in this volume, he argues that the prevailing neoclassical tradition in political economy is profoundly lacking in *scientific* attributes, judgmental warrant, and credible policies. Although an explanation of such deficiencies cannot be pursued in this context, the long-standing claims by neoclassicists to scientific dominion, credibility and relevance must be noted here. Is it possible to demonstrate, for example, that a "natural rate of unemployment" (nonaccelerating inflation rate of unemployment or NAIRU) is a constraint on policy making? Is macro-management policy by government actually made ineffectual by "rational expectations? "Should a balanced federal budget be the overriding policy directive? A neoclassically-grounded affirmative response to each question must explain the causal sequences that generate the outcomes presumed. We return to a critique of neoclassical orthodoxy in Chapter 3 and 7.

Moreover, since neoclassicism increasingly dominates economic inquiry in the Western World, Foster's critique of this tradition, and his advocacy of a scientific institutionalist perspective as an alternative, would appear to be even more timely now than when originally presented. The extraordinary magnitude of the conceptual revolution implied in an encompassing shift from orthodox neoclassicism to a heterodox institutionalism in economic inquiry and problem solving can hardly be overstated. Yet a substantial shift in this analytical direction is essential if the above-mentioned social ills and other economic afflictions are to be cogently addressed and effectually treated. Foster's view of scientific inquiry, as developed in this chapter, is not peripheral to the main body of his analyses; it is anterior, central, and defining. For Foster, science is the encompassing perspective within which particular constructs and theories are developed. But the nature of Foster's distinctively scientific social inquiry, especially in the area of economics, requires delineation. It is the purpose of this chapter to provide that introductory characterization.

In sequence, then, we explore Foster's views of: *(a)* the emergence of science, *(b)* science and non-science, *(c)* science and philosophy, *(d)* distinctions between social and physical sciences, *(e)* the logic of scientific social inquiry, *(f)* the primary processes of inquiry, *(g)* the object of social inquiry, and *(h)* the nature of scientific truth in social inquiry.

EMERGENCE OF SCIENCE

Science is a uniquely human perspective and product. Although we often presume that it is mainly the product of just the last couple hundred years, science, as a rational way of knowing, has for several millennia continuously and significantly affected the everyday life of nearly everybody. As a mode of reasoning, science is realistic and encompassing; for those holding conventional beliefs, it is a constant threat. The warranted knowledge of social science permits the identification and resolution of social problems, where problems are seen as a state or condition requiring change in beliefs and behavior for their resolution. Science is the continuously developing vehicle of comprehension through which the social order is understood, remedied and sustained and the physical order is explained, manipulated and augmented.

Foster perceives the development of science as a way of knowing to be co-extensive with the evolution of distinctively human beings. Malinowski concurs: "The scientific attitude is as old as culture." [(1944) 1960, 10]. The physical and genetic emergence of humanoids with attributes of erect stature, biocular vision, opposable thumbs, enlarged cranial capacities, et cetera, permits *(a)* the emergence, employment and enhancement of causal comprehension, *(b)* the creation and manipulation of conceptual and material tools and *(c)* the recognition that reflection may have a determinative bearing on conduct. The emergence of a developmental, social "human nature" reflects the human capacity deliberatively to create and, through habit to retain, interdependent modes of social conduct; that is, to create, absorb, reflect and accommodate prescriptive cultural conditioning. Thus social structure is constituted and cultural continuity is provided. People are, then, both products and creators of culture. Foster contends that:

> The most obtrusive distinguishing attribute of man is his rational capacity, and it is the degree of his use of this capacity which distinguishes man's effects on his environment.[1] Through his use of reason, man's operations on his environment may aptly be called control. He consciously modifies circumstances in which he finds himself, not only to attain an immediate end in view but also to provide easier or more efficient attainment of the same end when it reappears.That is to say, man generalizes his conception of his relationships with the remainder of his environment, and therefrom he generalizes the relationships between different aspects of the same environment. Thus man's comprehensions of the universe, including himself, are anthropocentric in the sense that he himself is the observer, and his observations are the materials of his comprehensions, including his observations of his own action of comprehending [(1963) 1981, 1009].

From the earliest periods of recorded history on, Foster says, a human being, exhibiting this rationality, "is distinguished. . .not only by his technological achievements but by his institutional achievements as well" [(1948a) 1981, 10]. The distinctive and peculiar characteristic of a person is that "he[/she] deliberately applies theory to the solution of. . .problems not only technologically but institutionally" (12). Foster's recognition that, historically, human reason and theory building are applied both to technological and to institutional dimensions of experience is a major insight. It undergirds his claim that the growth of knowledge not only encompasses new combinations and extensions of physical things but also encompasses new combinations and revisions of behavioral forms and connections. There is both a technological process and an institutional process to be examined in human history.

In sum, humans are the only theory-building organisms. Theories are causal explanations of observable phenomena; they tell us "which facts to gather and how to arrange them for analysis," as Foster repeatedly insisted. Theorists generate causal accounts of human origins, of productive determinants, of physical processes, of disabling impairments, of modes of governance, et cetera.

With the gradual development of languages, there emerged systematic ways of creating, ordering, and communicating symbols and their assigned referential content (Ogden and Richards 1946, 87-108). With the development of writing, human beings were able to record and share, linguistically and logically, detailed theoretical formulations. With the invention of printing, people became much more able to create, reproduce and distribute material, including theoretical materials (Randall 1940, 19-20). For Foster, Gutenberg's invention of movable type printing was particularly significant. With the development of organized theoretical inquiry, theory creation and expansion became endemic in the more tolerant human cultures. The more advanced the scientific learning, the more technologically advanced the culture, the more discretion people acquire in fashioning their own future. Says Foster,

> There are things which permit us to identify the category human being, among them deliberately organized theory and thus the capacity to teach, the capacity to do fine arts and/or sciences. The ability to find out theory and to transmit that to other members of the species, that is peculiarly human. . . .[O]ther species work out simple theories [understanding of elemental causal connections] but they can't teach them [record and lingually or cursively transmit] to others. . . .[T]hat's our peculiar advantage (1948a, 88).

Communities inherit the accumulated theories of the past and apply, revamp, augment, and/or abandon them as they see fit. "Our terrific advantage is that we can communicate theory and thus apply it to a problem effectively and thus solve problems so much easier than any other species that we have what we call civilization and the other species don't. We accumulate know-how as a species" [Foster 1948a, 89]. Other species, given genetic endowments, can "teach" their young but primarily by demonstrative mimicking and/or rudimentary audible communication. Some non-human species are also, in quite limited ways, "tool-using" but the development and accumulation of tool-idea combinations is distinctively developmental for humans. For non-human species, there is no significant accumulation of warranted understandings and explanations. The acquired capacity to create and transmit theory that explains in causal terms what it purports to explain is uniquely a human endeavor .

SCIENCE AND NON-SCIENCE

In the long tradition of distinctively human reflection and conduct, there has been, argues Foster, a continuing and vigorous struggle between those fostering a scientific mode of inquiry and those promoting non-scientific (magical) modes of thought. These profoundly differing belief systems and attendant behaviors are significant, and incompatible. He writes:

> [T]he evidence of modern anthropology, sociology, and economics is totally destructive of the "supposedly self-evident axioms or intuitions" which have served formal "logicians" during the long period of compromise during which science and magic tacitly. . .agreed on a division of man's experience into areas to be explained by one or the other.
>
> But science has constantly and persistently broken the compromise, claiming and conquering a greater and greater area of man's experience as its sphere of explanation. And finally, science comes to claim the last rampart of magic, the citadel of "value." The long struggle between magic and science, between apriorism and empiricism, has been continuous and bitter, often breaking out into violence. Indeed, violence is to be expected of a system of estimation based upon nothing more than the authority of arbitrary choice. It can find no other evidence of validity. But, without exception, when the evidence was in, science has won the victory. And this in spite of the fact that each major victory has been outlawed by the sovereign, denounced from the pulpit, lamented in literature, and deleted from polite, erudite discussion. This was the case when Galileo dropped various weights from the leaning tower of Pisa; it was the case when Harvey demonstrated the system of blood circulation; it was the case when the Darwinian cat devoured so many ecclesiastical pigeons; and it is the case now when Dewey explicitly demands the explanation of value in causal terms [1943a, 1-2, (emphasis in original)].

Foster's characterization of the nature of science is terse yet cogent. His reaffirmation of the interrelatedness of science, knowledge, and logic undergirds all of his encompassing analyses of both institutionalism and neoclassicism and their conflicting methodologies:

> Science is the conceptual apprehension of causal sequence; knowledge is the correct placement of items of experience in the causal sequences of which they are a part; logic is the effort at conceptual formulation of causal interconnectedness in conjugate correspondence with existential reality. These three, science, knowledge, logic, are inseparable, being merely several aspects of the same thing. Note that they all involve facts; an idea (conceptual formulation) is no more valid (true) apart from existential reality than a rail-road ticket is a journey. The one claim to validity is conjugate correspondence with the facts. No one has ever argued successfully with the facts; without exception, when the interconnectedness of a continuum is brought to light, the items in the continuum are found to fall into causal sequence. . . .In fact, that

> is what is meant by "brought to light," or "discovered," or "known." The theory of inquiry we call science. . .involves observation of facts in terms of causal interconnectedness, experiment, and conceptual projections of causal sequences in the form of hypotheses. The word "hypotheses" should be underscored [1943a, 2-3; (emphasis in original)].

Foster's references above to "existential reality" affirm an institutionalist conception that merits a further comment: Drawing on Dewey in particular, Foster's instrumental analysis rests on realist foundations. In words of Foster's student, Paul D. Bush:

> [I]nstitutionalist methodology. . .incorporates an ontological hypothesis that logically entails, among other things, the view that society as a system of institutions is real and not merely a figment of the intellectual imagination; that continuity in human experience is not only a convenient theoretical construct but is a real process, the disruption of which has consequences independent of our ability to conceptualize them in deterministic mathematical models; that social and individual value formation are real processes and, as such, must be subject to investigation rather than postulation; that the process of institutional change is not merely a matter of shifting ideologies, or changes in linguistic conventions, but changes in real habits of behavior that have real consequences which may or may not be captured in discourse; that physical and cultural processes are part of a contingent universe that guarantees nothing, thereby imposing the necessity of choice on the human agent; and, finally, that human choices have real consequences for the physical and cultural processes of which they are a part (1993, 73).

Foster and institutionalists, then, acknowledge their long identification with the scientific tradition of generating evidentially warranted, explanatory propositions that are rooted in, and purport to be consistent with, perceived generalities of the social and physical order. Such generalities may not be visually observable, but they are factually demonstrable causal connections the existence of which can be shown empirically, and/or causally. Institutionalists recognize the human developmental capability to demonstrate causal interconnectedness in the behavioral world of reflective agents and institutional prescriptions, and in the conceptual world of means-consequence connections, hypotheses formulations, institutional creations, and normative assessments. This conception of an existential world, and its disclosure through logical and empirical inquiry, permeates the whole of the institutionalist analytical tradition.

SCIENCE AND PHILOSOPHY

As is commonly understood, neoclassical economists perceive the subject matter of a scientific economics to be an analysis of the allocation of scarce means among unlimited ends. It is a positivistic analysis of the operations of an unfettered market pricing system. Their theorists do not presume to judge the character or the merit of the wants and tastes exhibited in market participation. They exclude normative queries regarding buyers judgments, sellers intents, or market outcomes; they allegedly eschew value judgments. In their texts, means and ends are divorced.

They are concerned only with means as the satisfaction of wants; their theory presumes no philosophic guidance or appraisal.

Institutionalists, in contrast, perceive a scientific economics to be a causal inquiry into how a community arranges its institutional structures in order to provide the maximal, noninvidious provision of the means of life for its members. Institutionalists, here Foster in particular, insist that value tenets are inherently incorporated in any proposals for institutional change in the economy and therefore must be included in any relevant inquiry agenda. This difference is revealed in the differing conceptions of the character and universes of application of science and philosophy.

As is already indicated, one of Foster's major, and atypical, foci of analysis is his bringing of conventionally normative concerns and constructs into the same universe of discourse as allegedly positive concerns and constructs. Normative tenets are historically thought to reside exclusively in the realm of philosophy. Positivistic tenets are the substance of the realm of science. Neoclassical economists have traditionally claimed that economics, if it is to be scientific, must be positivistic. In fact, however, neoclassicists in their advocacy are de facto normativists. The inherent normative-positive dichotomy implicitly defines the scope and content of orthodox economics. Thus, says Foster, it was thought that "where you are going is determined by philosophy; how you get there is determined scientifically" (1948a, 16). Philosophy and science, for the neoclassicists, are routinely presumed to be divergent loci of inquiry, theoretically and analytically. Foster vigorously rejects this conventional divorcement:

> Science is *(1)* the building of generalizations and *(2)* their constant verification and/or negation through. . .applications of those generalizations as working hypotheses. Numbers 1 and 2 are not separately operative, although they are separately identifiable. In fact, #1 is accomplished through the operation of #2. Neither can exist without the other, and the kinds of mental operations in each are generic with those in the other. Philosophy is a deliberate effort to think coherently over the entire field of human experience, i.e., a deliberately rational effort *(1)* to build generalizations which are inclusive of the whole of human experience and *(2)* to verify and/or negate the validity of these generalizations by observing . . .[their] applications. But these two statements of identification or, rather, of functional characterization, are substantially generic. And there is reason for this conformity: science and philosophy *are* the same thing as a kind of human operation. . . .[T]he only difference we can discern between science and philosophy is in. . ."universes." Philosophy is the all-inclusive science, and the sciences are . . .applications of philosophy. They differ only in the inclusiveness of their universes [n.d. Philosophy and Science, 1 (emphasis in original)].

Elsewhere Foster argues that science and philosophy "are mutually applicable. They are the same thing. They cover the same areas, they explain the same things in the same fashion. . . .[T]hey may both be mistaken; they both may be in error, but there can be no contravention by one of the other in fact (1948a, 23). For example, "the philosophy of atoms is exactly the same thing as the science of atoms. . .[T]he philosophy of human motivation is exactly the same thing as the science of human motivation."(15)

This means, says Foster, that philosophy and science "are not two extremes on the same attribute" (1948a, 22); they are not termini on either end of a conceptual axis. Neither are philosophy and science such different kinds of constructs that there is, comparatively, a "missing middle" between them. They cannot dualistically be presumed to have no common reality or content. Neither are they distinguishable "in regard to questions of fact or not fact, or more or less fact. . . .They are parallel in all of these senses in regard to all of these things" (22-23).

A major implication of this characterization is to demonstrate the interconnectedness and interdependency of the major areas of learning. Foster used different diagrammatic models of demonstration. The one that follows as Figure 1 is the familiar pyramidal construct with philosophy at the apex, social and physical science positioned below as the initial sub-set (less inclusive); the respective disciplines (e.g., economics, physics) beneath each as the second sub-set (still less inclusive); the areas of application (e.g., medicine, business, engineering) underneath as the third sub-set, and the trades across the base.

PHILOSOPHY

SOCIAL SCIENCE	PHYSICAL SCIENCE
Economics, Government, Psychology	Physics, Chemistry, Biology
Education, Business Mgmt, Politics	Medicine, Engineering, Meteorology
Skilled Workers, Childcare Givers	Technicians, Nurses, Artisans

[Enabling tools are language and mathematics]

Figure 1

The fundamental premise is that in any problematic inquiry, the inquirer is able to move freely among and between the differing areas, and/or levels, of inclusiveness, knowledge, and applications as needed. For example, an inquiry in biology may well require consideration of chemical elements, ecological influences, and philosophic tenets. An inquiry in economics may well require examination of business practices, psychological assumptions, and philosophical norms. Theories and tenets of warranted knowledge then vary both in content and in inclusiveness of the data, but "[n]o science. . .takes the position that it is not related causally to all. . .other sciences" (1948a, 14).

A second and even more compelling implication of Foster's joining of philosophy and science, is his explicit refutation of the alleged divorcement between economic and philosophic analyses. This positive-normative dualism, if accepted, would make rational analysis of normative premises impossible. Elsewhere, in a summarizing characterization of this distinction, as Foster perceived it, we wrote,

> Posited is a construct which divides and divorces some kinds of inquiry, knowledge, and activities from other kinds. Separation is alleged to be

> complete between the positive and the normative, between matters of "is" and matters of "ought," between means and ends, between the study of science and of art. . .between questions of fact and questions of value. . . between exercises in description and admonitions of prescription, between the disciplines of economics or politics and that of ethics, between the realm of the true or false and the realm of the good or bad (Tool 1985, 278-79)

Acceptance of this dualistic sorting of ontological and methodological attributes, obviously, moves important elements of inquiry outside the universe of causal demonstration provided by scientific inquiry. If these alleged "missing middle" constructs delimit and define the universe of social inquiry: *(a)* the purposiveness of inquiry is left ambiguous; *(b)* the logic of scientific inquiry is abandoned; *(c)* the relevance of economic analysis for problem solving is made indeterminate; and *(d)* the scope of inquiry is fatally truncated. Happily, Foster's analyses—here of inquiry, and in the next chapter of social value—reduce this dichotomy to a historically and analytically modest obstruction in the development of scientific social inquiry. It can and must be abandoned as a simplistic and illogical blockage to inquiry.

All significant inquiry, then, is purposive; purposiveness compels valuation; valuation requires a theory or criterion of value drawn from the inquiry process itself. Purposiveness in social and economic inquiry means problem-solving, otherwise "inquiry" is a mere charade of posturing, pretense and excuse hunting. Current commentaries, rooted in orthodoxy, that insist that the merging of large corporations enhances "price competition," is one example. "Rational expectations" analysis that contends that governmental macro economic adjustments are, because of private countervailing market actions, necessarily stillborn, is another. Valuation is a necessary and integral element in all economic judgments.

Significant economic inquiry must be logically credible. "Means and ends" distinctions, for example, are merely "if-then propositions" that identify means-consequence relations, or causal interconnectedness. They are procedural constructs of *explanatory* use to the inquirer. They are not dualistic realms of being or reality; neither are they incompatible categories of inquiry. It is Foster's view that "means" and "ends" are inquiry components purposely captioned to address the processual character of inquiry. What is" means" in one context may well be "ends" in another.

In response to a student's question concerning the divorcement of "means" and "ends," Foster pointedly observes that some authors claim that

> [W]e aren't concerned with ends, we are concerned with the means, and then [they] explain the validity of the ends. . . .[Evidences confirm that] the whole of human experience has been with the continuum. . . .Things never stop. Things happen. . . .We have never had an experience with cessation. There is no end so far as we can tell. . . .The whole of human experience. . .has been [one of] process, continuous, unceasing. . . .We are concerned with processes, with things happening, and causal relationships between them (1948a, 33-34).

Foster is emphasizing the processual character of inquiry in which means and ends are, in effect, mere designations to show provisional causal connections; their captioning shows tentative placement in a *continuum* of inquiry. Neither "means" nor "ends" has any conceptually autonomous inquiry status. Foster sees inquiry as the examination of the causal connections in the continuum of means and ends, causes and effects, means and consequences. The object of inquiry is the social *process*; analytical modes must then also be processual. Explaining the causal interrelatedness in and of that process is the task of scientific inquirers. This is the context and the content of "means" and "ends" in warranted inquiry.

SOCIAL AND PHYSICAL SCIENCE

One of Foster's more persuasive defenses of the possibility of economics becoming a legitimate and recognized science is his demonstration that the commonly alleged differences between the physical and social sciences do not preclude economics from becoming scientific in the same sense as, say, physics.

He perceives the physical sciences to "have, in most part, attained the state of inquiry that is logical," that is "they are carried on in terms of the causal interconnectedness of sequences of events and/or objects. The 'meaning' of any particular item in any sequence is in terms of its correlativity with other items in that sequence." The meaning of any affirmation, then, is in its referential content that identifies its place in inquiry and its connection(s) to items in the causal reality addressed. "'Meaning' in an ultimate, intrinsic sense just is not useful in the process at hand." Ultimate meanings, e.g. referential content for "Ends," as in "Maximizing Utility," do not arise from *within* the inquiry process; they are imported from *without* the context of continuing scientific inquiry. They are not products of warranted inquiry; they are not derived internal to existential sources of causal inquiry. Such items are unsustainable intrusions that corrupt, if they do not destroy, the process of warranted inquiry into the social process. Accordingly, the continuing inquiry function of the social scientist is "the determination of the places of the items in a [causal] continuum and in the extension of that continuum" [(1942a) 1981, 876]. As Foster explains:

> Logical analysis, or scientific analysis, has no need of an ultimate end-in-view . . . .In tracing a sequence in terms of the causal interconnectedness of the items in the sequence, the ends are *discovered* as the inquiry proceeds: they are not predetermined by immaculate conception or handed down from "on high." They are the items themselves; and short of some sort of magic, they can be nothing else. This. . .is not to say that scientists do not evaluate—they do. But the valuations are in terms of the consequences, not in terms of a predetermined ideal. Scientists have ends-in-view (Dewey's usage) all the time. These are estimates of value in terms of probable consequence of the then present state of affairs. The ends-in-view, that is, the expected consequences are stated in terms of hypotheses, each of which is more or less probable in view of past experience. They are not stated in terms of what the consequences must be, because, no matter how much they *ought* to be, when they *are* determined, they are, whether they ought to be or not. And when the ends-in-view are determined, they become items in the continuum and give rise to new and further ends-in-view, and so on *indefinitely*. Thus science continues to broaden, [and] extend. . . .Such is the nature of science [(1942a) 1981, 876-77, (emphasis in original)].

As any science broadens and extends, particular theories are necessarily and routinely brought into question. Their explanatory capacities are perceived to be, in some significant sense, inadequate or inaccurate, or both. They fail to account in causal terms for that which is claimed for them. Such "bad" theory can only be replaced with "better" theory—theory that explains *more* adequately, accurately, and/or *more* extensively the causal phenomena under review. The significance of any theory hinges on its capacity to explain in causal terms. If it has that capability, it is "good" theory and adds to current warranted knowledge. At any time, the appearance of new factual circumstances may well prompt, even require, the reassessment of the explanatory capacity of such prevailing theory.

In comparing social and physical science, it is sometimes argued that the basic data utilized in social inquiry are "abstract in the sense of being nonexistential, and are therefore not subject to being handled logically" [Foster (1942a) 1981, 877]. This is especially the case when neoclassical economists and their students take "'wants,' 'utility,' 'disutility,' and even 'happiness', as basic data." The function of a neoclassically-defined economy is to satisfy wants. But wants "cannot be considered in the abstract, although much social theory is built upon the notion that wants, as such, are being used as the beginning-and-end datum in explanation" of human conduct. On the contrary, "the notion that wants are basic data is functionally disregarded in all social theorists' demonstrations" (877).

It is sometimes argued that social inquiry cannot be scientific because, unlike physics, the inquirers have less deliberate control over conditions; they "cannot experiment in the same way;" they cannot repeat human operations as experiments. In many cases, it is true that "you cannot control conditions to the same degree that you can in a physics laboratory in reference to some things. But it is also true that you can control some things better in human relationships" (Foster 1948a, 30). For example:

> You can. . .[determine the level]. . .of national income over and over again going through the same operation, counting the same things, with appreciable confidence, confidence sufficient that you can operate on it without hesitation much more accurately than you can control and repeat over and over again the release of mesons from an atomic structure in a cyclotron. You can control the determining conditions (1948a, 31).

The control over conditions, ability to repeat experiments, and the scope of inquiry will thus vary widely in both social and physical sciences reflecting the diversity and magnitude of data developed that are pertinent to queries posed and hypotheses offered.

It is sometimes argued that social inquiry does not, in contrast with physical sciences, rely sufficiently upon and explain factual data. The concern is a genuine one. Scientific standing depends upon establishing "strict conjugate correspondence between factual data and conceptual description." And in social inquiry it may well be more difficult, than in the physical sciences, to bring causal relations of social phenomena into "correct apprehension and unified organization" [(1942a) 1981, 878]. As John Dewey observes: "the ultimate end and test of all inquiry is the transformation of a problematic situation (which involves confusion and conflict) into a unified one. That it is much more difficult to accomplish this end in social inquiry than in the restricted field of physical inquiry is a fact. But it is not a fact which constitutes an inherent logical or theoretical difference between the two kinds of inquiry" [Dewey, 1938, 491; quoted by Foster (1942a) 1981, 878]. In the physical sciences it may be relatively easier to isolate and identify some types of data. Indeed, disciplinary boundaries reflect such convenient divisions. But "in social inquiry, the items are, in causal terms, so complex and 'intricately interwoven that the difficulty of instituting a relatively closed system is intensified'"(878).

It is sometimes argued that social science and physical science differ in their respective ease of application to conceptual and social problems. Social theory is perceived to be more difficult of effectual application than physical theory. This is especially true where questions about, or revisions in, long standing institutional structures sustaining significant power centers (Veblen's "vested interests") are proposed. But it is also true that historically some physical theories have been violently resisted. "It is said that Galileo suffered official torture because the earth revolved around the sun"[(1942a) 1981, 879]. In any case, a condition of application of social science is that persons affected by social change have "a general understanding of the solutions as well as the answers. This is not as true of physical inquiry. People will accept physical changes, a gravity meter or a refrigerator, without requiring to know how it works or why its result is produced" (879). Not so with social inquiry; a "condition of application is understanding by the persons involved. . . .[T]he results of social inquiry cannot be accomplished in any large measure without the results themselves being a part of peoples' knowledge, and that knowledge must be operational, else the application is not accomplished"(879). We revisit this significant construct in Chapter 4 with the "theory of recognized interdependence".

It is sometimes argued that social and physical sciences differ in that the former is addressed to "ultimate ends" and "the character of the determination of those ends." The latter have no need for ultimate ends. The argument does hold if the social sciences are perceived to be directed toward the realization of an "ultimate and predetermined end" that is an anterior guide to, and directive of the nature of social inquiry [(1942a) 1981, 879]. But we have already observed that social inquiry from the institutionalists' position, makes no use of ultimates or absolutes, grounded on some pre- or non-inquiry presumption or preconception.

Finally, it is sometimes thought that the theoretical components of the respective disciplines in the pyramidal construct (Figure 1 above) generate quite different *kinds* of theory, e.g., that principles of inquiry in chemistry or physics are of a wholly different sort than principles of inquiry in economics or governance. Foster refutes this claim. He argues that the differing levels and disciplines of inquiry share a common concern to generate warranted assertions grounded in causal understanding. In the development of evidentially grounded inquiry in the various disciplines, and in the more particular areas of application and employment indicated, there will be dramatic differences, obviously, in the nature of the subject matter addressed, in levels of inclusiveness, in the contexts of theory building and problem solving. But the nature of the reasoning processes, the derivation of truth claims, the conceptions of relevance, the character of explanatory hypotheses are analytically uniform.

When Foster asserts, then, that "there is in fact unity of the facts and therefore unity of knowledge and therefore unity of theory in so far as it is applicable" (1948a, 84), he is identifying the myriad inter- and intraconnections of cohesiveness in scientific theory generally. Science explains fact, the demonstrable causal linkages; it reflects the interdependence of levels and models of warranted inquiry across the broad spectrum of human experience and reflection. Theoretical principles within and among the disciplines and applications, if generated by, and reflective of what we here construe to be a scientific perspective, will not be conflictual or incompatible. From a scientific perspective, an evidentially warranted principle in physics cannot be contradicted by a presumed non-evidential principle in philosophy or economics. Scientific knowledge, though disparately segmented, constitutes the aggregate fund of a community's warranted knowledge. It is both the basis of, and the continuing vehicle for, building human culture.

LOGIC OF SCIENTIFIC INQUIRY

Foundations

Implicit in the foregoing, is the conceptual substructure that undergirds the logic of Foster's theory of inquiry and that of institutionalists generally. That conceptual framework affirms an existential world, elements of which are continuing objects of inquiry. In the continuity of actual human experience, judgments of human agents are causally determinative of observable outcomes. Prescriptive and proscriptive stipulations of conduct, as institutions, define and redefine the social order. Indeed "human agency" is, in effect, "embedded intentional causality" (Lawson 1997, 63). Agents' discretion, created structures, observed performances, problematic conditions, experienced consequences are all demonstrably knowable as elements of the actual human experience continuum. The importance of this ontological avowal, although commonplace in most sciences, delineates the focus and conduct of social inquiry as a continuing exploration of an existential process employing scientific constructs and analyses. Causally-validated explanations of observable phenomena, and their coherent analytical ordering, constitute warranted knowledge. This is knowledge that can be, and is actually, used to guide and appraise conduct in the extant world of people, structure, functions, problems, and judgments,.

Instrumental Logic

Foster's characterization of the *instrumental logic* of a scientific mode of inquiry is sharply differentiated from the "logic" of non-scientific theories. This distinction between "instrumental logic," the inquiry mode of institutionalists, and deductivistic a priorism, the inquiry mode of most neoclassicists, merits additional comment. Dewey's theory of inquiry, as indicated in the following, is reflected in Foster's theory of the economic process.

First, we note that the modifier, *instrumental*, "stands for the relation of means-consequence as the basic category for interpretation of logical forms" [Dewey 1938, 14n, (emphasis in original)]. Instrumental inquiry, accordingly, is addressed to explanations of causal connections and consequent outcomes.

Second, we note that "the basic category of logic is *order*. . . .The universal order of material contents in every intelligently directed procedure is that of means-to-consequences; actual existential materials providing the 'stuff,' while the status of the material as means requires operations of selection and of re-arrangement so that special interactions may be instituted to effect the consequences intended"

[Dewey 1938, 385, (emphasis in original)]. Instrumental logic, then, consists of the ordering of existential materials to reflect means-consequence relations.

Third, we incorporate Dewey's *characterizations* of the theory of instrumental logic, on which Foster and other institutionalists draw; included are the following attributes:

(a). "Logic is a progressive discipline." As scientific ways of knowing advance, as mode and substance are revised, logic itself must be expected to adapt as necessary to order the inquiry process of exploring means-consequence relations. "The idea that logic is capable of final formulation is an *eidolon* of the theatre." [Dewey 1938, 14, (emphasis in original)].

(b). "The subject matter of logic is determined operationally." The inquiry process involves

> operations performed and to be performed. Logical forms are the conditions that inquiry, *qua* inquiry, has to meet. . . .The more material and instrumentalities are shaped in advance with a view to their operating in conjunction with each other as means to consequences, the better the operations performed are controlled. . . .Operations of inquiry. . .proceed by shaping, on one hand, subject matter so that it lends itself to the application of conceptions as modes of operation, and on the other hand, by development of such conceptual structures as are applicable to existential conditions. . . .Operations involve both material and instrumentalities, including in the latter tools and techniques. (Dewey 1938, 14-16).

(c). "Logical forms are postulational." Intrinsic postulates of and for inquiry are not "arbitrary" nor affirmed a priori; they are discovered in the course of inquiry itself. "Logic embodies stipulations that commit the inquirer to the observance of operations demonstrated earlier as conditions essential for any inquiry that seeks 'warranted assertibility'. . . .The postulational character of logical inquiry requires . . .the most complete and explicit formulation that is attainable of not only the subject-matter that is taken as evidential in a given instance, but also of general conditions stated in the rules and principles of inference and discourse" (Dewey 1938, 16-18).

(d). "Logic is a naturalistic theory. . . .There is no breach of continuity between operations of inquiry and biological. . .and physical operations. 'Continuity' means that rational operations *grow out* of organic activities, without being identical with that from which they emerge. . . .There is an adjustment of means to consequences. . . . Human beings in the ordinary or 'natural' processes of living come to make these adjustments purposely." Logic is "naturalistic in the sense of observability," not of mystic intuition (Dewey 1938, 18-19, emphasis in original).

(e). "Logic is a social discipline."

> Inquiry is a mode of activity that is socially conditioned and. . .has cultural consequences. . . .Any theory of logic has to take some stand on the question whether symbols are ready made clothing for the existence of meanings that subsist independently, or whether they are necessary conditions for the existence of meanings. . . .[E]very inquiry grows out of a background of culture and takes effect in greater or less modification of the conditions out of which it arises. . . .Language. . .is the medium in which culture exists and

> through which it is transmitted. Phenomena that are not recorded cannot be discussed. Language is the record that perpetuates occurrences and renders them amenable to public consideration. . . .Neither inquiry nor the most abstractly formal set of symbols can escape from the cultural matrix in which they live, move and have their being (Dewey 1938, 19-20).

Inquiry is conducted in a cultural matrix that includes symbols, languages and structures.

(f). "Logic is autonomous. . . .Logic as inquiry into inquiry is. . .a circular process. It does not depend upon anything extraneous to inquiry. . . .It precludes the determination and selection of logical first principles by an *a priori* intuitional act. . . .It precludes resting logic upon metaphysical and epistemological assumptions and presuppositions. . . .Knowledge is to be defined in terms of inquiry, not vice-versa both in particular and universally." In sum, "logical theory is the systematic formulation of controlled inquiry." Its "logical forms accrue in and because of control that yields conclusions which are warrantably assertible" [Dewey 1938, 20-22, (emphasis in original)].

Foster recognizes these attributes in instrumental logic when he makes the critical distinction between the perceptions of "ends" (ultimate) and "ends-in-view" (procedural, hypothetical). He writes:

> In all logical inquiry, hypothetical ends-in-view are a requisite condition. They are the criteria allowing selection of data to be used as means in resolving a problematic situation. Otherwise, any datum would be as meaningful in reference to a given inquiry as would any other datum. Selection of data is necessary; otherwise, there would be mere hodgepodge. The selection is made in reference to the ends-in-view. It should be emphasized again that the ends-in-view are hypotheses. If they are taken to be *the answer*, then inquiry ceases to be logical; it becomes mere excuse hunting. But the point is that the ends-in-view are beyond the boundaries of present existential knowledge; they are hypothetical resolutions of problematic situations. And until a problematic situation is resolved, the end-in-view remains a hypothesis; upon resolution, the end-in-view (in so far as it corresponds with the resultant facts) becomes an item of knowledge in the logical sense, that is, in the sense of its having a meaning in terms of its correlation with other items in the continuum of which it is a part. Social inquiry need not deviate from logical inquiry in this regard. It does so only in that, and insofar as, the actual conditions of its problem are not determined [(1942a) 1981, 879, (emphasis in original)].

Pure Logic

Non-scientific logic, in contrast, argues Foster, divorces "means" and "ends," and conceives the latter to be antecedently given goals that can be pursued only through non-causal or contra-causal routes. This non-scientific construct of a "reasoning" process may be characterized as follows: Foundation tenets are assumed; conjecture is accepted; reality is personal affirmation; origins of ideas are asocial; purposiveness is noncontextual; it is antecedent to, and unaffected by, inquiry; truth claims are non-causal. As Foster observes,

> Over against. . .[the] theory of logic that we call science is set "pure logic" which seeks to establish truth, validity, desirability, and/or value in a priorist isolation from observation of causal position. Indeed, its "purity" is supposed to connote disconnection from vulgar physical reality. Non-referential formulations of this sort may be of any number and have been very numerous. The reason they may be so numerous and varied is that there is no existential reality (conjugate correspondence) which requires uniformity. The operation in this case is magical in that it is in non-causal terms. The whole of the magician's art is, in fact, the camouflage of causal sequence. He brings a rabbit into position seemingly without causal antecedents. Our experience with rabbits prompts us to look for the "trick" that is being played on us when a rabbit is lifted out of an empty hat; we are not so well cognizant of the causal sequence in the valuation process. The difference between the "pure" logician and the magician is that the "pure" logician isn't aware of his own camouflage (1943a, 3-4).

The pure logician, of course, may enjoy the magician's skills of deception as entertainment; its fun to be fooled, at times. But the pure logician, by insisting that social value and valuation are extra-evidential, non-causal, outside the social inquiry process, is also engaged in deception by concealment, avoidance, or disclamation of the existential normative content of the process of social inquiry.

Role of Hypotheses

The role and significance of hypotheses in the process of instrumental inquiry require a further comment. At bottom, the creation and verification of hypotheses is demonstrably the preeminent focus and application of instrumental logic in pursuit of social problem solving. It is the heartland of scientific social inquiry. It is the critical vehicle for distinguishing between causal comprehension and cultural myth.

This hypothetical query is the imaginative fashioning of a provisional and/or exploratory causal explanation of observed phenomena. It is a plausible, but as yet unproven account that may have been stimulated by preliminary observation of causally induced consequences.

Hypotheses are preliminary formulations of causal interconnectedness. Given an observed inconsistency, problem or occurrence (emergence of doubt, inability to act habitually, perceived risk), the queries posed are: How did this happen? What generated these outcomes? How can continuity be reestablished? How can predictability be restored? How can the actual determinants of the problem be identified and modified? What is to be done? The mind strains and scrambles to find some tentative yet plausible and rational explanation of observable causal phenomena. Could A have caused B, and could B have produced C? Are A and B jointly causes of C? Instrumental inquiry is the search for demonstrable causal connections.

Initially then, hypotheses are speculative and approximate, but creative and credible, conceptions of causal linkages. They are initial conceptions of possible causal connections awaiting, through inquiry, confirmation, revision or rejection. Scientific social inquiry requires that hypotheses become instruments for guiding inquiry both in direction and in substance. They function as guidance mechanisms for the selection and ordering of evidence or data. When hypotheses are demonstratively shown to explain what they purport to explain in cause-effect terms, they become elements of warranted knowledge through placement in the continuum of which they are a part. Scientific inquiry is basically about the creation and testing of hypotheses.

An important addendum is provided by Dewey: "As a broad statement, no important scientific hypothesis has ever been verified in the form in which it was originally presented nor without very considerable revisions and modifications. The justification of such hypotheses has lain in their power to direct new orders of experimental observation and to open up new problems and new fields of subject-matter" (1938, 519).

PROCESSES OF INQUIRY

In more traditional language, instrumental inquiry of institutionalism incorporates what are commonly referred to as deductive and inductive processes. Either process may be instrumentally and/or hypothetically reflected in the initiation of interest in a problematic situation and in the inquiry process through which it can be explored. Inquiry may be set in motion then through the exercise of either of these processes; whatever the initiation, both will be operationally evident and logically essential in any subsequent warranted inquiry.

A deductive query may be provoked, for example, by some awareness of inconsistency or incompatibility of conceptual formulations. Perhaps, the "ifs" in "if-then" propositions are thought not to be well enough grounded empirically and are thus suspect. Perhaps, the "thens" cannot be shown causally to follow.

An inductive query may be prompted by the observation of data that do not fit current theoretical accounts. The relevant facts observed are seen as being at variance with prior and settled claims of generality or principle. Questioning the factual particular prompts exploration of the alleged empirically grounded generality.

But Foster's view of processual inquiry, drawing on Dewey, is *not* traditionally recognized or acknowledged: deduction and induction refer to the *direction* in which inquiry moves; not to discrete, necessarily sequential, exclusive processes. As Dewey explains:

> In science, the generic problem is promotion of controlled inquiry. . . .Since the required control can be obtained only through the intermediation of abstract interrelated conceptions, inductive existential determinations are conducted with constant reference to institution and application of conceptions deductively interrelated with one another, while the conceptions are chosen and ordered with reference to ultimate existential application. . . .As far as *processes* of inquiry are concerned, there is no difference between induction and deduction. Sagacity in evaluation. . .cherishing and development of suggestion, a keen eye for relevant analogies, tentative experimentation [et cetera]. . .are all demanded whether the subject-matter is observational or conceptual; that is whether the *function* of the subject-matter is. . .inductive or deductive. The distinction between induction and deduction does not lie then in the processes of inquiry but in the direction which the processes take—according as the objective is determination of relevant and effective existential

data or relevant and effective interrelated conceptions [1938, 484, (emphasis in original)].

Institutionalists, employing instrumental logic and methodologies, utilize deductive and inductive procedures as inquiry options that set directional pursuits. But each, by itself, is demonstrably *incomplete*. Logically and processually, inquiry is *neither* deductive *nor* inductive; it is *both*. What is missing is that strategically determinant element of instrumental inquiry, the creation and testing of *hypotheses*.

An hypothetisis, as noted above, is the imaginative fashioning of a provisional and/or exploratory causal explanation of observed phenomena. A plausible, but as yet unestablished, speculative account may be stimulated by preliminary observation of facts. We reaffirm that the central function of hypotheses in instrumental inquiry is to guide and direct inquiry in search of conjugate correspondence of theory and fact. The process of instrumental inquiry, then, consists in large part of the continued framing, testing, revising and affirming of generalities that originate as hypotheses. The process is unending; there are only tentative terminations. There is no final answer to an instrumental query. Every tentative conclusion can be brought up again for consideration and verification of its adequacy and relevance to social and economic problem solving.

In sum, deduction, induction, and hypothesis creation will most certainly be involved in any demonstrably scientific social inquiry. In drawing particular inferences from already affirmed basic constructs, deductive insights may be provided. In drawing inferences from particular, observed data, inductive generalities may be contributed. In fashioning initial and tentative accounts of causal phenomena, hypothetical explanations are created and operationally guide subsequent inquiry in quest of warrantable assertions. In Foster's conception of scientific analysis, the knowledge generated by this mode of inquiry is itself a continuum, a process. It never "arrives" except provisionally; it is always enroute. Its "givens" are never uncritically "taken." It is a processual, aggregative inquiry process that adds warrantable assertions to the emerging knowledge fund. This is the character of scientific economics.

OBJECT OF SOCIAL INQUIRY

As is indicated above, inquiry is and must be processual because the existential experience that is addressed in social problem solving, is itself processional! Human experience is a continuum, *unexceptionally*. The social process is the continuing and encompassing object of inquiry in social science. Inquiry tools, incorporating or reflecting that processual universe, must be fashioned and employed in recognition of that continuing reality. While the physical ("hard") sciences are directed to such physical processes as energy generation and dissipation, reproductive options and constraints, and chemical pollutants and removal, social inquiry addresses the processual functions of human culture and the implementing institutional structures that, through adjustments, provide for species development and cultural continuity. In Foster's words:

> Scientific principles, in whatever area, are statements of continuing factors which are uniformly applicable to all items in the area of inquiry. In social

> science the area of inquiry is the social process, and so any principle for which generality and foundation might be claimed must be applicable to all aspects of that process. . . .[T]he social science area of inquiry is a process; it does not present a static picture of any particular pattern of structural parts. Instead, no fact of human history is more obtrusive than that institutions change structurally. The only continuing factors involved are the functions which are carried on through institutions—the institutions themselves vary from culture to culture and over time in any particular culture. And so the general principles of the social process must be drawn in terms of the functions which comprise that process (1981, 931).

The distinction Foster makes between social function and social structure is fundamental in his social inquiry. Social functions are continuing *foci* of human activity. Social institutions are, for Foster, "prescribed (or proscribed) patterns of correlated human behavior" in the differing areas of activity. Social functions are broadly continuous; structures are potentially discontinuous and replacemental. Continuity is provided through institutional adjustments.

Foster identifies the continuing and encompassing economic function as the provision of the means of human life and experience. The correlative political function is the determination and administration of public policy. More particular foci of activity can easily be derived from the politico-economic functions, e.g. education, transport, communication. All human societies, in some measure, create and sustain institutional structures to carry on these and other continuing activities in the social process. That continuation is provided through institutional adjustments that create, modify, reconstitute "prescribed patterns of correlated human activity." (We consider Foster's theory of institutional adjustment in Chapter 5).

The structural fabric of any community, then, is extraordinarily complex; it is comprised of myriads of institutional forms and patterns that have become habitual. It is sometimes characterized as reflecting the mores principle: "Habits of action and thought constitute the established behavior patterns of individuals and therefore constitute the structure of institutions" (1948a, 111-12). Most behaviors necessarily are habitual; human lives are largely comprised of repetitious conduct, ordinary routines, accommodations to custom, observed conventions, et cetera. The mores principle, that people are products of culture, is descriptively correct.

But Foster is adamant in insisting that, while most behavior is in fact habitual, as the mores principle suggests, habits are not the *source* of changes in habits. Institutions emerge only as choices. Veblen is mistaken, argues Foster when he contends that "institutions are an outgrowth of habit" that the "growth of culture is a cumulative sequence of habituation, and the ways and means of it are the habitual response of human nature to exigencies that vary incontinently, cumulatively, but with something of a consistent sequence in the cumulative variations that so go forward" [Veblen (1919) 1961, 241; quoted by Foster 1981, 917]. On the contrary, argues Foster:

> The causal sequences involved and the determination of an institution. . .necessarily require initiation. . . .Initiation requires purposeful behavior. It requires the making of a choice and thus involvement of value theory. . . .The initial performance of a behavior requires choice and choice involves reason. Institutions are in fact initiated out of actions which are themselves efforts to

> solve problems. They are not and cannot be [the consequences of] incontinent habituation [1948a, 113].

One important implication of the foregoing is the contradiction of the view that institutions arise "spontaneously," that somehow they are inadvertent, unreflective, transformations of conduct. Foster is arguing that the modification of any habitual pattern *(a)* requires some conceptual comprehension of, and behavioral response to, demonstrated inadequacies present in current institutional structure; and *(b)* some conscious deliberative election of alternative structure or behavior. A criterion of choice is inherently and necessarily employed in any such judgments.

Accordingly, institutional structures that organize and facilitate the social process are being transformed continuously as new structures, new routines, new prescriptive arrangements are initiated and/or old structures, routines, or arrangements are abandoned or revamped. In some significant measure institutional forms are constantly undergoing adjustments or modifications through the exercise of discretion, e.g., the creation and implementation of governmental policies. The social process continuously incorporates institutional adjustments. Some new laws, statutes, procedural rules, et cetera, may restrospectively appear as wise or foolish. But that distinction itself depends on acquired knowledge and relevant experience. The source and character of institutional change is a continuing concern to those who are most directly affected by proffered adjustments. Initiations and applications of new knowledge are a major source of insights that bring existing structures under review as being in some sense demonstrably problematic. Other disrupting elements in the social process that may create pressure for institutional change would include, for example, *(a)* the use of power, by a political elite, that adversely affects the larger community generally; *(b)* environmental hazards, actual or perspective, that threaten community continuity; *(c)* applications of new knowledge as technological innovations the incorporation of which invalidates existing routines and structures.

NATURE OF SCIENTIFIC TRUTH

We are confronted continuously with the outcomes (physical and social) of scientific inquiry. That the impact of these outcomes on cultures is often dramatic, that their employment may or may not be constructive, needs no reinforcement here. Continuing reflection on, and assessment of, the character and application of those outcomes are essential if we are to gain increasing skills and capacities to create and manage our own futures. Foster's conception of the character and employment of scientific outcomes, the nature of scientific truths, will provide an epistemological basis for the remaining chapters of this exploration of his contribution.

We begin *(a)* with Foster's distinction between warranted knowledge (what he calls Knowledge 1 in his lectures) and private knowledge (his Knowledge 2), and their implications. We continue *(b)* by briefly distinguishing between the instrumentalist conception of truth as "warranted assertions" and various non-scientific truth claims. We consider *(c)* a heterodox institutionalist version of correspondence and coherence theories of truth. Truth claims can be appraised.

Character of Knowledge

Foster distinguishes between warranted and private knowledge. The former, "Knowledge 1" in his usage, is an emerging product of scientific inquiry. The latter, his "Knowledge 2," is non-public and ungrounded; it is logically and analytically irrelevant to causal inquiry, arguments to the contrary notwithstanding.

Warranted Knowledge

As observed above, warranted knowledge is created with, and consists of, the "placement of an item in the continuum of which it is a part." Its emergence is empirically identified as an element in process; it is connected to other elements in a context of causal linkages and continuity. Its referential content has meaning only in its relatedness to other items. Instrumental theory explains causal linkages. As Foster explains:

> Knowledge. . .is involved in all theory. . . .You can have knowledge of a theory, a theory can be knowledge, but so can an item of which that theory is composite. . . .You can have knowledge of something. . .only in so far as you can place it causally in the continuum of which it is a part. That placement we call knowledge. That placement involves comprehension of the causal relationships with the other items in the continuum. . .and that, of course is an operation of theory (1948a, 67).

Warranted knowledge is public knowledge in the sense that its contents can be and are communicated to and among persons. The causal continuum is no less than the cumulative and expanding fund of reliable knowledge developed, preserved and continuously revised as a social and public activity and responsibility. The reliability of Foster's "Knowledge 1," warranted knowledge, rests upon its capabilities of demonstrating causality. The functional operations of inquiry that generate warranted knowledge embody instrumental logic and causal analyses.

The growth of warranted knowledge, as perceived by Erich Zimmerman (1951, 7) and Clarence E. Ayres (1944, 112), is a consequence of the invention of new *combinations* of existing tools, physical and conceptual. These scholars were, in particular, trying to erase "the fallacy that invention is a matter of human genius, that it springs out of creative potency," that it is independent of culture, and that the social context and structure of communities is of little import. Foster accepts their view of knowledge growth, but suggests that it is incomplete.

> The fact seems to me to be that invention may also be not combinational but extensional, linearly extensional, not compositionally extensional. . . .[W]e do in fact extend, create, right down the line without combination. . . .[We] conceive new forms which are a modification of a particular form, not a combination of previously existing forms. . . .The most frequent invention, of course, is a combination of already existing forms, but invention also is a modification of a particular item only in reference to the function of the item

not in reference to other items which have other functions [1948a, 76, (emphasis added)].

By new combinations and extensions of tools, theories, constructs, the growth of warranted knowledge, social and physical, continues and accelerates especially where institutional controls are permissive and supportive. In sum, "the more you know [in the] Knowledge 1 [sense], the more you can learn. The more you can create, the more you can comprehend [in] addition. . .to what you now comprehend" (1948a, 77). When and under what circumstances, then, can the warranted assertions of "Knowledge 1" inquiry enjoy truth status? Can truth claims be made in a manner that is both logically credible and experientially pertinent? Foster rarely used the term "truth" in his own theorizing; he preferred instead to join Dewey in perceiving the outcomes of successful inquiry to be "warranted assertions." The quest for Foster's "truth" involves discovery, not excavation; procedures, not a priority; credibility, not presumption; creativity, not deference.

Private Knowledge

Private knowledge, Foster's "Knowledge 2," is perceived as an independent identification; its meaning is self-contained. It exhibits no causal linkages with any other items. The conceiver of private knowledge can discuss it with others but cannot empirically identify or causally place it. Neither its source nor its specific character can be communicated unambiguously. One can insist on its existence within his/her own head, but in no demonstrable way can it be shown to be a factual determinant of behavior. The question of its proof cannot be raised. As Foster observed: "It literally and exactly is impossible to know something independently of everything else. You can believe something on quite other grounds in private comprehension, but you can't operate socially on any . . .[such] grounds" [1948a, 70]. Words convey meaning as their commonly accepted referential contents are communicated and made part of the lingual currency of the culture. The "meanings" comprising private knowledge cannot be communicated in terms that disclose their character or content. There is no intellectual or social continuum of which they could in any evidential sense be a part. As we shall see below, neoclassicists' hedonistic preferences and utilitous satisfactions, per se, are affirmations of private knowledge and cannot be included in any inquiry model purporting to explain, in causal terms, social and economic phenomena, or to recommend or judge economic policy.

"Knowledge 2," then, is analytically sterile; it can generate no ideational progeny; it is irrelevant to substantive social inquiry. "You cannot in fact apply Knowledge 2 in. . .social analysis" (Foster, 1948a, 79). People do, and will continue to, hold elements of private knowledge. But the inability to verify, to demonstrate, to ascribe causality, to place in a causal context, moves this form of "knowledge" wholly outside the focus and realm of social scientific inquiry. "The effort at independent identification of anything is beyond the realm of social theory" (69-70). Taking "wants as given," then, as in neoclassicism, is to ground economic inquiry on "Knowledge 2," and therewith to abandon relevance to problem solving. In sum, "'Knowledge 2' isn't knowledge. It is not continuous. It plays out, it fills, it stops. It isn't knowledge because it has no possible verification in the sense of truth. Truth is inseparable from continuity" (1948a, 77).

Truth Claims

Foster, an ardent student of John Dewey, as noted, invokes and defends a theory of inquiry that incorporates Dewey's instrumental logic and generates warranted knowledge, "Knowledge 1," above. It will be helpful briefly to compare and contrast this instrumental theory of Foster with other, perhaps more conventional theories. In particular, our purpose is to better distinguish Foster's methodology from competing orthodox modes of inquiry and to bring an institutionalist process of knowing more sharply into view.

The Foster legacy may be perceived in part as an extension and application of Dewey's instrumentalism.[2] Accordingly, for Foster: "Science is the conceptual apprehension of causal sequence. Knowledge is the correct placement of items of experience (behavioral and conceptual) in the causal sequence of which they are a part. Logic is the effort at conceptual formulation of causal interconnectedness in conjugate correspondence with existential reality" (1943, 2). We seek here particularly to augment the referential content of the expression, "conjugate correspondence," already introduced, by contrasting it with neoclassical approaches.

Instrumental theory, "Knowledge 1," is not foundationalist.[3] It does not involve the formulation of "eternal verities, first principles, or essences." It does not abstract from the realities of actual human experience. It does not assume, nor provide an inquiry role for, the existence or relevance of idealistic utopias, natural law premises, Platonic absolutes, or of any other "quest for certainty" (Dewey). Dependence in inquiry on some preinquiry philosophical "given" that itself is not a product or an object of causal inquiry, renders the inquiry process irrelevant to the identification and resolution of human problems. Accordingly, the neoclassical assertions of natural economic "laws" of maximization, of tendencies toward equilibriums, of ordered preference functions, of alleged "in the long run" stabilizations, et cetera, are unacceptable tenets for scientific, institutionalist economic inquiry.

Instrumental theory, "Knowledge 1," is not dualistic, philosophically or analytically, unlike neoclassicism. The Cartesian dualisms reflected in neoclassicism are: mind-body (rational maximizing vs. utilitous satiating), knowing-doing (deductive logic vs. empirical behavior), value-fact (philosophical norms vs. evidential inquiry), normative-positive (what ought vs. what is), and ends-means (given ends vs. market means). They involve the assertion of, and the grounding of inquiry on, anterior metaphysical premises that divorce one paired construct from the other. That is, they share no common origin, content or reality. Such dualistic tenets and assumptions are rooted, then, in some version of "Knowledge 2." As Bush observes, "it matters not whether the neoclassical economist professes to be a positivist or a Popperian in methodological orientation because Cartesianism is common to both" (1993, 65). Postulated here is a world of dual reality: one part is non-evidential, presumptuous, revered, unexaminable analytically; the other part consists of evidential facts and experience. The former is presumed to define and guide the latter. This dualistic assumptive template proposes a fantasy world that is irrelevant to economic problem solving; indeed its dominion precludes both inquiry and problem solving based on "Knowledge 1."

Truth Theories

Finally, instrumental theory reflects both a correspondence and a coherence theory of truth, but each is a departure from the respective conventional characterizations of these positions: The conventional correspondence theory holds that "knowledge is achieved through the accuracy of representation of nature." Given the deference to the Cartesian dualism of objective-subjective, "the truth of a proposition (which is subjective) is established if it "corresponds" to the facts (which are objective)" (Bush 1993, 67). Dewey's unease with the conventional view is reflected in his "wondering at how something in experience could be asserted to correspond to something by definition outside of experience" (Dewey, quoted by Bush, 68). A leap of faith is required, manifesting Foster's "Knowledge 2." For Foster, the instrumentalist quest for correspondence is to establish "a conjugate correlation of ideas and facts." Provisional correspondence is disclosed if, in the proposing and testing of hypothetical accounts of observable phenomena, an item can be placed in the causal continuum of which it is a part; its causal linkage and processual role are identified. Knowledge via correspondence is achieved.

The conventional coherence theory of truth holds that the truth of a "proposition can only be determined by establishing whether it coheres with other propositions we already know to be true." But the nature of the "other propositions" are "metaphysical preconceptions of idealists" (Bush 1993, 69). They are philosophical assertions in the category of Foster's "Knowledge 2"—ungrounded, apriori, non-causally constituted premises. Coherence for Foster and institutionalists is an analytical linking of the experiential with the hypothetical, of the actual and the plausible. "Dewey's conception of the continuity of inquiry incorporates notions of coherence and holism. . .warranted assertions build on one another to achieve a coherent pattern that produces a unified whole" (Bush 1993, 69). Coherence is a function of causally perceived interrelatedness. Warranted generalities, then, may provide a pattern that discloses coherence. That pattern itself may serve as an analytical tool for subsequent inquiry.

Foster's model of inquiry, then, is devoid of foundationalist presumptions, Cartesian dualisms, idealist metaphysics, and a prioristic limitations. His quest, and that of institutionalists generally, is for "Knowledge 1." Instrumental inquiry can generate the warrranted knowledge and analytical tools needed to diagnose and reform non-functional, impeding, discriminatory institutional arrangements that sabotage the economic provisioning process.

In sum, Foster demonstrates that economics can be a science. "The subject-matter of economics is existential, and the causal relationships of the items in the continuum with which economics is directly concerned are subject to intellectual comprehension and conceptual formulation." In other sciences, "(r)elated causal sequences were conjoined. . .wherein each item had meaning in terms of its relation to the other items in its sequence. Thereafter, no magic revelation is necessary to give significance to the items whose correlativity with other existential items had been established" [(1942a) 1981, 880-81]. Economics is an inquiry mode generating "Knowledge 1." There are no "ultimates" (e.g. ,market equilibriums) in economics that are beyond inquiry. Neoclassicists' "goblins of childhood," e.g.,(market imperfections, intrusive governments); their "occult interpretations" rooted in utilitous feeling-states; their deference to innate maximizing rationality; their presumption of natural market forces; their evasion of accountability for "market driven" outcomes, combine to place orthodox neoclassical economics largely in the category of Foster's Knowledge 2. Contemporary economics can be, but is not yet, a social science.

ENDNOTES

[1]This conception of "rationality," obviously departs dramatically from the conventional neoclassical referent in which humanoids are perceived to be rational maximizers of utility rather than comprehenders and manipulators of causal phenomena. While we cannot pursue the matter in this context, we return to this distinction in Chapter 6.

[2]An exceptionally helpful exploration of these and related topics will be found in Paul D. Bush's "The Methodology of Institutional Economics" (1993).

[3]I draw especially on the Bush analysis (1993) in these next few paragraphs.

REFERENCES

Ayres, Clarence E. (1944) 1978. *The Theory of Economic Progress.* 3rd ed. Kalamazoo: New Issues Press, Western Michigan University.

Bush, Paul D. 1993. "The Methodology of Institutional Economics: A Pragmatic Instrumentalist Perspective." In *Institutional Economics: Theory, Method, Policy.* Marc R. Tool, ed. Boston: Kluwer Academic Publishers.

Dewey, John. 1938. *Logic: The Theory of Inquiry.* New York: Holt, Rinehart and Winston.

Foster, J. Fagg. (1942a) 1981. John Dewey and economic value. *Journal of Economic Issues;* 15:871-97.

———. (1942b) 1981. The approach to land use planning in a changing technology. *Journal of Economic Issues*; 15:985-1007.

———. 1943a. Uncertain objectivity, magic and logic: hedonistic goblins. Mimeographed 1-6.

———. (1943b?) 1981, The theory of institutional adjustment. *Journal of Economic Issues;* 15:923-28.

———. 1947. Syllabus for Problems of Modern Society; the theory of institutional adjustment. *Journal of Economic Issues;* 15:929-35.

———. 1948a. *Value and Its Determinants.* Lectures Notes (LN). Taped by Harry Brown; transcribed by Gladys P. Foster; computer printout, bound, 1-382.

———. 1948b. The character of the process and the specific identification of the theory of value. Typescript 1-4.

———. (1963) 1981. Environmental control. *Journal of Economic Issues; 15*:1009-12.

———. (1969) 1981. Economics. *Journal of Economic Issues;15*:857-69.

———. (n.d). Philosophy and science. Mimeographed 1-2.

Lawson, Tony. 1997. *Economics and Reality.* London: Routledge.

Malinowski, Bronislaw. (1944) 1960. *A Scientific Theory of Culture.* NY: Oxford. University

Ogden, C.K. & I.A. Richards. 1946 (8th ed). *The Meaning of Meaning.* New York: Harcourt, Brace & Co.

Randall, John Herman Jr. 1940. *The Making of the Modern Mind.* Cambridge: The Riverside Press.

Tool, Marc R. (1979, 1985) 2000. *The Discretionary Economy.* Piscataway, NJ: Transaction Press

Zimmerman, Erich. 1951. *World Resources and Industries,* rev.ed. New York: Harper and Brothers.

3 A CRITIQUE OF UTILITY VALUE

Veblen compelled. . . economists to search their hearts lest the truth be not in them . P. T. Homan

INTRODUCTION

For something over two centuries in the West, most of those engaged in formal inquiry into the economic process, have sought to demonstrate, in one fashion or another, that *utility* is the meaning of value in all manner of economic decision making and that *price* is its measure, its theory of valuation. Utility continues to be presented in neoclassicism, directly or by implication, as the inclusive and applicable criterion of judgment in the making of decisions concerning all aspects of the production and distribution of real income. Utility, in this context, is the ability of goods and services to generate satisfaction for participants in the creation and exchange of goods. Market participation, then, is thought to be driven by the quest to maximize utility and to minimize disutility. So much is, in general, familiar, but it has become a "familiarity that breeds contempt." It continues to corrupt and/or preclude genuine problem solving in the economic process.

Over the last century, beginning with Thorstein Veblen, and including John Dewey and Clarence Ayres, only the institutionalists have profoundly challenged this most basic tenet of orthodox economic inquiry. In recent decades, this institutionalist challenge has been mounted by Fagg Foster and other recent students of this alternate tradition. It is the purpose of this Chapter to explore Foster's comprehensive critique of utility value theory and its implications. It is the purpose of the following Chapter 4 to present and explore Foster's alternative theory of value, instrumental efficiency of the social process, as a necessary replacement for orthodoxy's utility value theory.

To present and develop Foster's critique of utility value theory we consider the following topics: *(a)* value theory in economic analysis; *(b)* avoidance and evasion of value analysis; *(c)* emergence of utility as a criterion of value; *(d)* an institutionalist critique of utility value theory.

VALUE THEORY IN ECONOMIC ANALYSIS

In social analysis, scholars require an explanation of the criterion (or criteria) that does or should guide the making of judgments in social and economic inquiry. If inquiry involves choice, and it does, the framing of, and the making of choices between or among alternatives, inescapably requires the employment of some standard of judgment, some criterion in terms of which the choice between or among options is made. *Value theory identifies and explains criteria of judgment.* If inquiry is to have significance in the sense of adding insight into, and comprehension of causal phenomena, it must include a credible and applicable criterion of value. Such a criterion is a critical analytical tool that provides an operationally employable distinction between "what is" and "what ought to be."

Foster briefly addresses the relation between value theory and social analysis as follows:

> The thing to look for in identifying "value" is the criterion of judgment applied in choosing between alternatives when solving problems. The successful continuation of human experience necessarily involves solving problems—resolving situations which infringe on the continuity of the social process and therefore necessarily involves value. To admit the character of the social process and to claim that value theory need not enter in as a determinant of human behavior is. . .[indefensible]. To assume that value theory need not be applied is to set up a paradox: to explain something without considering the determinants of that which you seek to explain. To describe something without consciously considering a part of the phenomenon being described is . . .[unacceptable]. That value theory, in the sense of [a] criterion of judgment, is applied to social situations is a fact. The problem is to establish the validity of the criterion being employed [Foster 1950 (LN) Value, 1].

AVOIDANCE AND EVASION OF VALUE ANALYSIS

Many conventional, orthodox economists and other social scientists seek for various reasons to avoid or evade considering the matter of value judgments in social analysis. One of the purposes of the present discussion is to demonstrate that value theory is inherently a part of economic analysis, claims to the contrary notwithstanding. Two examples of expedient but unsuccessful avoidance follow:

Avoidance of Value Analysis

First, many can accept that economics is concerned with providing the means of life, but some argue that it must be accomplished within an existing institutional order. Their support for the status quo, with whatever perquisites and power it generates and distributes, especially for elitist segments of the community, is insensitive to system deficiencies, inequities and blockages. Foster observes that: "The proponents of this expedient frequently take the position that economics cannot be concerned with economic problems, that economics may be occupied only with describing what goes on" [Foster (1949) 1981, 903]. Those who benefit substantially from the existing institutional array will be wary of any attempts at significant adjustments of institutional structure, in the private or the public sector, that threaten their present income, status and discretion. Economics is seen by them, then, as a description of "what is", not as a vehicle through which to reach "what ought to be" (903). This poses an irresolvable contradiction: Problem solving requires institutional change; the existing power groups oppose institutional adjustments that threaten the continuity of their status and power.

Second, a less obvious avoidance of recourse to value theory in general, and instrumental value theory in particular, Foster observes, is found in the prevalent practice of orthodox economists to *identify price and value* even as they also attempt to deny normative concerns in economic analysis. Value for the orthodox is properly a topic of concern for philosophers, not for economists. But note that their "etymological error" of identifying value and price very well serves their simultaneous claims and disclaims to normative analysis. Foster explains:

> Through this device [of identifying value and price] recent economic orthodoxy has managed to lay claim to generality and foundation, to lay claim to significance and at the same time to avoid all responsibility for doing more than describing relative prices. This conjoinment of unlimited significance and complete irresponsibility is accomplished by tacitly, and perhaps unconsciously, reversing the direction of identity between price and value, by asserting that value is merely another way of saying price, which means simply ratios of exchange, and then by proceeding as if price means value and therefore that price serves as the criterion of judgment in choosing between alternatives [Foster (1949) 1981, 903]. If the identification runs from *price to value*, and if price is used to mean simply and only ratios of exchange, then the identification has no significance beyond release from the tedium of a constant linguistic repetition [904, emphasis added].
>
> But. . .if the identification runs from *value to price*, then the equation takes on an importance that cannot be exaggerated. . . .[P]rice would be held to represent real worth (under whatever definition) and there could then be no necessity for economic analysis to go beyond the determinants of price. . . . [T]hen the revelation of the principles of price determination and the pattern of their interworking, the general price theory, would be the general theory of the economic process. And the revelation of the determinants of price would, *ipso facto*, be the revelation of the fundamental determinants of the economic process. It is this significance that is imputed to the identification of price and value by the insistence that economics be restricted to price analysis. . . .The insistence that economic theory be restricted to price theory must be either an abandonment of its function. . .and significance or. . .a claim that price measures real value [Foster (1949) 1981, 904, (emphasis added)].

Among those who identify value and price, are neoclassicists who "take the position that there is no need in economic theory to bother with value because wants can be taken as given, and that, since relative intensities of wants are brought toward equilibrium in an open market, no investigation and no theoretical formulation beyond the market is necessary" (904). Accordingly, for the neoclassicists, markets function to generate satisfaction of wants in a context where neither markets nor wants can be addressed in either an experiential or a normative context. Wants are given; orthodoxy purports to *eschew value theory.* Foster responds:

> [T]he things people want are a function of their social experience, and that is carried on through structural institutions that specify their activities and attitudes. Thus, the pattern of a people's wants takes visible form partly as a result of the pattern of the institutional structure through which they participate in the economic process. . . .[T]o say that an economic problem exists is to say that part of that structure. . .has ceased or failed to provide for the effective participation of its members. . . .We are necessarily. . .asserting that the instrumental efficiency of the economic process is the criterion of judgment in terms of which, and only in terms of which, we may resolve economic problems. In fact, we either must accept economic efficiency, in the instrumental sense, as the criterion of judgment, or we must revise the universally accepted conception of what constitutes an economic problem. Between these alternatives, there is only one rational choice because an economic problem is a conjuncture of factual circumstance, the effects of which can neither be avoided or denied [Foster (1949) 1981, 904-905].

Evasion of Value Analysis

Following is a prologue for the discussion and comparison, in this Chapter and the Chapter to follow, of neoclassicists' utility theory of value and institutionalists' instrumental efficiency theory of value. It may be instructive, however tersely, to consider some philosophical positions and characterizations that would, if employed, wholly preclude the fashioning and use of instrumental value, or any encompassing value theory. There is no presumption here of definitiveness. We wish only to locate, characterize and distinguish between the theoretical positions and postures of institutional instrumentalists and those of neoclassical utilitarians regarding value theory and its applications. Foster did not dwell at length on the following characterizations of nihilism, absolutism, positivism, and relativism except as comments "in passing" or as asides, in the course of identifying his general analytical positions. It will be helpful, even so, briefly to canvass and critique this array of philosophic characterizing constucts all of which perceive, but in different ways, value theory to be irrelevant or impossible of formulation and hence of no analytic or scientific significance. Value precepts are evaded and/or distorted in the following:

Nihilism

Nihilism will not long detain us. This "philosophy" of extreme skepticism denies all meaning in human life. It urges a comprehensive denial of value and valuation and of theories thereof. For nihilists, inquiry is pointless; human life is senseless; there is no meaning, no purposiveness in life, economic or otherwise. Alleged realities are delusional; judgments are illusions; morality is nonexistent. It offers no perception of social or economic problems. Searching for meaning in human existence is futile; widely shared beliefs are rejected. Value constructs are mere contrivances; value premises are irrelevant.

Neither instrumental theorists nor utility theorists accede or defer to these dicta. Foster did observe, however, that in some problematic circumstances, relativist theorizing, because of its normative ambivalence, can degenerate into nihilism.

Absolutism

For absolutists, value is a presumption, a given; it is not an object of inquiry. Absolutist criteria are reflected in dogmatic postures and rationalizations of power over other peoples' behavior: *(a)* Absolute tenets are imbedded in beliefs that sustain those in religious hierarchies who, as the "chosen" few, demand normative deference to an almighty supernatural being and to the "earthly" religious tenets and structures of divine rule. *(b)* Absolutist criteria are revealed in the a priori givenness of the natural rights doctrine, the natural-law principle, and its institution of private property. *(c)* Absolutist criteria are reflected in the dicta of a status-conscious ruler and the institutional givens of royal succession and autocratic hegemony. *(d)* The absolutist normative posture is exhibited also in the uncompromising ideology of a Platonic order as hierarchy, Marxist history as class conflict, and other Utopian models as panaceas. *(e)* The deference by utilitarians to free unfettered markets borders on the absolute.

For absolutists, scientific analysis of social value is pointless. Inquiry is merely a disclosure of antecedent assumptions and tenets. Absolutist dicta from lay or religious despots are not objects of inquiry or discussion; they are impositions. Their universe of "ought to be" is a world of command and obedience; not one of inquiry and cooperation. Achieved power is its own reward; value is defined as pursuit of invidious and self-serving interests. Status supported by power is the only social reality. The acceptance of, and deference to, absolute rule, idea, power or privilege is the fundamental tenet providing social order.

Positivism

Positivists acknowledge only the reality of empirical facts, of observable phenomena. They argue that virtually all intellectual propositions of significance can be scientifically verified or falsified. Indeed their inquiry is delimited by this distinction. Value is allegedly nonfactual, therefore it is not relevant to, nor a part of, social inquiry. Positivists, then, bifurcate the existential world. Knowledge and value have no common content; the former addresses what factually is; the latter addresses what ought to be. Ontologically, positivists are concerned with that which is empirically real; non-positivists explore the "un-real" world of hypothetical conjecture and public purpose. Methodologically, positivists explore the empirical reality of "what is"; normativists pursue the processual forms of "what ought to be." The positivist agenda for inquiry defines the character and extent of the universe of social inquiry. It specifies the character and extent of questions that may be posed and the sort of answers that are admissible in response. We extend this critique below in consideration of this normative-positive dualism .

Relativism

For relativists, knowledge, truth, and value, are relative to the culture accrediting them; they are not absolutes. Relativism, although a significant departure from nihilism, absolutism and positivism, is normatively ambivalent. Ethical relativists insist that there are no universal and objective ethical criteria available. No value premise can be accorded truth status. There is no generally objective standard of value, truth or beauty. Any value tenet is culturally specific to the sponsoring group; there are no cross-cultural criteria of analysis or behavior. Cultural realities are admitted, but they are specific to each particular community. The historical tradition of the utilitarians embodies ethical and cultural relativism.

In sum, traditional neoclassical economics is not necessarily nihilistic or absolutist, but it generally is both positivistic and relativistic. Institutionalists flatly reject the nihilistic and absolutist characterizations of earlier doctrines. Neither can their theory be characterized as positivistic and relativistic. Foster's theory of instrumental value substantively rejects all four as defining philosophical characterizations in social inquiry. Indeed it exhibits no common content with nihilism and absolutism and perceives positivism and relativism, respectively, to be grossly inadequate and quite unacceptable as well. The pragmatic instrumentalism of Foster wholly rejects the normative-positive dualistic contructs, identifies an experience-based value principle, locates it evidentially in the social process, and demonstrates its relevance for actual problem solving. Instrumental value theory brings objectivity, evidential substance and broad applicability to social problem analysis. For institutionalists, as we explain in the following Chapter, value in economics is instrumental efficiency of the economic process.

EMERGENCE OF UTILITY AS A CRITERION OF VALUE

It has historically been, and remains, commonplace for authors in the mainstream tradition of economics to disclaim interest in normative inquiry or value theory. They deny concern with criteria of value and their rationale. The historic belief has been that economics is a positivist science and analytically has nothing in common with normativist value theory. Value theory is perceived as inapplicable to scientific economics. They are alleged to be mutually incompatible constructs.

Actually, of course, this neoclassical tradition is one in which utility (satisfaction of wants and tastes) has long been the meaning of value and price has been its measure (i.e. the theory of valuation). Although scholars profess to eschew normative judgments, because they believe they rest upon philosophical and ontological tenets that are incompatible with those of scientific economics, they are and have been normativists all along. It is the *character* of their value theory that is at issue. Their contention is that value theory is inapplicable in economics. Foster vigorously refutes these disclaimers. In this section, we briefly explore *(a)* the historical development of utility as a criterion of value, and *(b)* neoclassical versions of utility value, In the following section, we review Foster's critique of utility theory and its successors in some detail.

Historical Development of Utililty Value

The Greeks

The utility theory of value, as with much else in formal social thought, evidently originated with Greek scholars, especially Aristotle, as they reflected on and wrote about "community policy and social analysis generally" [Foster (1942), 1981, 882]. Although Aristotle seems not to have formally identified a value principle, it is implied, for example, in his classic statement about the dual uses of possessions. As often quoted: "The uses of every possession are two, both indeed essential but not in the same manner, for the one is strictly proper to the thing, the other is not; as a shoe. . .may be either worn or exchanged for something else; both these are uses of the shoe"(882). For Aristotle, utility is the underlying, but unidentified, principle of value; labor is the measure. Use value reflects utility value; exchange value provides pecuniary access to utility value. The former is the "proper" usage; exchange value is "improper" usage but the latter is necessarily present. "He [Aristotle] seems to have had an idea of just price as the exchange of equal values in terms of labor"(882).

Foster indicates that "Aristotle anticipated the content and rationale of every subsequent theory of value" except for the instrumentalists' value principle. He was evidently not only the original source of the use-value and exchange-value distinction but he condemned usury, as did the Canonists; he offered, but disavowed, the Mercantilists' "bullion-wealth idea," and provided the "cue about land as the source of values," later eulogized by the Physiocrats. "Aristotle considered value incidentally in his major concern, which was 'justice.' He had no positive theory of value; value is an assumption taking the form of utility and measured by labor" (882).

The Canonists

The Canonists, drawing especially on Aristotle, offered and sustained the concept of "just price" through most of early Christian Europe even though its specific referential content was often unclear. The concept of "just price" seemed to imply exchange on the basis of labor cost. Given political control by the Church, however, as trade developed "the opposition of the churchmen managed to flex enough to allow practices which could hardly be done away with. Acquinas allowed variation from the 'just price' just as he allowed profit, on the basis of necessity resulting from the 'fallen state of man'. . . .The merchant was allowed profit as payment for his labor only, but it was to be enough to keep him at his *accustomed* standard of living [Foster (1942) 1981, 883, emphasis in original]. . . .A century after Saint Thomas, the justness of price was expounded by Saint Antonino on the basis of the concept of disutility. . . .With an occult ultimate, anything can be rationalized as a means" (883, emphasis in original). But Canonist doctrine was largely abandoned as a guide to economic conduct with the advent of the Reformation.

The Mercantilists

The emergence of post-feudal institutions (e.g., organized markets controlled by merchants) and technical advances (e.g., navigational instruments, farming techniques), facilitated the rise of merchants into discretionary control of both trade and de facto public policy, and fostered the appearance of an apologia for the exercise of that control. "The merchant was sovereign and what served the merchant became the order of the day, from constitutional monarchy to a forced favorable balance of trade. . . .Notions of value were consonant with the interests of the merchant" [Foster (1942) 1981, 884]. Trade was the route to wealth, especially pecuniary wealth. Wealth was perceived as a product of shrewd exchange. "This is not a theory of value as such: it is a theory of how a nation becomes rich, how it can acquire values, whatever they are. The utility concept seems to be assumed without sufficient challenge to make it articulate. . . .Labor was the source of value but that was inconsequential; what was important was that values could be accrued by sharp trading "(884).

The Physiocrats

Continuing change in the structure and technologies of production, in the 17th and 18th centuries, shifted the focus of inquiry from trade to production, perhaps most visibly in France. The Physiocrats' views focused especially on the agricultural sector where nature labors along with man to produce the annual output. This sector in particular exhibited, given the inherent reality of a natural order, an early version of supply and demand later developed by Smith. "Physiocrats recognized *prix fondamental* (labor-cost theory), but they were more interested in *prix courant* [going price], which depended, said Quesnay 'on the rarity or abundance of production, or the more or less competition of buyers and sellers.' This, of course, anticipates the supply and demand theory held by Smith" [Foster (1942) 1981, 885, (emphasis in original)]. Foster observes that: "Throughout this period, labor is presented as the source of value, although there is no unanimity of labor as the measure of value. Here again the measure and source of value are theorized, but the nature of value is not stated. Its character is assumed, and it seems to be of the nature of the utility concept. But its explicit statement as such had to await the neoclassicists' formulation in terms of the hedonistic calculus" (885).

The Classicists

In Foster's view, classical theory is a systematic characterization of the new economic order that was evident at the end of the eighteenth century, especially in Great Britain. The elements of a comprehensive statement were available but undeveloped. Adam Smith responded with *The Wealth of Nations* (1776). It is perhaps the most important work in political economy to that date. Methodologically, Smith never wholly became a formal logician. "He kept his eye on the economy. . . and felt the necessity for a theory's meaning and validity to be in terms of its conjugate correspondence with existential phenomena" [Foster (1942) 1981, 886]. This concern with "conjugate correspondence of concept and fact . . .kept him from forming a theory that held 'universally' and 'eternally'. . . . Smith's theories were 'according to the situation.'" Capitalism was perhaps a "natural " system, meaning "normal," but it was not "inevitable, everlasting, and necessary" (886).

Smith's explanation of exchange value in a primitive economy is "the labor-cost theory." "Where labor and capital are common to the same man. . .[n]o man will exchange an object requiring more labor for one requiring less" [Foster (1942) 1981, 887]. Where labor and capital are not common to the same man, Smith proposed his "labor-command theory." Any given market value was determined by the amount of labor each of the three factors in costs could command in exchange. "The distribution of 'embodied labor' on the basis of what each factor could command occurred in the market by 'higgling and bargaining'" (887). As with Ricardo and Malthus who follow, Smith assumed that the meaning of value was utility in the sense of want-satisfying ability.

Early in the 19th century, David Ricardo, a stock broker representing the interests of industrial capitalists, differed dramatically with Thomas Robert Malthus, a clergyman representing the landed gentry, in consideration of the Corn Laws—tariffs on grain imports. Ricardo argued against the imposition of such tariffs on grain; Malthus vigorously favored such tariffs. Ricardo thought that higher prices on grain, as a consequence of the tariff, would cause a rise in the wages of labor, as a consequence of an increase in the cost of labor subsistence, and hence a fall in profits for the industrialists. Falling profits compels the rate of accumulation out of profits to drop. For Malthus, "demand" was the determinant of exchange value. "Profits could be collected only if sufficient demand were extant to withdraw the goods from the market." And it was impossible for "labor to withdraw the goods because there would be nothing left for capital." Consequently, it was from unproductive groups, especially the landlords, that effective demand derived. "[I]t follows that the greater the rents, the greater the demand and hence profits; and the higher food prices were, the greater would be rent" [Foster (1942), 1981, 888]. Accordingly, the interests of the landlords were thought to be in harmony with the interests of society in general. Thus, "for both Ricardo and Malthus. . .the *meaning* of value was assumed to be utility in the sense of want-satisfying ability." (888-89, emphasis in original). So common was this deference to utility as the meaning of value, neither one raised any question about its substance or role in inquiry; it was just the common sense of the community.

The scholarly dependence on utility as value was further reinforced by Jean Baptiste Say in 1803:

> He stated that utility is the capacity to satisfy wants and that value originates in utility. . .[therefore] price is the measure of value and. . .value is the measure of utility. He [Say] went on to show that price is the measure of value and that value is the measure of utility. Hence, price measures utility, from which it originated. Price measures (determines the amount of) utility, and utility determines price--well. well, well! Taken together with Say's law of markets, [that supply creates its own demand] everything becomes equal to everything else. . . .[Even so] Say was the first to disavow effectively the labor theory of value and attempt a direct demonstration of the reflection of utility in price" [Foster (1942) 1981, 889].

"Nassau Senior sought to retain the Ricardian analysis, modified so as to answer the difficulties involved in the labor theory of value." He admitted the cost of production theory, "which had been developed out of Ricardo's labor-cost theory, together with allowance for utility and scarcity as determinants of value. . . .In his demand and supply explanation of price, he defines demand as utility, and he defines supply as the result of three factors: abstinence, nature and labor." He argues that "the 'obstacle' to supplying goods 'consists solely in finding persons ready to submit to labor and abstinence necessary to their production.'" "Here is the justification for profits which Ricardo had not furnished. . . .Here was something that put capital ownership on the same basis as labor." The two were equated "in terms of disutility, and the. . .[validation] of ownership was complete" [Foster (1942) 1981, 889].

Neoclassical Versions of Utility Value

As with the classicists, the neoclassical world of Jevons and Marshall, et al., in the latter part of the 19th century, continued and extended the basic normative commitment of economists to utility as the meaning of value and price as its measure. Utility becomes the articulated and general referent for value. The price system is the encompassing social instrument for its realization. Foster characterizes it as follows: "Beginning in. . .the 1870s, a new twist was given to economic theory. The new, of course, had its seeds in its parent. All the items in neoclassicism were to be found, at least in rudimentary form, in the classic formulations. . .but the new is sufficiently different to warrant a separate designation and similar enough to carry the family name. It is appropriately called neoclassicism" [Foster (1942) 1981, 890].

On one occasion, Foster sought to identify for his students the similarities and differences between classical and neoclassical theory. As for *similarities* they "both used logical deductions from reasonable assumptions"; "accepted existing institutional order as given data;" "had similar concepts of nature and natural law"; "of human motivation"; and "of prevailing institutional structure as natural." They held "similar preconceptions of the driving motive of economic affairs [as]. . .the desire for profit". . .[and] characterized individuals as atomistic units.

As for their *differences*, neoclassicists shifted "emphasis from the invisible hand to the laws of the market, made a "change in theory of valuation from labor to price." They "abandoned real substance" in favor of "the numerical aspects in market place." They abandoned the distinction between "man-made and non-man-made aspects of production", and made "explicit application of hedonistic calculus in marginal analysis [Foster (CN) Neoclassical Theory 1950, 7].

These forms of comparison are amplified in Foster's further characterization of neoclassicism:

> The core of neoclassicism is embodied in. . .Jevons statement that "value depends entirely upon utility". . .He stated the idea of marginal utility. . .and developed the converse, [marginal] disutility. As conceived by the neoclassicists, utility is a function of people not a property of goods. This anthropocentricity is. . .the same old utility looked at from the other end. Jevons and Aristotle both start from the same place: human wants and the

> means for satisfying them. Human satisfactions are maximized in terms of the greatest amount of utilities through the operation of free competition in an open market. Maximum [net] utility is secured when the [marginal] disutility represented in cost equals the [marginal] utility of the good. This equilibrium state is always reached in free competition. . . .[A]ssuming perfect bargaining, bidding would occur until [marginal] disutility and [marginal] utility were equalized before any goods changed hands. Either way equilibrium results. That is to say cost equals price, and demand equals supply, and values exchange for equal values. . . .Also it is a just price since equals exchange for equals. Jevons thought so, Ricardo thought so. Aquinas thought so, and Aristotle thought so. When equals exchange for equals, and in doing so maximizes human satisfaction, certainly no objection could be offered [Foster (1942) 1981, 890-91].

Thus for decade after decade, well into the twentieth century in the English speaking world, the neoclassical school with its utility theory of value and its price theory of valuation dominated economic inquiry.

In the last half century, orthodox economists, through a variety of approaches to research and writing, have sought to salvage the neoclassical tradition by finding less obtrusive and more persuasive ways of sustaining utility as the criterion of judgment in economic analysis and of employing price as the measure in valuation. Such efforts notwithstanding, Foster acknowledges that: "institutionalists dispute the utility theory of value operational in most presentations of economic theory" [(1975) 1981, 943]. While space does not permit an elaborate listing and sorting of orthodox inquiry approaches, it is useful and instructive to mention a number of these latter day evasions/extensions, all of which directly or surreptitiously, perceive utility to be the referent for value in economic analysis.

Paretian Optimum theorists seek an ethically neutral criterion. Their construct affirms that an economic change is validated if in consequence no one feels worse off and at least one person feels better off. But as Sidney Alexander observed, "As a normative principle, the Paretian optimality corresponds roughly to a cooperative egoistic hedonism plus the assumption that the individual is the best judge of what will make him happy, an alliance among monads. Whether right or wrong, it is normative to the core" (Alexander 1967, 94). Utility value is retained.

Indifference Demand theorists purport to drop cardinally measured utility in favor of ordinally ranked utility; maximization gives way to optimization. People have preferences that they are able to rank and order. The connotation of pleasures, utility, and hedonism is thought to be abandoned. The quest for satisfaction involves shifts to higher indifference curves but not necessarily to maximizing utility. Utility value remains embedded.

Axiomatic Choice theorists (Gerard Debreu et al.) suggest that "the formulation of choice theory involves the distillation of axioms that delineate the nature of choice as involving preference relations and indifference relations" that are designed to "complete the exorcising of utility constructs." "These basic and inclusive axioms take the form of logical imperatives for the construction of judgments" (Tool 1986, 95). Preference relations reflect utility value.

Public Choice theorists brashly extend the utility maximizing, egoistic tenets of economic orthodoxy into the realm of political analysis and conduct. Politics, in their view, is fundamentally a struggle of rivalries each participant in which judges on the self-interest basis of "what's in it for me?" Political activity then is warranted by personal goals and utilitarian and power-possessing desires.

Equilibrium theorists presume to characterize the economy as reflecting a continuing balance of forces, an equilibration of pleasure and pain, of supply and demand. The equilibriums struck are thought to be a positive reality of balanced market forces that conjointly provide normative solutions. As a descriptive analytical tool it requires recourse to anterior presumptions of pleasures and pains. Utility value is omnipresent.

FOSTER'S CRITIQUE OF UTILITY VALUE THEORY

Inadequacies of Utility Value

In seeking to explain why economics and its utility value theory have not been addressed scientifically by the neoclassicists, Foster offers partial answers that include "the complexity" and "intricacy of interconnections in subject matter," "recent accumulation of requisite data," and "the assumption of an ultimate end towards which the theory must point" [Foster (1942) 1981, 892]. Man perceives himself as living apart from nature, of being outside the stream of social causation. He is desperately engaged in an effort (now quoting John Dewey 1925, 394), to

> combine the obvious empirical *fact* that objects are qualified with good and bad, with philosophic deliverances which, in isolating man from nature, qualitative individualities from the world, render this fact anomalous. The philosopher erects a "realm of values" in which to place all the precious things which are excluded from natural existence because of isolations artificially introduced. . .they are gathered up into the realm of values contradistinguished from the realm of existence. . . .Values are values, things immediately have certain intrinsic qualities [(1942) 1981, 892, (emphasis in original)].

Foster extends the argument:

> Despite the fact that *every* item of empirical evidence that man has points him out as continuous with all the remainder of the world, he still persists in thinking himself a beginning and an end all rolled into one. Then, what he "wants," he wants. Thus "wants" are taken to be basic data and need no validation outside themselves. . . .And as long as man believed "wants" as basic data, as part of the "mystery that is man," he almost of necessity believed in value as "utility" or the capacity to satisfy wants. . . .When the requisite biological and anthropological data were available, man began to realize that he was part of the total and was in no logical sense the "chosen tribe". . . .As long as he was an end value as an individual and separate entity, he could and did arbitrarily impute, through belief, any number of qualities to himself. . . .He finally built utility economic theory, which directly explained himself in terms of his "basic" nature, "wants." But then social anthropology demonstrates that "wants" are almost altogether institutional. This destroys the basic datum of man's explanation of himself in his relations with other people and with his physical environment. What then? How can he evaluate

> in regard to himself? He cannot avoid the issue. He cannot evaluate without some basis for evaluation [(1942) 1981, 892-93, (emphasis in original)].

Foster continues:

> The institutionalists contend that the classical use of the utility theory of value has attained orthodoxy not because of evidence of its validity but because of its easy service as the philosophical foundation for the classical price theory, which has become the *modus operandi* of the classic tradition. In that tradition, price theory assumes as continuing factors particular institutional structures which have attained wide viability in only two comparatively short periods in the history of economy. Price and its theory are important matters, but to assign continuity and exclusive significance to price and to its associated institutions is an arbitrary imputation. As those institutions evolve and adjust, the use of the utility theory of value in the explanation of their determination becomes more and more difficult to accredit. In contrast [as we shall see in Chapter 4] the instrumental theory of value lays easy claim to developmental continuity. Its formulation in terms of the processes carried on through institutions, rather than in terms of particular institutional structures, allows its application in the analysis of any economy, irrespective of the institutional structure and irrespective of the stage of technical development of the economy [Foster (1975) 1981, 944, (emphasis in original)].

An example of Foster's refutations of orthodoxy's normative claims and postures appears in remarks prepared for a conference in 1975 in response to the query: "What are the institutionalist saying to us?":

> [I]nstitutionalists dispute the utility theory of value operational in most presentations of economic theory and analysis. The relation between the theory of value and economic analysis is simple and easily comprehensible. The difficulties that invariably arise when the problem is under discussion spring from other sources than novelty and complexity, although those attributes are often invoked. The institutionalists contend that the character of the criterion of judgment (the theory of value) is inescapably imposed by the problem-solving process. The process requires bringing into operational rapport the component elements of a problematic situation. In applying that dictum to the economic process, the character of what is thus imposed arises out of the requirement that any successful effort at resolution of a problematic situation remove the human incidences of the problem. Conceivably, attempts to apply any one of numerous criteria might be made through fiat or through persuasion, and successful resolution may be proclaimed. But, so long as actual instrumental disrapport remains, compulsions toward efforts at resolution continue. Thus, except through sheer accident, there is no escape from using instrumental efficiency as the criterion of judgment, because that criterion is the only one conceived precisely in terms of that concept of problem solving. Thus the instrumental efficiency theory of value is made secure [(1975) 1981, 944].

Foster observes that the:

> Reaction to the demonstrated inadequacy of [utility] value theory sometimes has taken the form of nihilism and its skepticism toward meaning in any sense. Out of this attitude may come complete mental letharargy. It also is humus for positivism in the sense that a set of values may be chosen arbitrarily, and any and all rationalization necessary to its attainment is made admissible. Out of such stuff has developed the Nazi set of dicta. [Foster (1942) 1981, 891].

Foster approvingly quotes Rosser B. Melton, a colleague at the University of Texas, who offers still another implication of the historic deference in orthodoxy to utility value theory:

> The conclusion, then, to which the evidence leads, is that value theory, in every form in which it has appeared in economic writing and thinking, has been a rationalization of social status; in no case has it been scientific explanation of economic phenomena. nor has it revealed "the law of motion" of any society. There is no essential difference, so far as its intellectual and social content is concerned, between the just price of the Canonists and the value theory which corresponded to it, and the cost of production price of classical economics and the value theory which corresponded to it. The status of different groups has been rationalized by the different schools of thought, but the means of rationalization have in every instance been the same theory of value [Foster (1942) 1981, 891].

It is clear from what has already been said that Foster and the institutionalists are seeking, with other pluralists, to displace, not just share, the dominion over economic scholarship held by the neoclassicists. If there is any remaining doubt about the extent of that dominion, a brief canvass of current Principles of Economics textbooks, a review of the mainstream economic journals, and/or a quick read of the editorials in the Wall Street Journal will reconfirm the assertion. If neoclassicism, as an inquiry perspective, is ever to be displaced, the disabling limitations of utility value in orthodox theory must be explored at some length. We turn then with Foster to the task of dismantling much of orthodoxy and its dependence on utility value. We begin *(a)* with Veblen's critique of the foundation characteristics of orthodoxy and *(b)* with Foster's assessment of Veblen's views. We continue with Foster's critique of *(c)* utility value and the mores principle, *(d)* utility value and equilibrium analysis, *(e)* utility value and equational justice, and *(f)* utility value and the normative-positive distinction.

Veblen's Critique of Neoclassical Theory

Foster generally shares and draws upon Veblen's critique of neoclassical orthodoxy. The claims to significance for orthodox utility theory were challenged initially and most vigorously be Veblen. As many are aware, this critique is presented most directly and extensively in his *The Place of Science in Modern Civilization* [(1919)

1961]. Veblen's contention is that neoclassicism could not be established as a social science because its perspective is, among other characterizations, hedonistic, teleological, taxonomic and tautological. We consider each briefly:

Hedonism

Veblen's characterization of hedonistic human nature in the utilitarian tradition may well be the most quoted passage in his *Place of Science*:

> In all the received formulations of economic theory. . .the human material with which the inquiry is concerned is conceived in hedonistic terms; that is. . .in terms of a passive and substantially inert and immutably given human nature. The psychological and anthropological preconceptions of the economists have been those which were accepted by the psychological and social sciences some generations ago. The hedonistic conception of man is that of a lightning calculator of pleasures and pains, who oscillates like a homogeneous globule of desire of happiness under the impulse of stimuli that shift him about the area but leave him intact. He has neither antecedent or consequent. He is an isolated, definitive human datum, in stable equilibrium except for the buffets of the impinging forces that displace him in one direction or another. Self-imposed in elemental space, he spins symmetrically about his own spiritual axis until the parallelogram of forces bears down on him, whereupon he follows the line of the resultant. When the force of the impact is spent, he comes to rest, a self-contained globule of desire as before. Spiritually, the hedonistic man is not a prime mover. He is not the seat of a process of living, except in the sense that he is subject to a series of permutations enforced upon him by circumstances external and alien to him [Veblen (1919) 1961, 73-4].

Veblen provides a concurrent and more scientific conception of human nature as the positive replacement for the psychological assumptions of orthodoxy:

> [I]t is the characteristic of man to do something, not simply to suffer pleasures and pains through the impact of suitable forces. He is not simply a bundle of desires that are to be saturated by being placed in the path of the forces of the environment, but rather a coherent structure of propensities and habits which seeks realization and expression in an unfolding activity. . . .The activity is itself the substantial fact of the process, and the desires under whose guidance the action takes place are circumstances of temperament which determine the specific direction in the activity. [These circumstances] . . .are the outcome of his antecedents and his life up the point at which he stands. They are products of his hereditary traits and his past experience, cumulatively wrought out under a given body of traditions, eventualities, and material circumstances. The economic life history of the individual is a cumulative process of adaptation of means to ends that cumulatively change as the process goes on, both the agent and his environment being at any point the outcome of the last process. His methods of life today are enforced upon him by his habits of life carried over from yesterday and by the circumstances left as the mechanical residue of the life of yesterday [Veblen (1919) 1961, 74-75].

Teleology

Veblen's critique of conventional orthodox economics extends to an assessment of economic doctrine, particularly of neoclassicism and physiocracy, that rest upon concepts of natural law and natural order. Inherent for the orthodox is the explicit affirmation of utility as value. Veblen challenges any view that presumes there is an inevitable trend or force in economic development. He describes the underlying teleology of orthodoxy as follows :

> The great law of the order of nature is of the character of a propensity working to an end, to the accomplishment of a purpose. The processes of nature working under the quasi-spiritual stress of this immanent propensity may be characterized as nature's habits of life. . . .The introduction of a mere mechanically effective causal factor cannot thwart the course of Nature from reaching the goal to which she animisticly tends. Nothing can thwart this teleological propensity of nature except counter-activity or divergent activity of a similarly teleological kind. . . .The laws of nature are in the last teleological: they are of the nature of a propensity. Conformity to these "immutable and unerring" laws of nature is the test of economic truth [Veblen (1919) 1961, 188].

Social science does not support the idea of natural institutions, nor laws of motion that purport to attribute social change to natural (non-discretionary) forces, nor to the naturally inherent drives to maximize utility. Foster identifies the social process as the causal continuum that is the object of social inquiry, but no causal potency for change is to be found in so-called natural institutions or natural processes. For Foster, recall, the locus of inquiry is the social process and that process, as a continuum, moves in consequence of purposive human choices among institutional options none of which are any more or less natural than any others [Foster (LN) Value 1948, 38]. In presuming to distinguish between natural institutional structures and discretionary structures, conferring an apriori, deferential, privileged, or divine status to the alleged natural institutions and the quest for utility therein, preempts and diverts attention from the existential reality of choosing instrumentally warranted, problem solving, institutions. Any such presumption would leave the substance of any problem of institutional adjustment unaddressed.

Taxonomy

Both the classical and neoclassical traditions of orthodoxy exhibit the characteristic of taxonomy, an assumption of, and quest for, a coherent naming and ordering of structure and behavior that constitutes the natural economic order. It represents one of the critical preconceptions, along with utility as value and price as its measure, that determines relevance and placement in an inquiry process. Following is an example of Veblen's characterization of this taxonomic neoclassical inquiry model:

> This school of economics stands on the pre-evolutionary ground of normality and "natural law," which the great body of theoretical science occupied in the early nineteenth century. It is like the other theoretical sciences that grew out of the rationalistic and humanitarian conceptions of the eighteenth century in that its theoretical aim is taxonomy—definition and classification—with the purpose of subsuming its data under a rational scheme of categories which are presumed to make up the Order of Nature. This Order of Nature, or realm of Natural Law, is not the actual run of material facts, but the facts so interpreted as to meet the needs of the taxonomist in point of taste, logical consistency, and sense of justice. The question of the truth and adequacy of the categories is a question as to the consensus of taste and predilection among the taxonomists, i.e., they are an expression of trained human nature touching the matter of what ought to be. The facts so interpreted make up the "normal" or "natural" scheme of things. . . .His task is to bring facts within the framework of this scheme of "natural" categories [Veblen (1919) 1961, 190-91]. . . . [Neoclassical economics] has never entered this field of cumulative change. It does not approach questions of the class which occupy the modern sciences,—that is to say, questions of genesis, growth, variation, process (in short, questions of dynamic import)—but confines its interest to the definition and classification of a mechanically limited range of phenomena. Like other taxonomic sciences, hedonistic economics does not and cannot deal with phenomena of growth except so far as the growth is taken in the quantitative sense of a variation in magnitude, bulk, mass, number, frequency. In its work of taxonomy this economics has consistently bound itself. . .by distinctions of a mechanical, statistical nature, and has drawn its categories of classification on those grounds. (192).

Foster does not dispute the need in inquiry for creating data, ordering data, for categorizing data, for analyzing data and for drawing inferences from ordered data. At issue, however, are the criteria for selection of data, the purposes to be served, and most importantly, the generation of causal explanations that actually account for observable phenomena. Inquiry dominated by and defined in taxonomic terms cannot become a major governing and ordering conceptual tool for inquiry into the social process and the institutional elements that are the focus of analysis. It implies neither the fact of change or the causal determinants of change. It shrinks the universe of discourse over change to apriori assumptions of purpose and significance. The generation of causal hypotheses to explain, to account for, and, if warranted, to direct social change, makes only minimal use of taxonomic concerns in quest for explanations of the causal determinants of the problems confronted. Taxonomy trivializes substantive social inquiry.

Tautology

Neoclassical orthodoxy is not only hedonistic, teleological and taxonomic; it is tautological as well, in Veblen's view. Foster agrees. That is, it assumes that which inquiry is intended to explain. This attribute has the effect of eroding (destroying?) any explanatory capacity of this general theory of economics. Veblen explains that "under the . . [neoclassical] natural-economic law of equivalence and equity, it is held that the several participants or factors in the economic process severally get the equivalent of the productive force which they expend. They severally get as much as they produce; and conversely, in the normal case they severally produce as much as they get" [Veblen (1919) 1961, 283-84]. "The equivalence between the aggregate factors of production in any given case and their product remains a dogmatic postulate whose validity cannot be demonstrated in any terms that will not reduce the whole proposition to an aimless fatuity" (282). "With some [recent] writers it is an equivalence of exchange values. . .but this. . .reduces itself to a tautology. . . .[T]he individual agent. . .normally gets as much as he contributes and contributes as much as he gets" (284). And thus equational justice is achieved.

What is this equilibration of equivalencies? What is given and what is received? What is brought into equality—wage and product, reciprocal servicibilities, units of marginal utility and marginal disutility? Some years ago Joan Robinson observed that "utility is a metaphysical concept of impregnable circularity; utility is the quality in commodities that makes individuals want to buy them and the fact that individuals want to buy commodities shows that they have utility" (1962, 47). In our view, "the alleged subjective quest to satisfy wants is not demonstrated by the objective fact of market activity; it is a tautological affirmation and attribution for which demonstration is impossible. Whatever occurs as market involvement is assumed to reflect a utility maximizing judgment of the participant" [Tool 1986, 91, (emphasis in original)]. Economic explanations must not be reducible to tautological circularities.

Foster's View of Veblen's Critique of Orthodoxy

In Foster's course on the American Contribution to Economic Thought, he responds more fully to Veblen's critique of orthodoxy. While Foster concurs with much of Veblen's critique, he finds it necessary to move well beyond Veblen in fashioning a warranted criterion of value. Given the complexity and significance of the discussion, we quote Foster at some length.

Orthodox Claims to Scientific Standing

Foster accepts Veblen's characterizations of neoclassical orthodoxy and their implications. "The preconception of the teleological character of the economic process (final causes worked out by unseen hand rather than by cause-effect relationships) is both taxonomic and tautological: assumptions and conclusions are the same, self-contained and self-warranting" [Foster 1974 (LN) AmCont, 2]. Orthodox claims to scientific standing, that requires continuing formulations and assessments of causal phenomena, are unsubstantiated. Inquiry for Veblen and Foster is processual and causally determinative.

Orthodox Presumption of Natural Order

Foster's assessment continues:

> Man's selfish nature leads him as if "by and invisible hand" to accomplish the general weal which is "no part of his intentions" but which is the inevitable result of the operation of the economic process in the natural pattern of human relationships which establish themselves of their own accord and which, therefore, are the natural order. This "guiding" is non-causal in its determination; it is outside the cause-effect continuum and guides the course of that continuum toward the natural end of human welfare. The outsideness . . . is "proven" by two "facts:" (1) [T]he natural course of [the social order] may be "deflected". . .by an outside interjection. . . .(2) [W]hen the natural course of events is deflected it recovers (heals) itself when the obstruction is removed and arrives at its natural outcome. Whereas a cause-effect sequence follows a different (conceptual) path after deflection and after removal of the interference. Since the course of events in the economic process resumes itself, the realignment of the determining factors must be outside the process itself. Veblen calls this "animistic prepossession," which is necessary to the conception of a natural order in institutional affairs [Foster 1974 (LN) AmCont, 2-3].

Veblen [in the] *Place of Science* . . .[says] "the mere cessation of interference will not leave the outcome the same as if no interference had taken place". . . .[Foster says] "and so in all continua, including one's personal life; one cannot not experience the results of current action; one cannot literally go back to the 'good old days'; therefore, one cannot escape responsibility for one's own behavior" [Foster 1974 (LN) AmCont 1974, 2-3].

Orthodox Presumption of Human Nature

Foster addresses the psychological underpinnings of the classical tradition as follows:

> The "economic man" is conceived in terms of the hedonistic calculus and framed parallel to the associational psychology. The older hedonism and classical theory proper were "naively" quantitative—Bentham, James Mill, Ricardian analysis of costs of production. The newer hedonism and neo-classicism of J.S. Mill replaced his father's association by passive agents on [the] basis of contiguity, with active agents on [the] basis of similarity. Alfred Marshall's formulation of the general theory attributed more and more to man and less and less to non-man's guiding. Thus man's alternative choices are the key to real costs. And thus the "law of reciprocal costs comes in to supplant the law of costs." But the character of economic man still dictated the same inclusive conclusions [Foster 1974 (LN) AmCont, 3].

Veblen's Criticisms of Marginal Utility Theory

Foster explains that:

> [Marginal utility] theory is limited to the theory of distribution and has only a secondary bearing on any other economic phenomena. Consumption is a cultural trait, and to explain either demand or supply you must go beyond the market process. The utility concept of value necessarily "is a matter of valuation." Valuation stems from choices of alternative utilities (anticipations of want satisfaction) which are a function of previous consumption, which is the direct concomitant of distribution [Foster 1974 (LN) AmCont, 3].
>
> Since this theory is necessarily concerned with adjustments of relative values to a given situation, it can add little, if any, to a theory of growth, change, or process, and thus can offer little to understanding the determination of the situation itself. One must take prices of commodities as given in order to reach answers about prices of commodities—tautology. But "to the modern scientist the phenomena of growth and change are the most obtrusive and the most consequential facts observable in economic life." The attribute intended in "most consequential" is applicability to the solution of real problems, and that can be accomplished *only* through change, since a problematic situation *means* something is "out-of-order" [that is, must be adjusted]. [Foster 1974 (LN) AmCont, 3, (emphasis in original)].
>
> [Veblen's] major criticism is that marginal utility theory has no way of getting at change within the institutions with which economics is directly concerned. The institutional structure must be assumed and the analysis made one of "wise adaptation to the demands of the main chance." Veblen is getting at the idea that all answers to economic problems take the form of institutional adjustment. He seems to be getting at this in several places but probably didn't see it very well; he never actually stated it. "[A] general theory must take the form of a life history of mankind drawn in causal terms," he said. The structure must be assumed in order to proceed with marginal utility analysis: wants [are] taken as given data.
>
> Veblen never could work out the theory of value because of his basic mistake, i.e. that institutions are a result of unconscious habituation. If that were true, one couldn't make institutional adjustments. But he did have some sense of the beginnings of value theory. [Foster 1974 (LN) AmCont, 3-4].

Foster identifies a conceptual blockage in Veblen's argument:

> Marginal utility analysis is confined to the ground of sufficient reason instead of proceeding on the ground of efficient cause. This is another revelation of Veblen's basic mistake. The only way that a cause-effect sequence comes into institutional structure is through becoming a sufficient reason, and so all effective cause at one stage in the process of institutional adjustments takes the form of sufficient reason. This blocked Veblen and his followers but is Ayres's contribution. A view must become a sufficient reason in the comprehension of the community so that they can modify their behavior. Veblen didn't see this; he thought a habit springs full-blown. But it is a matter of choice in the initial deviation from established pattern; it involves discretion. This mistake comes from applying what is true in the physical sciences: molecules don't think. But humans do have the power of discretion [Foster 1974 (LN) AmCont, 4].
>
> [T]he way people act in problem solving *is* on the basis of sufficient

reason. . . .This obstructs Veblen in trying to proceed to an organized theory. The contrary is true of modern science only in so far as that science is concerned with non-human affairs. But Veblen is correct even here in that non-utility comprehensions in human affairs do not enter the utility analysis. Veblen sensed the role of sufficient reason in human affairs. . . .[but] Veblen could not get beyond the mores principle in his articulate organization of economic theory although he proceeded far beyond it. Veblen couldn't articulate a theory of history, although he was applying one all the time. His position implied a different idea of habits than the one he took [Foster 1974 (LN) AmCont, 4].

Marginal utility is limited to individual motivation and action, and to their arithmetic sums as aggregates. [However, says Veblen] "such an inquiry can serve the purposes of a genetic theory only if and in so far as this individual conduct is attended to in those respects in which it accounts toward habituation, and so toward change or stability of the institutional fabric, and in those respects in which it is prompted and guided by the received institutional conceptions and ideals. . . .Veblen was asking for the theory of institutional adjustment, from which he had precluded himself by his confusion of the content (habit) and the determination (discretion) of institutions. But his point, that the exclusion of consideration of how institutional structures determines individual behavior, is well taken [Foster 1974 (LN) AmCont, 4].

Utility Value and the Mores Principle

A misunderstanding of the relation between utility value theory and the mores principle, observes Foster, is the source of profound and extensive analytical errors and difficulties in economics. The "principle" is rarely identified as such in the literature; when it is, it is frequently the source of confusion and misrepresentation.

Foster indicates that William Graham Sumner was mainly responsible for introducing the central construct of the mores principle into economic literature and debate. "The principle is that habits of thought and action constitute established behavior patterns of individuals and therefore constitute the structural character of institutions. . . .[I]nstitutions are made of patterns of behavior we call habits . . . . [T]he correlation of behavior which constitutes institutions is habitual" [Foster 1948 (LN) Value, 111-12)].

The mores principle is descriptively accurate; it is continuously affirmed by social analysis; it is a useful characterizing concept. There is, however, confusion surrounding the construct that arises from the mistaken view that "habits determine institutions. . .[that] habits 'cause' institutions to come about" (112). Veblen contributed to this confusion in, for example, the following passage: "The growth of culture is a cumulative sequence of habituation, and the ways and means of it are the habitual response to human nature to exigencies that vary incontinently, cumulatively, but with something of a consistent sequence in the cumulative variations that so go forwards—incontinently, because each new move creates a new situation"[Veblen (1919) 1961, 24].

As Foster observes, "institutions seemed to Veblen to be the development of, as he put it, 'incontinent habituation'. One might assume then that habits initiate institutions, that 'institutions' were in themselves nothing more than 'incontinent habituation'" [Veblen (1919) 1961, 241]. Indeed for individuals confronting a particular situation, they usually are given data. However, says Foster:

> [H]abituation is not even possible in the determination of institutions, the determination of course being a revelation of how they come about. The causal sequences involved and the determination of an institution (that is to say, pattern of behavior) necessarily require initiations. . . .Initiation requires purposeful behavior. It requires the making of a choice and thus the involvement of value theory. The constitution of the mores. . .being habitual, [are] commonly accepted. [They are] things you do as a matter of course, we say. . . .But in the specific determination of that pattern, the initial action of that pattern quite clearly could not be habitual, and if it is not habitual, it . . .certain[ly] can't be 'incontinent.' It involves making a choice. You may choose wrongly but you do make a choice. The initial performance of a behavior requires choice and choice involves reason. Institutions are in fact initiated out of actions which are themselves efforts to solve problems. They are not and cannot be incontinent habituation [Foster 1948 (LN) Value, 113].

Foster argues that,

> Any such initiated actions, become habitual, in the sense of wide acceptance—functionally widely accepted—before you can identify. . . [it] as an institution. Otherwise it would not have prescriptive force. If it does not have that [acceptance] we do not even allow a deliberate specification of it to be called an institution [Foster 1948 (LN) Value 114]. . . .It is only when that specification is imposed successfully so that persons do in fact act that way that we permit ourselves to call it an institution. It becomes an institution when it attains the status of habituation (114). . . .Institutions. . .are determined by behavior which in its initial execution is a matter of choice. Habit. . .is something which you do frequently enough to do it without calculation. . . .[Y]ou don't have to think about it to do it. . . .[F]or the individual, institutions are given data (115-117).

Foster adds:

> The mores principle is not a statement of function; it is nonoperational. It is a statement of what constitutes institutions (the habitual part). . . .Habitual behavior is subject to validation or refutation. Habitual behavior may not serve as an index of validity, but habitual behavior can be valid or invalid on other grounds. The customary response using the mores principle is that you cannot judge, that there is no way of deciding between and institutions or cultures [1950 (LN) Value, 7]

Foster, on another occasion, explains the significance for institutionalists of any use made of, or deference shown, to the mores principle:

> But to suppose that this dictum validates the various corollaries which have been imputed to it is to play havoc with the further development of institutional analysis, that is, to suppose that this dictum means that the

> structure of institutions is usually determined by "gradually acquired modes of unconscious habituation" (Veblen) is not only to impute through unwarranted conjecture, it is also to block all further rational and conscious application of social analysis. Veblen did not realize that all habits are instituted by deliberate choice. Initial performance cannot be habitual. And to suppose—the worst corollary—that this [mores] principle means that the criterion of judging between alternatives is a function of habitual modes of behavior is to preclude absolutely the use of institutional theory in the solution of any social problems whatever [Foster 1950 (LN) Value, 7].

An implication of the foregoing, is that any contemporary Hayekian-based notion that the creation of institutions is in any analytical and factual sense unreflectively "spontaneous" is unacceptable. Institutions appear as products of human decision-making, of choices made, of habits revised, of new directives generated, employing normative directions in one or another particular, of how individuals will relate to one another. Moreover, any remnant of the notion that some institutions are natural stipulations of behavior and changes in behavior, implying some extra-discretionary act, is without empirical support. There are no "natural" institutions in the givenness sense. Every institution at initiation is the product of choice(s) made by individuals. Institutional creation is unexceptionably an exercise of will, of purpose, of intellect, yes, of discretion. The manner of this creation, its incentives, the outcomes anticipated will, of course, vary over time and circumstance. We return to this theoretical debate in Chapter 5 addressing Foster's Theory of Institutional Adjustment.

Utility Value and Equational Justice

"The equational theory of justice," in Foster's view, "is a particular application of the utility theory of value" [Foster 1948 (LN) Value, 98]. It is Foster's descriptive caption for indicating in an accessible fashion the presumed desirability of balancing sacrifices and receipts, efforts and earnings, pain and pleasure, disutility and utility. In the creation of institutions, argues Foster, a persistent analytical and philosophical focus since the Greeks has been the normative concern with equational justice in the social order.

No such questions arise in the physical sciences. The exploration of nuclear physics or DNA structure, per se, does not address the normative substance of human interaction. The social sciences, however cannot evade the question. They can plead the case that justice is not their responsibility by insisting that events that occurred were simply consequences of Fate and beyond their control. But to walk out this "back door," as Foster characterized it, is to abandon any purposive notion of problem solving in social inquiry. "Fate excuses one from the necessity to comprehend" and thus to "escape the incidence of error" in social allocative decisions [Foster 1950 (LN) Value, 6] but no community can avoid this continuing normative area of judgments. Accordingly, a response to the query of "what is just" remains omnipresent in social problem solving.

Neoclassical economists uncritically incorporate what has come to be called by Foster, "the equational theory of justice" (G. Foster 1991, 1155-60). Indeed it permeates most social systems around the globe. For example: "a man pays his debt to society and we say justice is done—an eye for an eye and a tooth for a tooth." At the personal level, equational justice is a quest for equal shares and of getting and staying even, socially and financially. As Foster inquires: "what is price theory if it isn't an equational theory of justice in the economic process" [Foster 1948 (LN) Value, 93]. If price equals cost, if reward equals contribution, justice is served (93). And the vehicle for realizing equational justice is the free market system (capitalism)! The market allegedly brings contribution and reward into equivalence. Accordingly social justice is realized through the operations of free markets.

Neoclassicists are not unique in including the substance of this area of equational justice in their inquiry and analyses of social and economic orders. Marxists, for example, also make central use of the construct. To do so is to embrace one of the more profound elements of normative social analysis in its neoclassical version. The substance of their analyses (orthodox and heterodox) is to affirm that the quest for, and realization of, this basic equation of contribution equals participation is an indicator of substantial achievement in the economic process. Neoclassicists uncritically incorporate an equational theory of justice—that "contribution equal participation"—as a consequence of the operation of free markets. In their capitalist system, competitive markets, if left unfettered, balance out the utility of income and the disutility of work. Equivalence means that justice is done. Marxists also hold to this same equational justice construct in their insistence that workers, in a capitalist system, are deprived of income to which their labors entitles them. "Surplus value" belongs to the proletariat not to the capitalists. Capitalist systems are then inherently unfair and unjust from the Marxist prospective and must be replaced. Accordingly, equational justice becomes a vehicle for validating the institutional structure of both capitalism and Marxist socialism.

Proponents and opponents of equational justice have tended to question "the accuracy of factual observations and the logical consistency of various steps in the analysis" [Foster 1950 (LN) Value, 6]. Foster quotes Dewey as follows. "Failure to examine the conceptual structures and frames of reference which are unconsciously implicated in even the seemingly most innocent factual inquires is the greatest single defect that can be found in any field of inquiry" (Dewey 1938, 507). Foster in his examination of the equational theory of justice, finds that it is not congruent with the facts of the economic process and is devoid of logical consistency. Creating and equating want-satisfying capacities rests on the inadmissible bifurcated utility theory of value. Wants are not basic data; their referential meaning is imaginative not factual. Indeed, analysis "is driven toward nihilism." Evidentially demonstrating equivalence of contribution and participation, of feeling states (utility & disutility), is beyond the capacities of warranted inquiry.

With Foster's instrumental value theory, one wholly abandons equational justice. The instrumental concept of justice contributes to general welfare; "contribution = implementation of the social process = participation." [Foster 1950 (LN) Value, 5-6]. There is no equating of anything here; they are "in constant identity". Foster argues that,

> Using the instrumental theory, concepts like "needs", "wants", etc. come into meaningful use. For to meet instrumental needs of an individual means meeting more of the needs of everyone else—expanding production—whereas meeting the ceremonial "needs" of an individual requires, by definition, that others' needs be not so well met. For how else could invidious differentiation be evidenced? . . .And that. . .is what is wrong with most social theories, and

> that is why those same theories have been subject to disproof through revealing fundamental contradictions. In terms of the instrumental theory of value, our question about the equational theory of justice as a basis for warranting institutional structure simply disappears in that it is beside the point. Does equating meaningful participation with meaningful participation establish justice? The theory of justice becomes in fact identical with the theory of welfare and of progress [Foster 1950 (LN) Value, 7].

The foregoing does not imply that there is no "reciprocation involved in human relationships." Of course in families and communities we are engaged in "doing for each other. That's what constitutes civilization. That along with all of the things involved in it" [Foster 1948 (LN) Value 98]. But at issue is "what is being equilibrated." Does the punishment fit the crime? Does capital punishment solve any problems? Is the hedonistic calculus indicative of motive? Does not everyone gain from enhanced housing; what is the nature of the "cost" to the community? Should not access to education be supported? What is the negative of an educated populace? Are employment and unemployment to be viewed equationally? Who gains from unemployment?

The equational theory of justice is in fact an impediment to the creation of instrumentally warranted institutional arrangements that address the observed impairments in generating the flow and distribution of real income. The equational justice presumption is devoid of relevance in social and economic analysis. Efforts to balance utilitous and disutilitous behavior in judicial decisions, public policies, income distribution, political participation, et al, are doomed to failure in any instrumentally constructive sense.

> All of them are systems of valuation of the two basic things which are in fact conceived to be brought into equilibrium in the attainment of justice: utility and disutility, however conceived" [Foster 1948 (LN) Value, 103]. There is no escape from the consequences. The truth of Ayres's dictum that any community any member of which is in any degree crippled, to that degree cripples the community, cannot be made. . .[compatible with] the equational theory of justice. . . .Where, in the whole of human experience in so far as we have any evidence, do you find the problematic situation solved by the application of the equational theory of justice? (106)

Utility Value and the Normative-Positive Distinction

The basic analytical posture of the positivists is the ontological and foundational acceptance of the normative-positive distinction. This dualistic tenet was introduced briefly above. Foster observes that:

> Current social science inquiry is burdened with the normative-positive distinction. There is tremendous fear of going beyond this distinction, because its disappearance will remove validation of particular institutional structure. Social inquiry is held to become scientific when it becomes positivistic, assuming that value is unknown and unknowable. This position is invalid because all behavior, other than habitual or random, involves an effort to apply a theory of value [Foster 1950 (LN) Value, 8].

This distinction is exhibited as a dualistic separation of paired concepts that have no common content. In all cases of paired precepts, there is a missing middle. Lord Lionel Robbins's oft quoted and classic statement still has descriptive significance: "Economics deals with ascertainable facts; ethics with valuations and obligations. . . .Between the generalizations of positive and normative studies there is a logical gulf fixed which no ingenuity can disguise and no juxtaposition in space or time bridge over" (Robbins 1952, 148). Ergo "'positive' is that which is observable in a descriptive sense; 'normative' is evaluational, an operation of the mind."[Foster 1950 (LN) Value, 8]. In a version by Philip Blair Rice "'positive' refers to phenomena that are factual or evidential. . .'normative' refers to the privacy of direct observations, subjective knowing, personal feelings" (8). Still another version holds that: "'positive' is what goes on here; 'normative' is what ought to go on here" (8).

Neither item in the paired construct is presumed to have common content or purpose with reference to the other; they are mutually exclusive perceptions of reality. Additional examples of such constructs are legion: is vs. ought, fact vs. value, objective vs. subjective, means vs. ends, economics vs. ethics, description vs. prescription, and true or false vs. good or bad. Traditionally, neoclassical utilitarians have claimed the mantle of positivism. Instrumentalists reject this divorcement of means and ends and perceive social value to be analytically identified in the processual and successive choosing of ends that become means, that in turn become ends, indefinitely. Means and ends are appraised by institutionalists using the criterion of "instrumental efficiency" (as explored in the following Chapter). Foster argues that,

> Social analysis, if it is to be more than a catalog of descriptions, must involve the effort to apply a criterion of judgment. We are not concerned with what we would like to have as a criterion of judgment, but rather with what in fact is applicable as a theory of value. Since all purposeful behavior is initiated by a choice among alternatives. . .[that] seem to offer problem solving functions. . . [and that] become habitual and pass into institutional forms, [such choice necessarily]. . .involves the application of the theory of value. "What is" came to be by virtue of a deliberate choice, which is the application of a theory of value. Personal interest and social interests are different only under [the] utility theory of value: one member of the community can gain at the expense of the community. [But] instrumentally, there is no difference between individual and social interests.
>
> Scientific analysis cannot proceed without resolution of the value problem. To proceed in social analysis, we must have in view hypotheses to be used in purposeful behavior. We must identify the inclusive and continuing factors in the social process, which will permit selection and arrangement of data which must be correlated with instrumental efficiency. We must have a theory of [instrumental efficiency followed by a theory of] institutional adjustment [Foster, 1950 (LN) Value, 8].

We turn now to a consideration of Foster's instrumental theory of social value.

REFERENCES

Alexander, Sidney S. 1967. "Human Values and Economists' Values." In *Human Values and Economic Policy,* Sidney Hook ed. New York: New York University Press.
Dewey, John. 1925. *Experience and Nature*. Chicago: Open Court.
———. 1938. *Logic: The Theory of Inquiry*. New York: Holt, Rinehart & Winston.
Foster, Gladys, 1991. (ed.) J. Fagg Foster on the equational theory of justice. *Journal of Economic Issues;* 25:1155-1160.
Foster, J. Fagg. (1942) 1981. John Dewey and economic value. *Journal of Economic Issues; 15*:871-897.
———.1948. Lecture Notes (LN). *Value and It's Determinants* [recorded & transcribed).
———. (1949) 1981. The relation between the theory of value and economic analysis. *Journal of Economic Issues;* 15:899-905.
———. 1950. Lecture Notes (LN). Neoclassical Economics.
———. 1950. Lecture Notes (LN). Value and It's Determinants.
———. 1974. Lecture Notes (LN). American Contributions to Economic Thought
———. (1975) 1981. Current structure and future prospects of institutional economics. *Journal of Economic Issues; 15*: 943-47.
Homan, P.T. 1928. *Contemporary Economic Thought.* New York: Harper.
Robbins, Lionel. 19553. *The Nature and Significance of Economic Science*. London: Macmillan.
Tool, Marc R. 1986. *Essays in Social Value Theory*. Armonk, NY: M.E. Sharpe.
Veblen, Thorstein B. (1919) 1961. *The Place of Science in Modern Civilization.* New York: Russell and Russell.

4 THE INSTRUMENTAL THEORY OF VALUE

The determination of what ought to be is a constant part of what is.
J. Fagg Foster

INTRODUCTION

Foster's development of the instrumental theory of value, an explanation of the criterion of judgment in all scientific social inquiry, is one of his most original and important, if not revolutionary, contributions. He is attempting

> to clarify the meaning of the term value: All economists use the word, and this fact would lead one to suppose that value is subject to definition, or at least carries a constant core of meaning sufficiently peculiar to allow independent identification. A great many theories of how value arises and how it is to be measured clamor for attention, but the meaning of what it is that arises and what it is that is to be measured is seemingly assumed. This arouses suspicion. Perhaps value has been used to designate no particular concept—but [our inquiry discloses the contrary] [Foster (1942) 1981, 872].

The commentary in Chapter 2 on Foster's perception of social (and economic) inquiry indicates that the initiation, formulation and application of warranted knowledge requires that judgments continuously be made concerning the selection of topic, the choice of data, the logical ordering of data, and the plausibility, pertinence, and explanatory capacity of causal hypotheses. Since there can be no choosing among alternatives, no making of judgments in scientific inquiry, unless a warranted criterion of judgment is employed, *all social inquiry logically and continuously requires the employment of an applicable standard of judgment.* "Utility" as discussed above is an inapplicable standard. We shall argue here that Foster's instrumental theory of inquiry itself incorporates the criterion that enables the making of choices in any scientific inquiry process. Any such criterion of choice must itself be derived from, and remain compatible with, other distinguishing analytical aspects of instrumentally warranted inquiry introduced above.

Such warranted inquiry, argues Foster, employs the instrumental logic of science in identifying value; it does not, for example, employ deductivistic a priorisms or nonexperiential certitudes generated otherwise than through the logic of scientific inquiry. Value analysis is an integral and essential element in all scientific inquiry. It is a continuing element *inside* warranted inquiry, not a unique antecedent *outside* of inquiry. In the history of economic thought, economic analysts have offered an array of affirmations of what "goodness" is, *none* of which, in Foster's view, can be validated through recourse to the logic of scientific inquiry. He writes:

> The ancient Greeks sought to analyze their economy in the light of "justice"; the Canonists explained economic intercourse on the basis of "God's will"; the mercantilists used "national honor" as the sum end of economic analysis; physiocratic doctrine explains the "natural order" of the economic world; classical theory showed the working of "human nature" toward the establishment of the "natural order"; neoclassical theory explained how "happiness," maximum "utility," and "equilibrium" were attained through the functions of the current economy. [Foster (1942) 1981, 894].

None of the above characterizations is derived from, or warranted by, the logic of scientific inquiry. Indeed, each is incompatible with what Foster perceives as scientific inquiry. He argues that the logic of scientific economic inquiry, in contrast, permits one to provide a functional analysis and characterization of the process of generating real income.

> People have always been engaged in activities contributory to sustaining human life in its total[ity]. . . .The total existential function of human beings is what is meant—no mystic, self-contained entity is. . .[connoted] in the word *life* as used here. Human life *means* functioning as a human being; it is the function that is life, not an expression of life. . . .Human life in this sense can be handled logically as part of the total inclusive continuum. . . .In the logical sense, life has no 'ends' in the ultimate. Ultimates are, from the logical view. . .[inadmissible in warranted inquiry]; life is a continuum, any item in which has meaning in terms of the other items with which each is causally related, and in no other terms can any item be said to have logical meaning [Foster (1942) 1981, 894, (emphasis in original)].

Foster affirms the nonavailability of ultimates in the logic of scientific inquiry. He locates value, in contrast, within the existential reality of the social process and the economic function embodied therein:

> Economics is concerned with that aspect of human experience called making a living—the production and distribution of goods and services. What, then, is value in the economic sense? . . .[I]t cannot exist as a separate entity. It must exist. . .[in the existential evidences] in the continuum that is the economy, and the run of the facts therein is a technological process. No imaginary situation ever produced one nail, or delivered one letter, or composed one song. The existential economic realities can be considered logically only in terms of their interconnectedness. And there is where value makes sense. Consider any item, either in the present situation or in the projection of the present situation: Does it add to the function that is called economic? If so, it has economic value; if not, it does not have economic value. Economic value

> is the degree of technological efficiency. It is as simple as that. This is, and always has been, the actual, functioning theory of value. People have always acted upon it in their economic functions, not forgetting that ritualistic functions are frequently confused with economic functions. In the actual provision of the means to function as a human being, each item in the process has value in proportion as it implements that provision. That is the logical meaning of economic value; that is the *only* real meaning of economic value that permits logical treatment in economic analysis and upon which a science of economics may be built [Foster (1942) 1981, 895, (emphasis in original)].

As Abraham Kaplan observes, all social inquiry is purposive: "what we call 'facts' all involve an element of value. For purposes are embedded in all our meanings, and every purpose determines a value. Discourse, even the most theoretical and abstract, is a segment of purposive behavior" (Kaplan 1961, 35). Inquiry is addressed to a query about, or condition in, the social process that has generated doubt about present understandings, behaviors or outcomes. The undertaking of any effort to explain the origins and impact of an initiating question or observed condition must generate reflective effort to determine "what goes on here" and by implication, "what ought to go on here." The normative dimension of inquiry reflects this purposiveness. A criterion of judgment, a theory of value, is necessarily implied in the pursuit of purpose to change "what is" into "what ought to be."

It is commonplace to employ implicit criteria in distinguishing between social purposes that are constructive and those that are not constructive. Social inquiry, for example, that: *(a)* explains and extends our understanding of causal connections in behavioral contexts; *(b)* pushes out the frontiers of warranted knowledge and enhances our comprehension of observed behavioral phenomena; *(c)* recommends adjustments in the current institutional structure to assure productive performance, and/or *(d)* reduces invidiously discriminatory treatment of people, are constructive. It promotes the life process; it serves instrumental purposes in pursuit of the community's well-being and continuity.

Social inquiry, however, that: *(a)* reaffirms antecedently acquired, but unappraised, beliefs; *(b)* reaffirms the discretion of unaccountable economic power systems; and/or *(c)* provides apologia for sustaining the flawed status quo, are all normatively viewed as being destructive, that is, they serve ceremonial purposes that threaten the community's well-being.

The intent here is to reemphasize that since all inquiry is and must be purposive, the character of inquiry pursued *inherently* has normative elements and implications. Foster's value theory should be understood, then, as providing a warranted criterion of judgment in social inquiry that distinguishes between constructive and destructive purposes. This value theory is derived through scientific social inquiry; its character reflects its standing as an existential scientific generality; it plays a critical and continuing role in such social inquiry; its application guides judgments of economic and social policy.

To present and develop Foster's value theory we address in this Chapter the following topics: *(a)* value theory and economic analysis, *(b)* instrumental value theory: locus; *(c)* instrumental value theory: sources; *(d)* instrumental value theory: substance; and *(e)* instrumental value theory: implications.

VALUE THEORY AND ECONOMIC ANALYSIS

Foster offers a largely unique theory of value reflecting and extending the theoretical contributions, especially of John Dewey, Thorstein B. Veblen and Clarence E. Ayres. This value theory, Foster argues, is a necessarily integral and essential element of all scientific economic and social theory. If inquiries into public policy are, in Foster's view, to be credible, robust, substantive and directive, they must employ the methodology of scientific inquiry. In the application of instrumental value theory to the construction of public policy options, the choosing of pertinent and constructive institutional adjustments must be guided by the continuing employment of pragmatic instrumentalism, as explored in Chapter 2. All such inquiry, then, is value-laden.

The following encompassing analytical affirmations of fact, as offered by Foster, provide an introductory overview of the critical linkages between value theory and economic analysis. He is, in effect, redefining the nature and significance of inquiry in economics:

Economic Inquiry

Foster insists that "economics is and always has been concerned with the process of providing the means of human life and experience." It is the continuing task of economists. . .to explain it, to make it understandable to the community so that the community may proceed to a solution of its economic problems." But, as a social science, economics "is concerned primarily with the institutional aspects of the social order, not with the physical-engineering aspects, except as the latter bear on the former. . . .Economics is. . .concerned with. . . the prescribed patterns of human relations, patterns of correlated activities and attitudes, among groups of persons who are organized for the purpose of carrying on the process of providing the means of human life and experience [Foster (1949) 1981, 899-900].

Economic Problems

The community supports inquiry in economics because "it is and always has been confronted by real economic problems" and has presumed that extended inquiry might contribute to their understanding and amelioration. "The significance of inquiry," then, for Foster

> lies in its applicability to the solution of real problems. Our conception of what constitutes significance and importance. . .remains fixed on the possibility of solving real problems confronting real people, and we concede significance to any inquiry in any field only on the basis of that possibility. A problem arises when that process ceases to be carried forward at the level of efficiency indicated by the current state of the industrial arts. It becomes an economic problem when that failure is caused by the failure of any one, or several, of those patterns to contribute to the economic process or when any institutional arrangement interferes with its on-going. . . .An economic

> problem appears [then] when disrapport arises between two or more patterns of human activities that are supposed to be correlated toward the effective continuation of the productive process [(1949) 1981, 900-01].

For Foster, then, "[E]conomic problems are situations of instrumental dislocation. [I]t follows that answers to economic problems must take the form of institutional judgments—modifications of prescribed patterns of human relations looking toward the instrumentally effective correlation of those organizational patterns with each other and with the noninstitutional aspects of the economic process." The identification of an economic problem is clearly, then, a "recognition of a discrepancy between 'what is' and 'what ought to be', between 'what goes on here' and 'what ought to go on here'. Problem solving would destroy that discrepancy" [(1949) 1981, 900-901].

Institutional Change

"If the dictum that 'whatever is , is right' holds true, then most certainly there could be no such thing as an economic problem." Trying to sustain the status quo at a time when the community is confronted, for example, with maldistribution of income, invidious discrimination or underutilization of available resources, is unproductive effort. "[T]he community finds repeatedly that the economic process does not go forward at the level of efficiency that the noninstitutional factors indicate is available. [T]he economic general theory must be the theory of institutional adjustment. Otherwise, economic theory can have no significance insofar as significance is a function of problem solving." And no scholar or advisor has successfully argued the contrary. "Since the physical circumstances that converge to bring on an economic problem remain just what they are, there can be no way of resolving the problem except to adjust the institutional structure so as to bring the two phases [physical, social] into instrumental rapport [Foster (1949) 1981, 901].

Value Theory

So long as there are persons with reflective capacity and social concern, "there is no way, short of forceful destruction, to *prevent* recognition of a discrepancy between 'what is' and 'what ought to be' in terms of instrumental efficiency of the economic process. . . .[T]he problematic situation is a matter of factual circumstances the human incidences of which *cannot* be escaped except by 'making up our account' with those physical circumstances. This requires adjusting the relevant institutional structures so as to remove the inefficiency; there is no other way to remove the human incidences that comprise the compulsions toward adjustment" [(1949) 1981, 902 (emphasis added)]. It follows, then, that

> A criterion of judgment independent of any particular institutional structure is necessary if an economic problem is ever to be recognized. . .the substance of that criterion is the instrumental efficiency of the economic process. [S]ince 'what ought to be' in economic affairs is nothing less than

> the application of a theory of value, and since no economic problem can be conceived or resolved without some comprehension of 'what ought to be'. . . significant economic analysis necessarily involves the application of the theory of value. This is the simple and apparent relationship between value theory and economic analysis [Foster (1949) 1981, 902].
>
> [T]o say that an economic problem exists is to say that part of that structure, that particular pattern of human relationships, has ceased or failed to provide for the effective participation of its members. In so saying, we are necessarily in the position of asserting that the instrumental efficiency of the economic process is the criterion of judgment in terms of which, and only in terms of which, we may resolve economic problems [Foster (1949) 1981, 905].

INSTRUMENTAL THEORY OF VALUE I: LOCUS

The continuing existential universe in which value theory is developed and utilized is perceived by Foster to be the encompassing social process. This social process is the locus of Foster's value theory. This process is a universally continuing phenomenon of interaction of structure and function under the deliberate, normative, and continuing discretionary guidance of members of the social order. Instrumental value theory, then, is grounded in the *continuum of actual experience of human agents* encompassing the following loci of interest and concern: The social setting compels a genuine recognition of the physical and emotional status of the community. The physical setting provides the context in which identified problems are exhibited in particular places and times where the provisioning of actual individuals and communities is being directly determined. The cultural setting assures recognition that all those affected by problems are themselves products of lifelong behavioral conditioning. The conceptual setting provides the source from which analyses, beliefs and convictions acquired over long periods are brought into evaluative consideration. The judgmental setting reminds all inquirers that choice making pervades the whole of human experience and that all such choice making *compels* recourse to criteria of choice.

Institutions are structural stipulations organizing the behavior, and often the thinking, of members of the human community. In Foster's view, institutions are prescribed or proscribed patterns of correlated behavior and attitudes directed to the performance of one or another social function. Institutional structures that have demonstrably failed adequately to provide for the community's well-being must become the objects of inquiry and perhaps revision or abandonment, if the continuity of the community is to be assured and its efficiency in applying warranted knowledge is to be enhanced.

Inquiry categories of *social functions* that comprise the social process, as viewed by Foster, would particularly include, among others, the following continuing areas of major human interest and concern:

provision of the means of life and experience,
determination and administration of public policy,
continuing education in critical thinking,
creation and communication of warranted knowledge,
creation and equitable distribution of real and money income,
provision for public health and safety.

These and other major loci of social functions are developed in, and given effect through, organizing and coordinating institutional structures. Such structures are the vehicles through which intellect and judgment guide the conduct and performance of functions comprising the social process.

Mal- or non-performance of these functions in institutions on which the community depends creates problems of disjunction, disrapport, disintegration and/or recourse to invidious distinctions. Solutions to institutional problems require, obviously, changes in institutional structure. The instrumental theory of value provides the criterion that identifies the determinants of problems in and among these functional areas of human activity. Note that all references to utilitious concepts are abandoned as intrusive and irrelevant in the identification and resolution of instrumentally defined human problems. We turn to the particulars of the theory of institutional adjustment in the following Chapter 5.

INSTRUMENTAL THEORY OF VALUE II: SOURCES

Although over the last 100 years or so a large number of scholars have formulated, continued, and extended the inquiry discipline of institutional economics, we focus here on three scholars whose contributions were particularly significant in the development of Foster's perspective on the normative aspects of his theory of economic progress: Thorstein Veblen, John Dewey and Clarence Ayres.

Thorstein B. Veblen

Introduction

Veblen was generally perceived as someone well outside of the general culture of intellectuals in the late 19th and early 20th centuries. As Foster views him:

> Veblen was never really able to become a part of American culture, he never understood the idiom. This gave him both advantages and disadvantages. He was influenced by Spencer's sociology, by Hume, Kant, and Darwin. As always he took what he could use and discarded the rest. Dewey and Veblen took from each other. [After contact with Dewey] about 1921 there was a different tenor in Veblen. But he. . .discloses only the most rudimentary beginnings of his general theory [Foster 1974 (LN) AmCont, 2].

Foster was intimately familiar with the Veblenian literature; indeed he once remarked that institutionalists, following his own practice, should reread the Veblenian library every few years. More particularly, it seems evident that Veblen's *Theory of the Leisure Class* (1899), *The Instinct of Workmanship* (1914), and his *The Place of Science in Modern Civilization* (1919) were the most important sources of insights for Foster in developing his scientific mode of social inquiry that encompassed his instrumental theory of value. In addition, he often alludes to Veblen's *The Nature of Peace,* as an indicator of the predictive significance of Veblen's analyses.

Foster surveys and assesses the contributions and limitations of Veblen's work in institutional thought in various places, but most directly, perhaps, in his course entitled "The American Contribution to Economic Thought." Both the contributions and the limitations are instructive in understanding the instrumental theory of value in institutional economics. But perhaps the most significant contribution for Foster is Veblen's fundamental distinction "between the 'institutional' and the 'technological' aspects of the economy" [Foster (1943) 1981, 926]. This Veblenian distinction or dichotomy is the initial and primary construct on which Foster's scientific instrumental theory of value is built. This dichotomy between science and nonscience in social inquiry, is still a profound and significant undergirding construct for contemporary institutionalist analyses of social value and its applications.

Somewhat ironically, however, Foster observes that Veblen himself was theoretically blocked by the value problem. He made judgments about institutional structure; he acknowledged the fact of, and sought to explain the determinants of, economic change. But he did not develop a theory of value rooted in his basic commitment to a scientific approach to inquiry. He was blocked by his "basic mistake. . .that institutions are a result of unconscious habituation" not of deliberate selection [Foster 1974 (LN) AmCont, 4].

Veblen frequently disclaimed that he was generating and applying social value theory. He insisted that about tastes "there is no disputing" [(1919) 1961,29]; that " in making use of the term 'invidious', it may perhaps be unnecessary to remark that there is no intention to extol or deprecate, or to commend or deplore any of the phenomena which the word is used to characterize" [(1899) 1934, 34]; that in discussion of the leisure class, "'right' and 'wrong' are of course here used without conveying any reflection as to what ought or ought not to be"(207). Disclaimers notwithstanding, Veblen was an inveterate "judger" of social and economic conduct and institutions. As Foster observes, Veblen was blocked by the value problem; he seemingly never escaped the contradiction of his own making. He disclaimed use of normative criteria while he was, in fact, offering normative assessments.

Veblen, despite his blockage, was extensively and consistently engaged in evaluation. "He was applying value theory in distinguishing between institutions that exhibit 'compatibility or incompatibility with the effective evolutionary process.' He distinguishes between institutions that are 'imbecile' and those that are not. . . .Veblen's inquiry is purposive; it is value laden" (Tool 1986, 34-35).

The Veblenian Dichotomy

Some years ago, the present author attempted more fully to identify the Veblenian dichotomy as a normative premise. We here draw upon that analysis (Tool 1986, 36-37):

> In Veblen's *Leisure Class* we are offered this descriptive statement: "Institutions—the economic structure—may be roughly distinguished into two classes or categories, according as they serve one or the other of two divergent purposes of economic life. . . .they are institutions of acquisition or of production. . . .they are pecuniary or industrial institutions. . . .they are institutions serving either the invidious or the non-invidious economic interest (Veblen (1899) 1934, 208). Veblen used the term "*invidious*" to

describe a "comparison of persons with a view to rating and grading them in respect of relative worth or value [Tool 1986, 34 (emphasis in original)].

But the forms or versions of the distinction extend well beyond the three mentioned above. Indeed, the distinction appears in all of Veblen's published works in one form or another; it was for him a *general* principle. Note the following diverse additional examples:

salesmanship —— workmanship [(1914) 1946, 216ff]
vested interests —— common man [(1919a)1946, 85ff & 159ff]
business —— industry [(1904) 1932, 20ff]
ceremonial —— technological [(1915) 1964, 26ff]
ownership —— production [(1923) 1964, 65ff]
free income —— tangible performance [(1919a) 1946, 63ff]
sabotage —— community serviceability [(1917) 1945, 167ff]
pecuniary employment —— industrial employment [(1904) 1932, 313ff]
invidious emulation —— technological efficiency [(1899) 1934, passim]
competitive advertising —— valuable information [(1904) 1932, 57]
business prosperity —— industrial efficiency [(1904) 1932, 178ff]

"And the foregoing does not exhaust the list. Entries in the left-hand column refer to individuals, behaviors or institutions [and/or attributes, practices, and outcomes] that are different in kind from those in the right-hand column; the distinction is a dichotomy" (Tool, 1986, 37.) As I argue earlier:

> The *normative* use, by Veblen, of this set of distinctions can hardly be in doubt. "The interest of the community at large demands industrial efficiency and serviceability of the product, while the business interest of the concerns as such demands vendibility of the product" [(1904) 1932, 157-58]. It is scarcely morally colorless to contend that "all business sagacity" in the final analysis "reduces itself. . .to a judicious use of sabotage." "Captains of industry" through owners' discretion give "authoritative permission" and "authoritative limitation" to the industrial process. It is Veblen's lament that such authority is not used with "an eye single" to produce the "largest and most serviceable output of goods and services, or to the most economical use of the country's material resources and man-power, regardless of pecuniary consequences." "The volume and serviceability of the output must wait unreservedly on the very particular pecuniary question of what quantity and what degree of serviceability will yield the largest net return in terms of price" [(1917) 1945,168-69, emphasis added)].
>
> Veblen characterizes a "vested interest" as a "prescriptive right to get some thing for nothing" [(1919) 1946, 162]. He sees the objective of competitive advertising as the establishment of "differential monopolies resting on popular conviction" which are of "slight if any immediate service to the community" [(1904) 1932 57-58]. Can these observations be considered devoid of normative content? Obviously not. (Tool 1986, 37, emphasis added).

Accordingly, disclaimers notwithstanding, Veblen was engaged in normative inquiry. Foster identifies his problem. Veblen perceived and articulated the continuing (indeed inescapable) need to judge institutions with applicable criteria but was never able to formulate a theory of value that would provide a continuing criterion that itself was drawn from the warranted inquiry process. Foster, as we have seen, is able to provide the warrantable value theory that continuing discretionary involvement in the social order requires. Value is instrumental efficiency, as Foster has cogently and persuasively affirms.

Foster's Views of Veblen's Contributions

> Veblenian economics is the only [approach to]. . . economics that is peculiar to America. Americans [tend to] talk ismatically and generally act instrumentally [Foster 1974 (LN) AmCont, 5].

Foster contends that

> [his] distinction between technology and institutions,[was misunderstood]. Critics said [that] since he was not going toward any ism he was not going anywhere; he was directionless and meaningless. But Veblen recognized that the identification of direction cannot be stated validly in terms of institutional structure. That is, the criterion of judgment cannot be in terms of institutional structure. To Veblen, an ism exists as an idea, and it is a useful structure as identifying a pattern of ideas in reference to a theory of value. He noted that these patterns were accepted as natural, but they were not so [Foster 1974 (LN) AmCont, 4].

Moreover, says Foster,

> Veblen realized that given data must be taken from technology (state of industrial arts), but he didn't go far enough. . . .[He did not] distinguish between instrumental and ceremonial [functions of] institutions. Veblen knew of no way to determine the validity of an institution, implying that technology is valid and institutions invalid. But all institutions are partially valid, and there is a criterion of judgment for evaluating them. That is what makes social science significant. Without a criterion there is no significance [Foster 1974 (LN) AmCont, 5].
>
> What Veblen started is the development of a theory of institutions, of which economics is one phase. We have been devoid of a general theory; Veblen gives us a chance to work toward one. He does away with ismatic criteria for the judgment of direction. Ayres works from Veblen with what he calls a technological theory of value [Foster 1974 (LN) AmCont, 5].

Clarence E. Ayres

Fagg Foster studied formally and informally with Clarence E. Ayres for a decade and a half from 1931 to 1946; he wrote his doctoral dissertation under Ayres's supervision; he remained a good friend and professional colleague until the death of Ayres in 1972. Ultimately, in some areas, Foster even reversed the roles of teacher and student. Ayres seems to have had a greater impact on Foster's professional development and intellectual maturation than any other scholar. Accordingly, Foster's perception of Ayres's work reflects this long interactive association. Perhaps Ayres's most important publications for Foster were his *Theory of Economic Progress* (1944) and his *Toward a Reasonable Society* (1961).

"Veblen left his general theory at the stage of 'making up one's account' with the material conditions that converge to bring it [institutional] (adjustment) on" (Foster 1946, 96). But how is this "accounting" to occur? A clarification of the concepts of "institutional" and "technological" and their relationship, was undertaken by Ayres. Indeed, Ayres extends, in two directions, Veblen's early-on perception of a theory of institutional adjustment:

The first of these extensions concerns the theory of value, "the theory of that in terms of which the account may be drawn" (Foster 1946, 97). Ayres recasts the Veblenian distinction between the technological and institutional aspects of institutional performance in the economy by emphasizing the continuity of tool making, conceptual and material. Ayres explains:

> Social analysis has not stopped with the discovery of the diversity of ceremonial practices and conventional evaluations. There is also the continuity of tools, in terms of which—in spite of ceremonial diversities—a basic continuity of judgment has always prevailed. This continuity still prevails and is the basis of valid judgment today as it has always been. For every man the real and valid judgments of economic value are those he makes between purchases, judgments of value in use as economists once said, tested and verified by the way things work in the continuous effort of existence. It is to this test that all economic values are in fact submitted, those of public policy affecting the industrial system as a whole no less than those of private life. For every individual and for the community the criterion of value is the continuation of the life-process—keeping the machines running. That is what we have in fact been doing throughout the ages, and that is what we must continue to do and do continually better—technologically better—if we are to continue and exceed the achievements of the past [Ayres (1944) 1978, 230].

Ayres is affirming the normative content of "the run of the physical facts" and, says Foster,

> [I]t is obvious that any criterion of value in terms of which action is taken which contravenes the continuity of the economic process thereby cancels all human action, including the action taken under those terms. It is proposed, then that economic estimation be made directly in terms of the criterion which the run of the facts dictates. Professor Ayres' views the character of that dictation much as the curvature of a lens is dictated by its function in the process in which it plays a part. The problem posed by any disrapport between the lens grinder's predilections concerning proper concavity or convexity on the one hand and the dictation of the facts on the other hand can be resolved only by an adjustment of the predilections. In this sense Professor Ayres points out that the locus of economic value is in the economic process, not in predilections drawing warrant from any other source (Foster 1946, 98).

Foster continues:

> Something of this same conception of value is implicit in most of Veblen's work, and he tacitly applies it in almost all of his discussions. But his view

> of science as being motivated by 'idle curiosity' blocked any logical way to a theory of value drawn in terms dictated by the run of the facts. [I]f science is valid only as an exercise in idle curiosity, although its content is dictated by the run of the facts, there is no way to base the validity of science itself in the sort of mental processes with which it examines and explains the facts [Foster 1946, 98-99].

A second area in which Ayres extends the Veblenian theory of institutional adjustment, in Foster's view, has to do with what Ayres calls "the power of ideas." Some readers of Veblen "got the impression that institutional adjustments, being changes in the 'settled habits of thought common to the generality of men' are altogether a matter of unconsciously modified habituation." Some have drawn the conclusion "that changes in structural institutions are exclusively unreasoned change in habits." Ayres, drawing on his concept of "the power of ideas" argues that "*ideas* are the immediate point of departure for adjustments in structural institutions, that is, in the prescribed relations of a group of people organized for definite purposes"[Foster 1946, 99 (emphasis added)].

Indeed, Foster observes, Ayres "points out. . .[that] two kinds of ideas are involved"

> On the one hand, conceptual formulations based on the authority of personalities serve toward maintaining the existing rules of the game. On the other hand, ideas arising as conceptual formulations of the material economic process serve toward changing the rules of the game as the material conditions of the economic process change. Either way, the pattern of *ideas* is the immediate prescription of the pattern of *human relations*, and any change in the former is the immediate prescription of a change in the latter.
>
> Professor Ayres's contribution at this point is that the causal potency of an idea based on the authority of personalities is a function of the coercive power of those personalities whereas the causal potency of an idea based on the run of the facts in causal terms is a function of the correctness of the idea (Foster 1946, 100, emphasis added).
>
> The former, Professor Ayres identifies as non-causal or metaphysical; the latter, he identifies as science. Metaphysical ideas have no potency in themselves; the source of their potency is exterior to the ideas. Scientific ideas are potent as such. Then it is the interplay of these two forces that determines the pattern of any adjustment. Professor Ayres concludes that there is no way, short of total destruction, in which metaphysics can prevent the encroachment, however gradual, of science as a way of understanding and therefore specifying the patterns of human relationships. And the reason for this is that the inherently developmental character of science means that it constantly proliferates beyond its immediate boundaries. As a way of explanation, science encroaches upon new areas and therefore specifies the trespassed area (Foster 1946, 100-101).

Before moving on to Dewey's contribution to the instrumental theory of social value, it will be instructive briefly to indicate the conceptual transformation of the Veblenian distinction as it was addressed subsequently by Ayres and Foster.

Veblen's dichotomy characterizes institutions as being bad or good: bad institutions are concerned with acquisition rather than production; they exhibit imbecilic rather than reasoned conduct; they operate incompatibly instead of harmoniously with the evolutionary process. Veblen sees institutions as being distinguished by one or the other of two generic purposes. Some promote production and well-being; some promote acquisition and prowess.

Ayres's version of the dichotomy characterizes institutions as dominantly ceremonial. Technology, per se, is non-institutional. "The business of 'getting a living' includes. . .activities of a technological character and. . .activities of a ceremonial character" (1978, 99). Ayres, then, sees two generic social systems each of which claims warrant but only one, technology, has it.

Foster, as noted, distinguishes between instrumental and ceremonial functions in *all* institutions. Any institution will likely have elements of each in its makeup, although the relative proportions vary widely. Foster, then sees two generic but divergent, functions in each and all institutions. Progress means inhancing the instrumental functions and diminishing the ceremonial functions in institutions.

Baldwin Ranson, a student of Foster, suggests the following characterization of the Veblenian dichotomy for contemporary purposes of normative inquiry:

> Human beliefs, behaviors and artifacts generally contain: (a) elements that are serviceable to the continued life of mankind in society, and (b) elements that are not so serviceable. To apply the Veblenian distinction, ask of any object of inquiry: What elements promote the life process? What elements obstruct the life process? The first elements are called instrumental, developmental, serviceable, and/or productive. The second elements are called ceremonial, acquisitive, invidious, and/or wasteful (Ranson 1999).

John Dewey

As indicated in the previous Chapters, Foster, in fashioning his instrumental theory of inquiry, draws heavily on the philosophical contributions of John Dewey, perhaps the most prominent and productive philosopher in the United States in the 20th century. Of Dewey's work, *Logic: The Theory of Inquiry* (1938) and *Theory of Valuation* (1939) are clearly the most relevant and significant for Foster. But Dewey was an extraordinarily productive scholar; several other publications were also important sources of insight: e.g. *Human Nature and Conduct* (1922), *Experience and Nature* (1925), *The Public and Its Problems* (1927), and *Problems of Men* (1946).

Foster draws on Dewey to reset the analytical context for value inquiry:

> [T]he existing state of discussion shows not only that there is a great difference of opinion about the proper theoretical interpretation to be put upon the facts, which might be a healthy sign of progress, but also that there is great disagreement as to what the facts are to which theory applies, and indeed whether there are any facts to which a theory of value can apply. For a survey of the current literature of the subject discloses that views on the subject range from the belief, at one extreme, that so-called "values" are but emotional epithets or mere ejaculations, to the belief, at the other extreme, that a priori necessary standardized, rational values are the principles upon which art,

> science, and morals depend for their validity. [Dewey 1939 ; quoted in Foster (1942) 1981, 872].

Foster's conception of value is *not* derived from either extreme. Drawing on Dewey, he develops instead a logically acceptable and empirically demonstrable theory of social value.

> John Dewey comes into the picture because of a failure on the part of the economists. They have failed to produce a theory of value which does not violate every requisite of scientific reflection and explanation; this despite the fact that all economic theory has, of necessity, to do with value in some connotation or other. This side of nihilism, some concept of value is a necessity in dealing with any problems at all. But this is not to say that value must be an occult, all-pervading "something" that is *inherent* in any object or event. The failure by the economists to produce an acceptable theory of value has led to [a] "lament for economics" by those who recognize the inadequacy of orthodox theory. And these persons' failure to continue on to a positive reappraisal of economics results in the meaninglessness and doubt of nihilism. The character of that reappraisal is most maturely stated by John Dewey. [Foster (1942) 1981, 872-73, (emphasis in original)].

Foster explains why social value theory is such a forbidding area of inquiry for economists to address:

> The problem of value. . .is very difficult to handle in "economic" terms. Its difficulty does not derive from complexity, but from novelty. It is new in its full realization, if indeed it is yet fully realized. The new is always difficult, and particularly so if it replace old concepts or habits, and very much so if the new cannot be handled in terms habitually used in handling what it replaces. There is an "inalienable and ineradicable framework of conception which is not of our own making, but given to us ready-made by society—a whole apparatus of concepts and categories within which and by means of which all our individual thinking, however daring and original, is compelled to move (Cornford 1912, 45). The "apparatus of concepts" requisite to handling the problem is at hand, but it is so new in the field of economics that much blundering is occurring and is to be expected. Even an economist of the caliber of J. M. Keynes, with his . . .[awesome] erudition, fails to see his key problem, although he does realize the inadequacy of his habitual "apparatus of concepts." [(1942) 1981, 873].

Scientists in any field, Foster contends, must concern themselves with ethical implications of their work and any social opportunities or responsibilities arising therefrom. A scientist (social or physical) must become aware of the "widening circle of consequences" generated by, and emerging from, his/her inquiry and policy recommendations. As Dewey observed: "Just as the validity of a proposition in discourse, or of conceptual material generally, cannot be determined short of the consequences to which its functional use gives rise, so the sufficient warrant of a judgment as a claimant to knowledge (in its eulogistic sense) cannot be determined apart from connection with a widening circle of consequence (1938, 490).

But the outcomes that derive from "the continuum of the widening circle of consequences" of inquiry are, of course, social as well as physical. Foster explains:

> In a very real sense, scientists determine the social environment. Technological development which is continuous with inventions in "pure" science. . .is the most obviously changing aspect of man's environment. And it is this changing which, "at bottom" gives rise to the inadequacy of institutional arrangements instituted on the basis of former technological situations. . . ."[T]he notion of the complete separation of science from the social environment is a fallacy which encourages irresponsibility on the part of scientists regarding the social consequences of their work" [Dewey 1938, 489; quoted by Foster (1942) 1981, 875].

Dewey would agree with Hogben that

> [T]he recognition by scientists of their social responsibility would not render to logic all the plain and fancy superstitions. The results of the development of physical science are, in large measure, not in the hands of scientists. . . .They are the result of all the items in the panorama of organized human relations. That is why "science is an important part of education, not because it satisfies curiosity, but because intelligent citizenship is no longer possible unless we understand the place of science in the everyday life of everybody" [Hogben 1937, 55; quoted by Foster (1942) 1981, 877].

Foster shares Dewey's view that technological change "is the chief determining condition of social relationships and, to a large extent, of actual cultural values in every advanced industrial people, while they have reacted intensively into the lives of all 'backward' people. Moreover, only an arbitrary, or else purely conventional point of view. . .can rule out such consequences as these from the scope of science itself" [Dewey 1938, 487; quoted by Foster (1942) 1981, 876].

INSTRUMENTAL THEORY OF VALUE III: SUBSTANCE

Foster's Concept of Instrumental Efficiency

Because of its incisiveness, and given its comparative brevity, we present here Foster's summarized characterization of his instrumental efficiency theory of value as he drafted it for his students. That it draws on his precursors, Veblen, Dewey and Ayres, will become evident: We consider in sequence, *(a)* value in process, *(b)* condition vs. direction, and *(c)* measurement.

Value in Process

Foster explains:

> Since truth lies or is identifiable only in continuity, and since the only continuity which is not self-contained, and therefore not tautological, is the

evidentially determined (scientific) progression of human devices, then the true criterion of judgment must be identified in terms of that process. And the kind of thinking which characterizes it in conjugate correspondence with that process must be the kind of thinking which can bring into view the referent in question [Foster 1950 (LN) Value, 2].

The notion that *any* theory of value can be applied even though only one is in fact applicable, is a paradox. It is not that others are applied; it is rather that we try to apply others. The apparent paradox is resolved by discerning correctly the relationship between the facts ("what is") to "what ought to be".

That relationship is as follows: the activity of judging alternatives (which necessarily involves the application of value theory) is one of the most obtrusive facts in the continuum of events, and that activity connects the present and the future through the efforts to resolve problems, and thus the choosing among alternatives, and thus the determination of the course of events, etc., etc. Judgment is the connecting link between the present and the future [Foster 1950 (LN) Value, 2 (emphasis in original)].

Foster affirms instrumental value:

[T]he concept of value must be in terms of process because the *whole* of our experience has been with process. . . .[T]o be a true concept, it must display the attribute we call continuity. Therefore, a true concept of value must be in correspondence with the evidential facts of continual process. But the only identifiable continuum in our whole social experience is the progressive causally-determined sequence of events we call the social process. And so it is in that process itself that we can correctly identify the locus of value. But even yet, the character of the identification which we seek is not in view because the locus of value (Ayres's terminus) does not identify its character and because that locus, the social process, may be and is gauged in two ways: *(a)* direction, *(b)* condition [Foster 1950 (LN) Value, 2 (emphasis in original)].

Condition versus Direction

Foster continues:

"Direction" may be and is used in the sense that judgments may be and are made with reference to whether the process is toward or away from a particular pattern of invidious differentiation, a particular institutional structure, a structure within which the process goes on. But in this instance, the structure must have its validity outside and irrespective of the character of the process which goes on within it. And, to attain such a separate identification, the institutional structure must in fact be determined independently of the remainder of the process. But all of the facts of history and of common experience prove beyond any . . .doubt that the character of the process and the structural institutions are not independent of each other; they are causally related, although separately identifiable, phases or aspects of the same process [Foster 1950 (LN) Value, 2-3].

Not only is the "direction" concept of the criterion of judgment invalid because the referent for direction cannot be separately established in fact, but also that criterion is devoid of truth because its referent is discontinuous. Nothing is better established in human history than the fact that the institutional structure itself constantly changes, and not only the remainder of the process. And so we shall have to discard "direction" as value [Foster 1950 (LN) Value, 3].

"Condition," in the sense of how efficiently the social process is proceeding, is the other way to gauge the process. But here again the referent we seek for the term "value" is not yet specifically identified. For "condition" also can be conceived in two ways. First, it can be thought of as a degree of efficiency in maintaining or attaining a particular pattern of invidious differentiation, a particular institutional structure. But this concept displays all of the defects of the "direction" concept; it is, in fact, fundamentally the same idea. Thus the condition of efficiency alone does not end our quest for a true identification of value [Foster 1950 (LN) Value, 3].

The second way in which "condition" can be conceived is instrumental in character. The social process can be judged in terms of how efficiently the non-invidious function is being carried on. But . . .it is this very aspect of the social process which we have identified as the continuum which does not change in character, but only in degree and in quantity. . . .[A]lso. . .it is this function that is continuous—inescapably so. This concept of value, like the ceremonial concept of efficiency, is applicable to the whole or any part of the social process at any time or over any period of time. But it differs from the other in that its referent remains the same—it is continuous. It has real and uninterrupted continuity. Its referential content at any time and in reference to any item is continuous with all that has gone before and with all that exists concurrently, and what succeeds that content can be conceived only as causally continuous with it. It has uninterrupted continuity and it has unexceptional applicability throughout the universe of its application [Foster 1950 (LN) Value, 3].

Measurement

The application or employment of the instrumental efficiency criterion of value is neither obvious nor automatic. What *theory of valuation* accompanies the instrumental theory of value? Is it possible numerically to measure more or less efficiency in the scientific sense?

In the orthodox neoclassical general theory and tradition, the referent for value, as noted, is utility. Since units of utility, "utils," defy both identification and measurement, price became and remains the *surrogate* measure of utility. The theory of price determination comprises the only orthodox theory of valuation. It permits the use of numerical calculations of price movements and therewith by imputation, the determination of greater or lesser utility, i.e. value. One could assume, then, that utilitious satisfaction varies inversely with price for consumers and directly with price for producers. Recourse to mathematics to "explain" price determination provides the allusion of factual certainty for the analysis offered

For institutionalists, there can be no scientific credibility for the orthodox theory of valuation. But an institutionalist view of the theory of valuation remains to be considered. Foster asks, "How do you know what is more or less [instrumentally] efficient?" A concept of more or less efficiency would appear to be necessary. He responds: " in science, there is no common unit of measurement for efficiency. . .comprised of different items, events, and/or objects" [1948 (LN) Value, 362]. The efficiency of a combustible engine is not measured in the same way as that of a telescope. Efficiency relates to differing functions and the adequacy of performance thereof.

In instrumental social inquiry, then, there is no singular theory of valuation; "there is no unit of measurement of social value"(363). "Every problem specifies the units of measurement; the facts of the problem specify the theory of valuation applicable to it. It is from those facts, and reference to relationships of those facts, that that unit becomes available or not available" (362). For example: the instrumental efficiency of the function of teaching children to think critically and clearly about substantive social issues would be measured differently from the instrumental efficiency of the function of achieving full and meaningful employment.

Foster's concluding value affirmation:

> This concept of the criterion of judgment satisfies all of the requisites of truth; it is true. Value is instrumental efficiency. It is as simple as that. Fundamentally, social value cannot be anything else, because with anything else the very process being judged ceases to be, and thus all worth in it and of it ceases to be; continuity becomes a meaningless sound, and truth is a lie [Foster 1950 (LN) Value, 3].

Characterizing Attributes of Foster's Value Theory

Following are some hallmark and derivative characterizations of Foster's theory of instrumental value, the criterion of judgment in social analysis. Foster did not fashion the following attributes in the form presented here; they are derived from Foster's general normative position. But they are, we believe, logically credible and empirically grounded characterizations that are helpful in understanding how the processual and evidential instrumental value principle identifies problematic conditions and determinants and guides the fashioning of corrective institutional adjustments.

Pancultural, not Parochial

Foster's instrumental value theory incorporates a conception of scientifically warranted knowledge that is universal in social analysis generally. Social inquiry is addressed to the causal determinants of breakdowns in the social structure. This inclusive theory of inquiry is not delimited by time, by place, or by culture. The principles of instrumental value theory are continuously pertinent, warranted by scientific generation and validation, and are panculturally applicable. With continued warranted inquiry, the defining principles of this inquiry mode must be expected to be revised in consequence of that inquiry, but the substantive methodological content and problem-solving relevance will continue indefinitely, even if in modified form. As we noted in the previous Chapter, science is a continuously emergent and universal way of generating and employing warranted knowledge. The data change; the problems change; the hypotheses change; the institutional policy formats change; the scope of institutional applications change; the consequential impacts change; the loci of discretion over policy change. But Foster's basic causal inquiry model of social valuation should be thought of as a continuing analytical construct that remains itself a potential object of inquiry.

The degree of success in instrumental institutional problem solving will, of course, vary over time and place. But the instrumental value principle is as pertinent in Washington as in London, in Tokyo as in Delhi. However, a considerable degree of intellectual freedom must exist in relevant private or public bodies if there are to be any pertinent proposals for modification of institutions in search of more instrumentally efficient operations. Accordingly, instrumental value theory is not the intellectual property of any one national or cultural group. But its continued development does depend, as indicated, upon permissive, if not supportive, governance structure that facilitates and supports warranted inquiry and its institutional applications.

Degrees, not Directions

Foster's instrumental value theory addresses degrees and/or levels of instrumentalness in appraising institutional structure. It has no directional constant in the sense of installing and/or implementing otherwise warranted (ceremonial, invidious, coercive) institutional adjustments. It has no teleological "drivers" (e.g. natural laws) that inherently shape the direction and implementation of institutional adjustments. It offers no ideological institutional recipes—capitalism, communism, fascism—to serve as all-purpose, all encompassing, institutional solutions for problems confronted. [See Chapter 7 below.] Indeed, these isms have proven to be theoretical and behavioral cul de sacs. They do not and cannot guide a processual economy in any constructive direction. The instrumental theory of value does require knowledge about and assessment of the condition and performance of existing structure. One may ask: does the proposed institutional adjustment create conditions that are less invidious and/or are more instrumental in the performance of a social function? Do the changes envisioned enhance the mechanisms of democratic governance?

Continuous, not Episodic

Foster's instrumental value theory is processual and continuous in form and substance. For inquirers, value analysis is always "on the way;" its "arrivals" are tentative and provisional. Its relevance and applicability must be determined anew in every particular problematic context. This normative inquiry mode then has no a priori beginning and no preconceived end-in-view except for enabling continual provisional assessments generated by inductive, deductive and/or hypothetical inferences about institutional structure and performance.

Episodic inquiry, in contrast, rests on an anterior and unexamined use of an analyzing and organizing conceptual frame whose character is determined and established prior to and/or outside the conduct of inquiry itself. An episodic presumption implies inquiry movement through an a priori succession of preconceived stages or sequence. These stages shape and delimit the structure of inquiry. For example, the data may be developed and sorted with reference to the anterior function of reinforcing the status quo. Experience is guided and shaped by the process of making and assessing consequences of institutional adjustments. Instrumental inquiry is cumulatively developmental of warranted knowledge and its application, as institutional adjustments, to problematic areas of political economy.

Evidential, not Conjectural

Foster's instrumental value theory is grounded in existential and experiential phenomena, evidentially affirmed. The quest is to seek, through inquiry, to establish conjugate correspondence between theory and fact. Evidentially grounded theory does explain what it purports to explain. To confirm this accounting, one must demonstrate logically and empirically that the explanation offered and the institutional adjustments proposed are grounded in the perceived run of pertinent evidences, both as to cause and to consequence. There is no place in instrumental value theory for idle conjectures, ungrounded speculations, or positivist affirmations. Inquirers have a continuing task to secure pertinent facts and theoretical accounts which demonstrably explain what they purport to explain.

Conjectures, then, are not stand-ins for hypotheses. The latter are the major creative dimension of all warranted inquiry. The significance of hypotheses (as we noted above) derives from their contribution to the ordering of data, the defining of focus, and the offering of causal accounts. They provide for social inquiry addressed, for example, to real problems of income generation, growth in warranted knowledge, and equitable distribution of money and real income. Conjectures, on the other hand, are speculative guesses not necessarily based on warranted knowledge. They may well be suppositions that consist of inferences drawn from false, non-existent or inadequate data. It is not inconceivable that a surmise, guess or conjecture may, *through inquiry*, ultimately become a relevant and purposive hypothesis or be validated as a construct capable of being included in scientific social inquiry. But this, surely, is an infrequent outcome. Conjectures generally are devoid of context placement, evidential grounding, and explanatory capacity. Conjectures, per se, are not capable of being integrated into processual instrumental analysis of observed phenomena.

INSTRUMENTAL THEORY OF VALUE III: IMPLICATIONS

Choice and Habit

Foster's instrumental value theory, in application, relies on both choice and habit.

Habits are Conservative

Habits represent an acquired disposition to think or behave in a particular way. They fortuitously preserve judgments, canons and tenets of conduct made earlier in response to then pertinent concerns. Habits order our lives and provide predictability. They are critical attributes of learned behavior and critical reflection.

Habits, by permitting one to economize on time and effort, are an essential precondition for choice making. The role of instrumental value theory is continuously to provide for a running appraisal of habits even as they are indulged and exhibited, often uncritically and routinely. Habits are critical in inquiry and in problem solving. They represent previously found solutions to problems. By economizing on inquiry efforts, they enhance the probable intellectual focus on problems that do currently exist. Habits are stabilizers; they may be simple or complex. But they are imbedded in institutions. In economies, most of the structural fabric consists of habits, routines, established patterns, concerning the creation of goods, the marketing of goods, and defining roles each plays in the economic process. Skills become habitual; speech patterns become habitual; inquiry modes become habitual; responses to external stimuli may well be habitual. But a habit does not create a habit. A habit does not attain significance merely in consequence of it offering a familiar response; the consequences it invokes must continuously be appraised ; habits do not provide criteria of appraisal.

Choices are Pivotal

Habits, however, need not preclude the application of criteria of appraisal. But the construction of choice requires the employment of some criterion of choice. Value premises are inescapable in choosing among options or patterns of conduct. One cannot select among two or more options with out some standard, some criterion, some value premise that indicates what ought to be. When we contend that prevailing habits produce unacceptable consequences we are evaluating conduct with an appraiser's eye on what "better" conduct might be. Choice-making formally but minimally permits the choosing among two or more options. But choice making, employing the instrumental value principle, does direct that social choices non-invidiously enhance social reconstruction, solve economic problems, and/or restore instrumental functions of existing institutions.

Problem Solving

Foster's instrumental value theory, in sum, functions to direct the resolution of institutional problems. Indeed, one cannot even define a social or economic problem without engaging in normative assessments of institutional behavior. Solving problems requires institutional change; a directed modification of the structural fabric that has become non-functional, non-instrumental, or invidious in some significant operations or impact. Problem solving means adjusting or modifying institutional patterns in pursuit of a more productive, less ceremonial, and/or more technically efficient institutional fabric.

Problems originate and appear, then, as disjunctions, malfunctions, and/or disrapport in the institutional structure that organizes the social and economic processes. The perception of a disjunctive gap occurs between what is going on and what ought to go on. For discernible reasons, instrumental functions have been abandoned, precluded, rejected, reduced, impaired or ignored. Ceremonial functions may have become dominant, pervasive and destructive. The economy may confront problematic conditions of inflation or deflation, impeded growth or stagnation, structural and/or cyclical unemployment, technical retardation or misdirection, environmental destruction and/or invidious discrimination, skewed distribution of income and product, and other impediments in the provision and distribution of the means of life and experience.

Accordingly, it is Foster's instrumental value principle that provides for an economic problem to be identified and resolved through instrumental reasoning and institutional adjustment. The solution of problems, then requires the continuing adjustment of institutions to enhance their instrumental functioning and to diminish the invidious or ceremonial impairments of one or another instrumental function in the social process.

The following Chapter addresses Foster's theory of institutional adjustment, and the democratic mechanisms that make its application possible and desirable.

REFERENCES

Ayres, Clarence E. (1944) 1978. *Theory of Economic Progress*. Chapel Hill: University of North Carolina.

———. 1961. *Toward a Reasonable Society*. Austin: University of Texas Press.

Cornford, Frances M. 1912. *From Religion to Philosophy*. London: Edward Arnold.

Dewey, John. 1922. *Human Nature and Conduct*. New York: Henry Holt

———. 1925. *Experience and Nature*. Chicago: Open Court.

———. (1927) 1946. *The Public and Its Problems*. Chicago: Gateway Books.

———. 1938. *Logic: The Theory of Inquiry*. New York: Holt, Rinehart & Winston.

———. 1939. *Theory of Valuation*. Chicago: University of Chicago Press.

———. 1946. *Problems of Men*. New York: Philosophical Library.

Foster, J. Fagg .(1942) 1981. "John Dewey and economic value. "*Journal of Economic Issues*; 15:871-897.

———. (1946). *Theoretical Foundations of Government Ownership in a Capitalist Economy*. Ph.D. Dissertation, University of Texas (unpublished).

———. 1948. Lecture Notes (LN). Value and It's Determinants [recorded & transcribed).

———. (1949) 1981. The relation between the theory of value and economic analysis. *Journal of Economic Issues*; 15:899-905.

———. 1950. Lecture Notes (LN). Value and It's Determinants.

———. 1974. Lecture Notes (LN). American Contributions to Economic Thought.

Hogben, Lancelot. 1937. *Retreat from Reason*. New York: Random House.

Kaplan, Abraham. 1961. *The New World of Philosophy*. New York: Random House.

Ranson, T. Baldwin. 1999. Personal Correspondence.

Veblen, Thorstein. (1899) 1934. *The Theory of the Leisure Class*. New York: Modern Library,

———. (1904) 1932. *The Theory of Business Enterprise*. New York: Charles Scribner's Sons.

———. (1914) 1946. *The Instinct of Workmanship*. New York: The Viking Press.

———. (1919) 1946. *The Vested Interests*. New York: The Viking Press.

———. (1919) 1961. *The Place of Science in Modern Civilization*. New York: Russell and Russell.

———. (1921) 1965. *The Engineers and the Price System*. New York: Augustus M.. Kelley.

———. (1923) 1964. *Absentee Ownership*. New York: Augustus M. Kelley.

> Economics is concerned with the living-getting process. The area of that process for which economics seeks to provide explanation and understanding is the pattern of human relationships. The pattern of human relationships takes visible form in structural institutions.
>
> Structural institutions serve two kinds of functions: on the one hand, they serve to express and to give effect to the pattern of invidious distinctions among the persons who make up the institution; on the other hand, they serve as the organizational devices through which human activities are directed to, and given material effect in, the process of providing the means of life.
>
> These two functions are the visible results of two different kinds of mental operations: the invidious-differentiation function and the "rules of the game" which give it effect are the result of conceptual operations which are based on, and seek optimum correspondence with, a preconception of the ultimate correctness of a pattern of invidious differentiation; the material-effect function and the "rules of the game" which give it effect are the results of conceptual operations which are based on, and seek optimum correspondence with, the run of the facts in the process of providing the material means of life.
>
> Therefore, the character of a structural institution is the resultant of the interplay of these two ways of thinking, the former seeking optimum fidelity to a preconceived situation, the latter seeking optimum correlation, or efficiency, in an inherently developmental process. The adjustment-determining power of the kind of thinking based on a certain pattern of invidious differentiation is a function of the coercive power of the persons giving active support to that pattern; the adjustment-determining power of the kind of thinking based on the efficiency of the economic process is a function of the scientific correctness of the pattern of ideas.
>
> The points of encroachment are specified by the emergence of the scientific understanding of any particular relation in the institutional structure on the part of the persons whose relations comprise the structure of the institution. Therefore, the pattern of adjustment is prescribed by the pattern of encroachment on the non-efficiency-determined portions of the structure by the scientific method of explanation and therefore understanding and therefore verification and therefore specification in the minds of those persons whose relationships are specified in the structural institution. This general theory is an explanation of the process of institutional adjustment (Foster, 1946, 101-103).

Foster's theory of institutional adjustment, accordingly, is an explanation in some detail of the inquiry route specified to incorporate and utilize the instrumental theory of value in the continuing process of social change.

Setting for Theory of Institutional Adjustment

Foster acknowledges that other scholars, obviously, have commented at length on differing aspects of social change, but evidently no one has formed a coherent theoretical construct approaching his three principles of institutional adjustment and "nowhere is there an effort to indicate their interrelationship" in the context of solving economic problems. Indeed, "the inclusive principles have not heretofore been given names" [Foster (1943) 1981, 928]. The formulation of this Theory of Institutional Adjustment, then, is a most provocative and significant contribution of Foster. Its analytical role is to guide and facilitate problem solving through modification of established institutional behavioral patterns that have become nonfunctional (stagnant, irrelevant, inefficient) and/or dysfunctional (ceremonial, coercive, invidious) in some significant respects. The embedding of Foster's instrumental value theory in his theory of institutional adjustment permits the joining of normative and substantive elements for guidance in problem solving. He has distilled and formalized a most pertinent, credible and significant theory of institutional adjustment. In Foster's words:

> [S]ince the agreed assignment of economics is to explain the institutional determination of the level and character of real income, economists cannot avoid analyzing all of the cause-and-effect relationships among whatever institutions exhibit such relationships. . . .[I]nnovations in the technological aspect and other non-institutional aspects of the economic process often stimulate and even compel changes in one or more components of the institutional fabric. . . .[T]he effects of such innovations and changes must be brought into the analysis [Foster, (1975) 1981, 945].

The need for a warranted and general theory to explain structural change in any economy is made evident by Foster. He suggests that technical innovations and archaic behaviors prompt much institutional structural change. He explains:

> Whether the initiating influence is in the technological sector or in the discovery of instrumental disrapport among existing institutions, efforts to resolve the problems which are created thereby force the adjustment of those institutions. For example, if the technological capacity of the economy be easily and markedly superior to the current level and quality of real income, then, clearly, the institutions must be adjusted if the problem is to be resolved. Or, for another example, if a disturbingly large portion of the population be unable to attain meaningful participation in the economic process, then numerous and obvious problems arise, and, again, the only recourse . . .is to adjust the existing institutions to permit that participation.
>
> The immediate realization is that all answers to all real economic problems necessarily take the form of institutional adjustments. Then, since theory is assigned significance in relation to its applicability, economic theory must, if it is to attain accredited significance, be addressed to the process of institutional adjustment [Foster, (1975) 1981, 945-46].

What sort of revisions should be sought if the adjustments in institutional structures are actually to contribute, e.g., to more extensive use of warranted knowledge or enhanced noninvidious participation in the economic process? What aspects or elements of institutions create problems? What aspects or elements contribute to the removal of problems? To respond, we must in this context examine the structural content and the particular functions carried on in these correlated activities perceived as institutions.

Foster contends that *all* prescribed patterns of behavior within and comprising institutions can be sorted into one or another of two analytical and behavioral categories:

> [E]very institution serves to bring the activities of individuals to bear in a contributory way. . .which is the collaborative activity of the group. . . .For example, through such institutions as contract, the market, the wage system . . .the activities of a large number of persons may be correlated so as to result in the erection of building, or the provision of foodstuffs. . . .[This is] the category [of] instrumental function[s] of institutions.
>
> [E]very institution [as well] serves a completely different kind of function: It serves to differentiate between persons and groups in invidious terms. The boss may be identified in terms of his instrumental function, but he also may be identified in terms of prestige, honor, deferential attitude or power. His "standing, we say, is "higher." By saying "higher" we do not intend to signify any superior instrumental contributions; in fact, the higher rating may stand on contrary grounds, on the power, for example, to obstruct the social process [Foster, (n.d.) 1981, 908].

Again, we observe that problem solving requires the enhancement of instrumental functions and the erosion or abandonment of invidious functions through institutional change.

Accordingly, following this introduction, we turn directly to Foster's theory of institutional adjustment beginning with *(a)* the character of scientific principles, followed by *(b)* his principle of technological determination, *(c)* his principle of recognized interdependence (alluded to above); *(d)* his principle of minimal dislocation, *(e)* his illustrative applications of the theory to the problems of land use planning and of government ownership. The Chapter concludes with *(f)* his principle of democratic implementation. For Foster, the actual achievement of institutional adjustments to resolve social problems is contingent upon the availability of, and recourse to, democratic precepts and practices.

THE CHARACTER OF SCIENTIFIC PRINCIPLES

Foster presents three *principles* of institutional adjustment. His referential content for the term "principles," then, is crucial to his argument. Moreover, this clarification of the nature and meaning of "principles" further distinguishes the institutionalist perspective in economics from that of orthodoxy. He explains that:

> Etymologically, the word [principle] refers to an inclusive and continuing operational proposition to which there are no exceptions in the universe of inquiry. In economics, then, the principles presumably set forth the determinants of the processes through which human beings provide themselves with the means of life and experience. . . .[T]he principles are supposed to explain the determination of the level and character of real income. But in the "mainstream" of economics, the term has become restricted to the determination of comparative prices through the interplay of forces called supply and demand which in turn are presented as the effective expression of the controlling factors in human nature; thus the claim to generality and foundation in the study of a particular . . .institutional variable. In compliance with this claim, all other institutional variations and adjustments are treated as exogenous to the central cause-effect sequence defining the economic process.

> [This]. . .general pattern of analysis of the economic process is usually referred to as neoclassical economics. [Foster, (1972) 1981, 938].

For Foster, "mainstream" neoclassical *principles* of economics are not scientific principles; claims to their exclusivity, relevance, and sufficiency cannot be substantiated. Such "principles" are neither general nor foundational. They "do not appear to be inclusive and continuing factors in all aspects of the economic process. They appear rather to be tenets which may apply to a lone institution [price] under very specific and restricted circumstances. . . .Price is indeed an important economic phenomenon." But it is "untenable" for economists to "assign it the position of foundation and generality in the economic process" [Foster, (1972) 1981, 939]. In the social sciences generally, as well as in economics, institutions of various kinds: families, unions, corporations, governmental constraints and subsidies, et cetera, are necessarily objects of investigation by inquirers. But such scholars "find no evidence that price is exempt from any generic quality that can be observed in the determination of other institutions. . . .There is nothing unique about price" (940). What scholars have observed is "the mutual interplay of adjustments in related institutions consequent upon changes in either the institutional or the technological aspects of the social process" (940).

> Both kinds of initiating changes are consequences of the process of inventing, of contriving new means, ways, or devices. But the principles governing invention and discovery emerge out of the process of problem solving; they do not resemble the principles of supply and demand. Indeed the initial proffer of an innovation typically is regarded as something of an affront. The first inventor of the bronze ax probably was sacrificed to the gods in the volcano by the holy order of flint workers [Foster, (1972) 1981, 940].

In institutionalist inquiry, *principle*s have scientific warrant; they are fundamental generalities; they are evidentially validated; they identify and disclose continuing economic functions and factors. They exhibit evidential grounding. Situational elements, in contrast, are not continuous; institutional patterns and structures change over time. Cross-section views of the economic process do not disclose processual functions. "The only continuing factors involved are the functions carried on through institutions—the institutions themselves vary from culture to culture and over time in any particular culture" [Foster, (1946) 1981, 931]. The inclusive economic function, as noted, is the production and distribution of real income. Instrumental functions are continuous; "they are validated on the evidences of contribution to the efficiency and continuity of the social process"; invidious functions are discontinuous; they are "validated on some assumption of authority" (931).

Principles, then, are instruments of explanation. "[I]f they are to be applicable to social problems, they must disclose what kind of data are pertinent to the problem at hand, and they must disclose how those data are related to one another so that the data can be arranged for analysis" [Foster, (1946) 1981, 932].They must order and shape inquiry into the social process and disclose continuing functions and processes. As Foster explains: "Scientific principles. . .are statements of continuing functions uniformly applicable to all items in the area of inquiry. In social science, the area of inquiry is the social process, and so any principle for which generality and foundation might be claimed must be applicable to all aspects of that process" (931). Foster's three Principles of Institutional Adjustment meet this test of applicability to the social process.

THE PRINCIPLE OF TECHNOLOGICAL DETERMINATION

The roles of science and technology in affecting social change are central. Foster writes:

> "[T]echnology determines how the instrumental functions are carried on. . . . And, since technology is simply the application of scientific physical theory, there is no way to undo technology short of destroying the actual persons with the know-how. . . .We cannot "unknow" something which we do know in the scientific sense. Therefore, we cannot escape from taking scientific know-how as a given datum in social problems. And we thus cannot escape from adjusting our institutions so that their instrumental functions are carried on so as to make tolerably efficient use of that know-how. . . .Technology is determinate of both the character of our experience in providing the means of life and the character of our experience in making use of those means. . . . Invention is, indeed, the mother of necessity [Foster, (n.d.) 1981, 912].

In a Syllabus on "Institutional Adjustment" prepared for social science students at the University of Denver, Foster offers perhaps his most succinct statement of the principle of technological determination:

> The principle of technological determination is simply that social problems can be solved only by adjusting the institutional structures involved in the problem so as to bring them into instrumentally efficient correlation with the technological aspects of the problems. What is meant by "instrumentally efficient correlation" is that the instrumental functions of the institutions in question be carried on at a level of efficiency tolerable to the members of the institution in view of the possibilities indicated by those same technological factors. The members of an institution cannot "unknow" anything which they do know as a technological or physical fact; and no amount of coercion, short of complete destruction, can alter that situation. The members of an institution cannot avoid seeking adjustments because they cannot avoid the human incidences of a problematic situations which require adjustment. And, since they cannot "unknow' their accomplishments in the technological area, they are driven toward institutional modifications so long as the problem and they remain.[Foster, (1948) 1981, 932].

There is a continuing compulsion, then, as new warranted knowledge (inclusive of technology) is generated and made available, to explore its pertinence for incorporation into the existing knowledge fund, and its consequential creation of, and/or impact on social and economic problems as perceived by persons affected therewith. We ask: What problems exist? What has gone awry? What institutional structures have become inadequate, obsolete, irrelevant, or oppressive? What kind and extent of institutional adjustments can be recommended?

Always, technological determination creates both options and limits. For example, what existing systems of medical authority and direction have become discernible and which judgments therein are subjected to question? What recent additions to medical knowledge and its delivery have made previous practices (technical and institutional) obsolete? Consider, e.g., the health delivery implications of medical and surgical technologies and knowledge in heart by-pass surgery, in organ-transplants, even in cloning capabilities. Questions of normative merit and value, of entitlement, of relevant medical skills, of adequacy of facilities, of governmental promotion and/or regulation, of public and/or private methods of payment, involve and require a continuing deliberation on how to bring new medical knowledge effectively and fairly into use. Of what would actual instrumentally efficient recommendations for institutional adjustments in the provision of medical care consist?

We acknowledge, from what has already been said, that "adjusting the institutional structures involved in the problem so as to bring them into instrumentally efficient correlation with the technological aspects of the problem," is in no way a trivial pursuit, an ideological panacea, or a historical recipe. Technological determination not only creates problems; it also "is determinate of the solutions in the sense that it constitutes the basic data which must be taken as given in social problems" [Foster, (1948) 1981, 932].

THE PRINCIPLE OF RECOGNIZED INTERDEPENDENCE

We have already observed that Foster explains how actual changes in behavior can occur only when there is some recognition on the part of those affected of the need for institutional change and a willingness to accept that change as indicated by an instrumental assessment of the problematic conditions to which inquiry is addressed. His more formal statement follows:

> The principle of recognized interdependence is simply that the immediate pattern of any institutional adjustment is specified by the pattern of interdependencies recognized by members of the institution. Institutional structures are made up of habitual behavior in most part, but an adjustment in any such structure requires that a deliberate choice be made among the possible alternatives recognized by those who must alter their behavior. A new pattern of behavior requires that the behavior be "directed" in its initiation. It becomes habitual through repetition, but its initial performance requires conscious direction. Since all adjustments, and therefore the whole of institutional structure, are specified at initiation, it necessarily follows that conceptual apprehension *precedes* the course of action differentiating the new pattern from the old [Foster, (1948) 1981, 933, emphasis added].

The principle holds as well in situations where *members of the institution* have not acquiesced in the establishment of their own institutional structure; where self-determination does not exist. It also holds in situations where *those affected by policy* have not been actively involved in its initiation.

> In either or both cases, the fact still remains that the new pattern of behavior must be specified in conceptual form before it can emerge into the new pattern of behavior. However unwillingly the persons involved accept the new pattern and however little discretion they may have in specifying the adjustment, they must recognize their actual relationships as specified in the new pattern.

> Otherwise the pattern simply does not eventuate into action. No one can perform a new activity without deliberately directing his efforts in the novel activity [Foster, (1948), 1981, 933].

As we observed above in Foster's comments on Veblen, "patterns of human relationships we call institutions are [indeed] 'made up of' habitual actions and attitudes, but they are not *determined* by habit. Their determination is a matter of deliberate and guided action. The habituation follows; it does not precede. Constitution is not the same as determination" [Foster, (1948) 1981, 933, emphasis in original). We initiate institutional adjustments, then, that *become* habitual. The initiation may be self-originated or otherwise directed, but individual recognition of a newly introduced prescriptive rule, and a consequential incorporation of altered behavior, are required if any structural change is actually to be realized. The distinction between "self-originating" and "otherwise directed" changes in conduct is a critical one that bears on the acceptance or rejection of institutional adjustments. To repeat, institutional patterns are constituted of habits but they are not determined by habits. At bottom, human agents are discretionary beings whose very continuance requires the making of choices among and between alternative institutional adjustments in view of the consequences that can reasonably be expected from recourse to one, rather than another.

THE PRINCIPLE OF MINIMAL DISLOCATION

We have now acknowledged Foster's understanding of the origins of circumstances and conditions which singly or conjointly generate the need for institutional adjustments. We also have acknowledged that a new pattern of behavior "must be specified in conceptual form at initiation" and be understood by those affected if it is to provide direction for institutional change. What remains is the Principle of Minimal Dislocation. This principle affirms that all institutional adjustments must be capable of being incorporated into the remainder of the institutional structure without significantly disrupting instrumental functions of nonproblematic structure, if they are to be contributive to problem resolution. This principle "discloses the limits of adjustment in terms of rate and in terms of degree and area" [Foster, (1948) 1981, 934].

Pose these queries: How rapidly can changes in institutional structure be introduced? Fairly rapidly, perhaps, *if* the first two principles are observed. How extensive will the disruption of existing patterns be if the new structures are introduced? Minimal dislocation means that overreaching must be avoided. Changes should be limited to instances where invidious and ceremonial judgments are significantly impeding the economic process. What changes in behaviors and attitudes can be anticipated? Only those fashioned with an eye on the most significant and encompassing recognitions of the need for adjustment.

The minimal dislocation premise implies and affirms that communities *cannot* stop and start over. Utopias fail precisely because no human agent can comprehensively *abandon* an extensive and intricate pattern of beliefs and accompanying behaviors and remain a contributive member of the community. No ideological recipe for an ideal social and economic order has any scientific merit or validation. Individuals and communities cannnot, in matter of a few days or even weeks, *comprehensively* alter its habitual behavior and institutions. Maximal dislocation will sabotage the constructive economic functions on which all communities individually and collectively must depend. As Foster observes:

> In the first place, the adjustments must be in tolerable rapport with the noninstitutional factors. Attempted adjustments must make instrumentally better use of the technological factors, else they simply increase the human incidences that initially motivated the adjustments. In this sense, there is compulsion toward progress. In the second place, attempted or contemplated adjustments must be brought as problematic factors into the comprehension of persons involved; and those projections must do no violence to the factors not considered problematic. Otherwise, it would be impossible to initiate the new pattern because of its disruption of the social process [(1948) 1981, 934].

Foster summarizes his theory of institutional adjustment with the following comments and contentions:

> The principle of technological determination discloses what data are required, both institutional and non-institutional, to grasp any particular social problem. The data encompassed in this principle constitute the requirements for recognizing the difference between "what is" and "what ought to be" in terms of institutional structure as judged by its performance of its instrumental functions. It discloses what information must be in hand to determine what adjustments should be made [Foster, (1948) 1981, 934].
>
> The principle of recognized interdependence discloses the immediate character of institutional innovations which are attempted. It therefore identifies what must be done to get from "what is" to "what ought to be." In application, it specifies the pattern of understandings which must be accomplished in order to solve any particular problem. The actual content of its specifications in reference to any particular social problem is disclosed by the data used in "filling in" the first principle (934-35).
>
> The principle of minimal dislocation discloses what limitations, in terms of rate and extent, are in effect (935).
>
> Filling in the data specified by the first principle when applied to a specific problem discloses "what is" and "what ought to be"—it sets up the problem so that the. . .[inquirer] may anticipate what *will* be the course of adjustment as well as what *should* be the course of adjustment. The application of the second principle to the same data as understood by the persons involved discloses what should be done as well as the probability of its eventuation. The application of the third principle sets forth what can be done. Together with their pattern of interrelationships, they constitute the theory of institutional adjustment [Foster.(1948) 1981, 935, emphasis added)].

APPLICATIONS: THEORY OF INSTITUTIONAL ADJUSTMENT

Land Use Planning

In a paper written in 1942, Foster applies his then newly constructed theory of institutional adjustment to the area of land use planning in the United States. He is concerned to examine empirically and analytically problematic conditions that prevail in agriculture with reference especially to governmental land use policies, and to existing and growing technological developments in and for agriculture.

With the closing of the physical frontier in the late 19th century, the government's policy of "bestowing titles to public lands on anyone who contemplated any enterprise calculated to be of ultimate public benefit," and the government's emerging interest in conservation and water use, forced its "recognition of the interdependence of the various groups in the nation's economy." It consequently was obliged, indeed compelled, to address the general topic of land use planning. The government's historic land use policy had been based on grants of public lands in "constant physical units without regard to soil types or the most appropriate use" i.e. "so many acres per person" or per enterprise recipient. Many of these beneficiaries were speculators. The land grants to railroads, were, of course, enormous by any standard [Foster, (1942) 1981, 990-91].

The technological revolution in agriculture was at least as significant as that in industry. The advent of agricultural colleges, experimental stations, and the expanding role of the Department of Agriculture, in the late 19th century prompted a major escalation in productivity that continues into the present. "The activities purporting to develop agricultural technology have expanded to every part of the nation and offer direct contact and service to every farmer" (991).

In Foster's words, "the real problem is how to use the soil in terms of present state of technological development. . .so as to realize the greatest general welfare" (993). But to identify the substantive content of the expression "general welfare" compels recourse to value theory.

Technological Determination

Productive use of land is necessarily a major and continuing concern in any operative economy of any size. Land use is, and must remain, a continuing component of the economic process. Land use planning, therefore, remains high on the agenda of any discretionary management of the economic process. Foster acknowledges its significance and applies his value theory to this area of concern:

> [L]and use is a function of the state of technological development. It is recognized that institutional obstructions exist and that they enter in a negative sense into the problem. But they offer no basis for a logical approach to the problem; they merely inhibit accommodation of organization and operation to the technological situation. The problem in regard to the institutional obstructions is an educational one, not an economic one in the strict sense. The approach to land use planning must be on the basis of how to attain the greatest summation of economic values, and the summation of values is what is meant by welfare. This objective, welfare, can be attained directly in proportion as the approach to the problem is based on the most efficient land use as determined by the state of technological development [Foster, (1942) 1981, 1000].

Recognized Interdependence

As we noted above, Foster quite correctly contends that "In deliberate economic changes, people require to know the solutions as well as the answers. . .[T]he application of economic planning of any sort *means* the operational participation of the people, and they cannot engage in economic activity without some comprehension of what they are to do and the purpose for so doing. . . .[L]and use planning cannot be applied without the participation of the people whose relationship to the land is thereby affected [Foster, (1942) 1981, 1000, emphasis in original].

Land use planning as a process depends on the use of instrumental inquiry in the identification of problems of underdevelopment or impairment in the production and disposition of agricultural output. Factual inquiry must disclose the substantive differences between "what is" and "what ought to be." Hypothetical ends-in-view provide the criteria that guide inquiry in the selection of data and in its analytical ordering. As with all instrumental inquiry, the quest is for causal comprehension of the determinants of the conditions that are perceived to be problematic. These conditions are the causal determinants of the identified problem, but the application of these insights and outcomes remains. As Foster puts it:

> [A]fter determination of the conditions that constitute the problem of land use planning and after logical resolution of the problem in terms of welfare, the application of the solution remains. The application can be initiated by the sovereign, whether [it be] the people, as in a democracy, or an individual, as in an autocracy, but the successful operation of the solution necessitates that the people involved understand what is happening and why. The degree to which the people involved in cooperative enterprise such as land use planning will function interrelatedly is determined by the degree of their recognized interdependence. . . .Successful application is not to be expected if the plan does not stay within the limits of recognized interdependence. . . .The principle of recognized interdependence is, in a sense, a derivative of the principle of technological determination. It is the "state of the industrial arts" that determines the degree of specialization of which this principle is a function. The degree of specialization in land use has constantly been increasing, and in the discernible future gives promise of continuing the same trend. This means greater interdependence if our theory of welfare in terms of technological efficiency is valid. And this indicates a continuously greater need for logical land use planning. But application of any plan must be within the limits set by recognized interdependencies. [Foster, (1942) 1981, 1001].

Minimum Dislocation

Foster well understood that technological enhancement in the production of food and fiber provided by land use planning could, and probably would, be dislocative. Those involved in or affected by the institutional adjustments advanced are called upon to modify habitual and common practices and perhaps even beliefs. For example, workers' habits, workers' options, workers' income, workers' discretion over employment, conditions of employment, technological displacement of labor, et cetera. may well be proposed and anticipated with much insecurity. Discretionary roles over policy may be increased, decreased, and/or relocated. Some dislocation is therefore inescapable, but such disruptions of habit and practice should be kept to that minimum which is sufficient to achieve the implementation of the new knowledge, new instruments, new concepts and material. Remedial provisions and adjustments must also be included on the land use planning agenda.

Not only is the *character* of land use planning of concern but the *implementation* of such planning also bears on what is and is not a "minimal dislocation." Foster's view follows:

> In the present state of technological development and the consequent widespread interdependencies, if any planned adjustment is made there must be a commonly accepted agency to make the planning effective. The only agent in modern society that can be empowered with this function is government. This is a necessity since the adjustments necessary to efficient land use are beyond the power of farmers to effect, even if they all worked in voluntary harmony and cooperation; adjustment must be made in part by groups whose interests are antithetical to efficient land use and who would, therefore, not cooperate [Foster, (1942) 1981, 1003], [Veblen would likely identify such "interests" as "vested"].

Following is Foster's own summary of the employment of his three Principles comprising the theory of institutional adjustment vis-a-vis land use planning:

The Principle of Technological Determination "is the direct application of the [instrumental] theory of value and its concomitant theory of welfare to the problem of land use planning". . . .The Principle of Recognized Interdependence "is correlative with the first and derived from it. It. . .points out the fact that any planning of land use necessarily starts from 'what is' and can be applied successfully in proportion as the persons involved realize the degree of their interdependence in terms of welfare as the objective." The Principle of Minimal Dislocation "is conceived in terms of the first. It points out that technological efficiency may be violated. . .in deliberate change . . .and that therefore planning must take into consideration the means whereby this will be at a minimum" [Foster, (1942) 1981, 1005].

Government Ownership

In his doctoral dissertation, entitled "Theoretical Foundations of Government Ownership in a Capitalist Economy" (1946), Foster presents an explanation of how and why economies ostensibly capitalist in design and validation, nevertheless exhibit productive enterprises and economic institutions that are governmentally owned and operated. While most of his demonstration cannot be pursued herein, his explanation of how and why public productive organizations are *chosen* as institutional options in economies ideologically committed to the promotion of private enterprise and minimal governments, is most instructive. The rationales that justify the shifting of the operating structure of a productive function from private to public, or from public to private control and operation, must at bottom, be other than ideological mantras.

Briefly, Foster examines the divergent historical circumstances that led the community to establish or convert streets and highways, harbors and waterways, waterworks and sewage disposal, schools, forestry and housing to governmental ownership (1946, 8). That is, "processes have been carried on directly by bodies politic through their duly organized governments" (1946,1). What he demonstrates, not unexpectedly, is that in each case the institutional context and difficulties therewith are in some sense unique. Causal antecedents of the shift to public control of roads and canals differ from those encountered in explaining the growth of pubic schooling, for example. Clearly, then Foster must fashion and employ an encompassing *theory* of institutional adjustment to account for the initiation and/or acceptance of governmental performance of economic functions. That *theory* was introduced above.

In the following illustrative example, the theory of institutional adjustment is employed: Foster asks, "did streets and highways become government-owned for reasons which find expression through the market process?" His reply is negative across the board: There was no deficiency in private capital. The users could have paid for the service. The returns would not have been excessively postponed. "Consumer surplus" would not have been foregone. Controlling traffic was not at issue. "The government ownership of streets and roads seems to have been occasioned by situations which do not find expression through price" (1949, 137-38).

On the contrary, "roads became a physical necessity and were recognized as such. . . .The market process did not keep up with the recognized need. . . .The physical need of roads could be better met by payment through taxes than by sale of the service. . . .The general pattern of the institutional adjustments relating to streets and roads has been in the direction of setting up the control devices which permit the optimum physical correlation between roads and the remainder of the economy" (1946, 138-39). Foster argues that the basic issues were not particularly those of ownership but involved the quest to get more and better roads, locally and nationally. Foster explains:

> [T]he general pattern of the causal sequence seems to have been as follows: *(1)* the development of a physical need, *(2)* recognition of that need by the people involved, and *(3)* selection of the most efficient, available control-device. The first step was a matter of people and geography and invention. It was occasioned in some measure by people pushing beyond the area of the price-determined economy because of comparatively superior living-getting possibilities in the relatively non-price frontier economy. Thus price determinations may be thought of as a causal factor. But that relationship was one of restriction and limitation rather than one of positive dynamic. The first step bears out the principle of technological determination. The second step was a matter of enlightenment. It bears out the principle of recognized interdependence. The third step was a matter of accommodation with the limits imposed by the first two steps and by those aspects of the total institutional structure which did not enter the problem as items on which choices could be made. For example, the decisions to place roads under government ownership did not entail any prospect of abandoning payment by the people who used the roads generally, nor did it involve any idea of the roads not being paid for in money terms. Thus the government ownership

of roads was made with minimum dislocation to the institutional structure generally (1946, 139-40).

THE PRINCIPLE OF DEMOCRATIC IMPLEMENTATION

Foster's commitment to democratic theory and practice is optimistically inclusive and conceptually unambiguous. If it seems unusual for an economist to be profoundly concerned with political theory and applications, with the way in which public policy is created and implemented, perhaps the following commentary will be instructive. We will argue that it is not an exaggeration to assert that, in Foster's view, his principles of institutional adjustment *can not easily serve* as guiding constructs addressed to problem solving *unless* the social order and its economic processes are developed and operated with democratic concepts, in pursuit of democratic purposes.

Democratic Concepts

Democratic Rule Making

With and since the end of the Cold War around the globe, "there is," argues Foster,

> a tacit admission that the idea of democracy has already won. No one now seriously dares to bid for the active support from the rest of the world under any other banner. . . .It would seem that democracy must be the spelling on whatever banners are carried into the struggle. . . .The ordinary peoples conceive democracy to be the popular determination of public policy. . .and they are correct. . . .[T]he actual popular determination of public policy and therefore of institutional structure is nothing. . .unless the people themselves have the right to determine which things the people will act upon and how they will go about acting. There is no safer—indeed, there is no other—effective guardian of the fundamental sovereignty of the people than the actual exercise of that sovereignty. If history has disclosed anything with certainty it is that arbitrary power begets arbitrary power; it is that dictatorship, under whatever name and to whatever degree, never willingly adjusts toward democracy [Foster, (1949) 1981, 976-77].

What Foster makes clear is that his referent for democracy does not imply any *particular* institutional structure as such. It does not defer to or abide a dictatorship of the proletariat, a republican form, a capitalist system, a competitive corporatism, a tripartite government, a utopian commune, or a plutocratic elite. Lincoln's concept of "government by the people," extended for clarification into "the popular determination of public policy" (i.e. the institutional structure must be determined by popular judgment) is Foster's characterization of the democratic process [Foster. (1949) 1981, 979]. He argues that when American's "have judged that a particular institutional structure is resulting in a contravention of the popular conception of proper policy, we have changed that structure" (979). The democratic process is then both a practical and a pertinent vehicle through which to seek problem-solving institutional adjustments.

Freedom versus License

We are, then, in search of rational theory which will permit, if it does not ensure, that institutional adjustments introduced will typically have more cogency, relevance and credibility if they are generated through open inquiry and implemented through democratic means and measures. But our conceptions of what a democratic system is, and how it functions to facilitate communal problem solving, have often been confused because of a failure to distinguish confidently between *freedom* and *license*. If democratic procedures are to be employed, we need to clear away this troublesome conceptual underbrush so that we can carefully distinguish between the *freedom* to propose institutional adjustments and the *license* to corrupt and destroy that process. Foster clarifies this distinction:

> License has [sometimes] been defined for the community as overextended freedom. Thus, since almost everyone is against license, almost everyone concludes that the way to exclude license is to limit freedom. . .the [alleged] problem is where to draw the line [between the two ideas]. . . .[F]reedom is conceived as a sort of midway position on the axis of an attribute running from slavery to license [Foster, (1966) 1981, 972].

For Foster and institutionalists, however, freedom means *discretion*, "the genuine right to choose among available genuine alternatives. . . .The conception of freedom as discretion involving genuine alternatives operates through understanding and is founded on integrity." In contrast, "license is *privileged impairment of the social process*. . . .It necessarily involves infringement of the continuity of choice among the alternatives. Its operating factor is propaganda, and its cornerstone is power" [Foster, (1966) 1981, 972, emphases in original). Accordingly, as Foster sees it,

> [F]reedom and license, so conceived, are not opposite extremes of a single attribute. They are not opposite extremes of the same thing. . . .These two things are different in kind; they are not merely different degrees of each other. Likewise their corollaries contrast in kind rather than degree. Understanding and propaganda, the respective *modi* of freedom and license, are not opposite poles of a common axis. Understanding is the comprehension of causal relationships; propaganda is excuse-hunting for a predilection. . . .Neither is a smaller or larger degree of the other. And a parallel contrast exists between integrity and power. Certainly, no extension or contraction of either constitutes the other. . . .Freedom does not become license when its boundaries are extended, and license does not become freedom however much constricted. Each is antithetical to the other at all levels or degrees of either or both [Foster. (1966) 1981, 972, emphasis in original].

Accordingly, for Foster and institutionalists, democratic freedom means an expanding area of discretion for members of the community over the creation, operation, and adjustment of institutional structures in the social process.

Power versus Authority

For Foster, *power* means exercising discretion over other peoples' behavior *without responsibility* to such persons. *Authority*, for Foster, in contrast, means exercising discretion over others *with responsibility* to them, validated by their comparative ignorance and dependence. The exercise of authority is instrumental where the recipient lacks relevant warranted knowledge and where the discretion of the authority is guided by the non-invidious interests of the recipient (Ranson, 1999). For example, the discretion exercised over children's conduct by, as we say, *responsible* parents, would be perceived as an exercise of authority. The exercise of discretion over children that served only the invidious or ceremonial interests of the parents would be perceived as an exercise of power; it would be widely acknowledged as *irresponsible* judgment and conduct. The children are controlled in either case, but the normative credibility of authority hinges on the character of and purposes served by the exercise of discretion.

Foster reiterates: "Does not the useful distinction between power and authority disallow the use of the word power to include both? Since both words connote discretion over the behavior of others, they are easily inter-changed. . . .But since power means that exercise without responsibility to those whose behavior is directed and authority includes that direct responsibility, does not the latter offer avenues toward Jefferson's idea of equality?" [Foster 1964, 1162, emphasis added.]

The response is affirmative. A democratic process provides for the popular determination of public policy. Those elected to serve the community by exercising discretion on its behalf have contingent and delimited authority, and thus the responsibility, to make choices of structural change on behalf of the community. But the contingency is reflected in *accountability*. In a democracy, the irresponsible exercise of authority can be abated or reversed by political means. Equality in this context means non-invidious participation in holding elected leaders to account.

Noninvidious Participation

Foster argues that democratic determination of policy requires that the members of the community participate without reference to, or being the victim of, the *invidious* use of distinctions among persons. Recall that Veblen's referential content for "invidious" is the "comparison of persons with a view to rating and grading them in respect of relative worth or value" [Veblen, (1899) 1934, 34]. Accordingly, to deny access to political participation with the invidious use of such indices of "worth" as race, age, gender, color, wealth, ancestry, or power is to preclude and/or corrupt the adjustment of institutions in pursuit of instrumental ends-in-view. Denying access, marginalizing participants, intimidating activists, and imposing misinformation all have the effects of forestalling and/or corrupting an instrumental comprehension of what the demonstrable nature of a problem is and of aborting any serious efforts at institutional adjustment to resolve the problem.

Attention, then, must continuously be focused on the character of the political process of developing popular policy to facilitate institutional adjustments across the broad spectrum of the political-economy. The heart of the matter is that all members of the community generally must continuously have the freedom, as identified above, to participate non-invidiously in generating the institutional structures that facilitate informed judgments, to create and sustain institutional adjustments that provide and preserve political participation, and to make the structure of governmental institutions, and those engaged therein, continuously accountable to the larger community. Democratic forms and constraints should permit the community regularly if not routinely, to undertake institutional adjustments reflecting instrumental attributes, when and as needed as perceived by the community. As Foster continuously reminded his students, *democracy*, because of its continuous promotion of reasoned discourse and instrumental design of institutional adjustments, *is the most instrumentally efficient approach to social policy-making known.* Accordingly, all other approaches are less instrumentally efficient because in one form or another, invidious and/or ceremonial judgments and structure get in the way of making the corrective instrumentally warranted institutional adjustments needed. Through democratic means it is both possible and desirable to determine the institutional character and the instrumental functioning of all aspects of the social process.

Indeed, in a democracy there is a continuing *compulsion* toward instrumentally warranted progress. So long as democratic means of deliberation and social action are available, the community is prompted to continue its experimentation with alternative institutional forms until the most efficient options, on present warranted knowledge, are chosen. Policies, for example, that would ensure the maintenance of intellectual freedom, that would provide educational access for all who can benefit therefrom, that would develop responsibility of print and visual media for enhancing instrumental understanding, that would fund political campaigns through public rather than private sources, that would treat access to employment as a human right, are instrumentally warranted functions the implementation of which would help create, facilitate and sustain the popular determination of public policy, that is, democracy.

We turn now, in Chapter 6, to the American Contribution to social and economic inquiry, some cultural and intellectual resources in the United States, on which Foster's draws in formulating his general theory of institutional economics.

REFERENCES

Foster, J. Fagg. (1942) 1981. The approach to land use planning in a changing technology. *Journal of Economic Issues;* 15:985-1007.

———. (1943) 1981. The theory of institutional adjustment. *Journal of Economic Issues;* 15:923-928.

———. 1946. *Theoretical Foundations of Government Ownership in a Capitalist Economy.* Ph.D. Diss. University of Texas, Austin. 1-188.

———. 1948. Lecture Notes (LN). *Value and Its Determinants.* (Taped, transcribed, bound. 1-382).

———. (1948) 1981. Syllabus for Problems of Modern Society: The theory of institutional adjustment. *Journal of Economic Issues;* 15:929-935.

———. 1948. Lecture Notes (LN). History of Economic Thought.

———. (1949) 1981. The United States, Russia, and democracy. *Journal of Economic Issues;* 15:975-980.

———. 1949. Lecture Notes (LN). Comparative Economic Systems.

———. 1950. Lecture Notes (LN). Comparative Economic Systems.

———. 1964, Book Review of *Wealth and Power in America,* by Gabriel Kolko, *Monthly Labor Review*, Oct: 1162.

———. (1966) 1981. Freedom and license in higher education. *Journal of Economic Issues;* 15:969-973.

———. (1972) 1981. The fundamental principles of economics. *Journal of Economic Issues; 15:937-942.*

———. (1975) 1981. Current structure and future prospects of institutional economics. *Journal of Economic Issues;* 15:943-947.

———. (n.d.) 1981. The effect of technology on institutions. *Journal of Economic Issues;* 15:907-913.

Ranson, T. Baldwin. 1999. Personal Correspondence.

Tool, Marc R. 1995. *Pricing, Valuation and Systems.* Aldershot: Edward Elgar.

Veblen, Thorstein B. (1899) 1934. *The Theory of the Leisure Class.* New York: Modern Library.

6 THE AMERICAN EXPERIENCE AND CONTRIBUTION

The frontier gave validity to the ideal of human equality without reference to economic status. J. Fagg Foster

INTRODUCTION

Fagg Foster comes to a consideration and assessment of the American experience unabashedly as an American patriot, but certainly an atypical one. He seeks to identify primary attributes of that experience that contribute to its emergence as the world's leading political economy. Some examples: He regards the three-century experience with the American frontier to be fortuitously and significantly unique in important and continuing ways. He considers the American Declaration of Independence and the Constitution of the United States to be historically peerless and dramatically consequential in their stipulations of the structure and function of democratic governments. He reminds us of the extent to which these documents have been copied, mimicked and adapted for use elsewhere by those in pursuit of non-invidious self-governance. In his emeritus years he reads the autobiographical literature of Jefferson in search of the latter's early recognition of distinguishing attributes of the American experience and its relevance for contemporary inquiry.

This Chapter is addressed, accordingly, to Foster's characterization and assessment of aspects of the emergence and development of the American political economy and to selections of American institutionalists' contributions to analyses of the economic process and problems arising therein. In Part One, the distinguishing attributes of the American experience, as perceived by Foster, are considered: Topics included are: *(a)* stimuli for change, *(b)* the influence and consequences of a three hundred year frontier experience, *(c)* existential compulsions toward problem solving, *(d)* institutional inventions and innovations (institutional adjustments) as a necessarily continuing function. In Part Two, we explore Foster's assessment of the analytical and interpretative contributions to American institutionalist economics of: Thorstein B. Veblen, John Dewey, Clarence E. Ayres (an extension of earlier considerations above), John R. Commons, Wesley Clair Mitchell, and John Maurice Clark. Summary observations conclude the Chapter.

DISTINGUISHING ATTRIBUTES OF EXPERIENCE

Stimuli for Change

People left for the New World from one or another European community in the 17th, 18th and 19th centuries, via a long and threatening voyage, for a variety of reasons, of course. Some sought to escape political oppression or religious prosecution; others sought relief from outright famine or conscription into military service. Some were willing to sign on as indentured servants in the expectation that after the indentured period they would have opportunities unconfined by status, income, or ancestry. The movement of captive Negro people from slave status to discretionary status, of course, was legally accomplished only in the post-Civil War period. Perhaps the "prisons of Europe" were emptied; perhaps many were malcontents, ne'er-do-wells, or outsiders. The fact of their removal—coerced or voluntary—from a known community and environment into one that was largely unknown, confronted individuals with major and continuing demands on their knowledge, capacities, resources and adaptability. They were seeking increased discretion over their own lives and livelihood—eventually if not immediately.

If the old habits did not work (i.e. function), expectations had to be modified. The institutional structures through which the lives of immigrants would be ordered and their work arranged would almost certainly be different. They were compelled by force of circumstance to engage in and/or respond to institutional prescriptions that were for them often novel and unfamiliar. But what they came to confront and acknowledge is that institutions are not "fundamental data. These things, in any particular form and however dearly apprised, are assumed to be subject to change at will and invention." [Foster (n.d.) 1981, 981]. They came increasingly to realize that "particular patterns of institutions have to be changed as the 'state of industrial arts' changes" and that "the continuing factors in social analysis are the social processes carried on through the use of material things and the use of institutional structures" (981-82). This *realization*, argues Foster, was of extraordinary significance:

> It prompted the American Revolution, and it found expression in the fundamental blueprint of the body politic and body economic: in the Declaration of Independence and in the Constitution of the United States, the two most revolutionary documents in the history of mankind. Those documents specified what has now become the oldest political organization of any large community on. . .earth. The US. government is now the oldest government in the world. And its continuity during the most revolutionary period of world history has been maintained. . .because of the realization that the criterion of judgment is not the sanctity of particular institutional structures; it is rather the efficiency of the social process. That is to say that the theory of value is the quality of human life and that human life is correctly judged in terms of developmental continuity [Foster (n.d.) 1981, 982].

Foster continues:

> This idea is now spreading around the world, with all the upheavals and with the quagmire of mistakes now so obtrusive. . . .[A]mong the most revolutionary effects of the American experience is the arrangement through which changes in institutional structures, however revolutionary, can be brought about without the unfortunate accompaniments which occur in less fortunate communities. The last serious remnant of the contrary opinion [in the US] was settled in the Civil War in the 1860s, and that settlement was conclusive. These ideas about the criterion of judgment—about the theory of value—and the consequent ideas about institutional adjustment became actually operational in a large community for the first time in the United States [Foster (n.d.) 1981, 982].

The Role and Significance of the Frontier

What emerged as a political reality that fostered democratic determination of policy, as alluded to above, was reflected as well in the economic reality of new and adaptive institutional forms organizing the economic process. The quest for enhanced discretion over one's political participation was paralleled by the quest for enhanced discretion over one's economic options in pursuit of the sufficiency of, and continuity in access to, the flow of real income. Indeed economic options are necessarily interdependent with political options.

For Foster, the social flexibility alluded to in the foregoing generalities, was largely a consequence of the physical and quite novel presence of a nearly three century long *land frontier*. Foster explains: "[W]ith the exception of small areas along the extreme eastern seaboard, Americans developed their economy and their formative ideas about it in the effective presence of a land frontier. Land was available to anyone who could and would make use of it in the absence of effectively organized power structures" [(n.d.) 1981, 982].

It was this "absence" that was permissive; institutional experimentation and creation were possible, even typical, because, until near the end of the settling, there were no centralized, effectively organized, control structures. On the frontier, settlers were institution-creators; they were not compelled to model a community in accord with some external and established governmental body. They could, and did, create their own proscriptive and prescriptive stipulations of option and conduct. They could and did establish their own initial instruments for governance.

On the frontier, "there were natural resources outside the market process; [i.e.] you did not have to pay for them; you could get them by just going to work on them" [Foster 1949 (LN) CompEconSyst, 127]. "The presence of free or easily attainable natural resources is the circumstance in terms of which the frontier's influence may be explained." This influence is reflected in "the ease of acquisition and accessibility of its resources," and the character of its influence is reflected in "the classes and types of people to whom the resources were available" (Foster 1942, 5). That presence, the pervasive frontier, was the forcing bed, the primary conditioning influence that fostered the appearance of the frontiersman.

But as Foster observes:

> [T]here is and was no such thing as "the frontiersman" in the sense that all who successfully encountered the frontier portrayed the same personality and character. Individuality was perhaps their most striking common characteristic. But the conditions under which they lived necessarily brought forth new mores and folkways. Their range of honesties was different; their attitude toward authority was different; their concepts of fair practice were different; their hospitality was different; even their language became different. In a sense, they created a new civilization and in large part reflected it as individuals. . . .A common characteristic of the frontiersmen was their belief in man's right to be different. (Foster 1942, 9).

Foster perceives this emergent frontiersman to be a unique participant, a discretionary agent, exhibiting atypical conduct and beliefs:

> He was distinct. He developed a large array of skills and techniques. He was his own trapper, his own farmer, his own barber, his own tailor, his own carpenter, his own tanner, his own brewer, his own freighter, his own cook, and not least of all his own policeman. . . . [H]e was in almost every instance the first one there. As effective community caught up with him, he became the founding father, the old man to whom the community could turn for know-how and advice in the earliest adjustments to community in a frontier setting. And they often had to refer to him since he sometimes had acquired some sort of claim to the land in the area [(n.d.) 1981, 983].

Foster continues:

> The American frontiersman's experience was almost altogether with the natural resources; he had relatively little experience in human conquest. His energies, efforts, and time were occupied with making a living through his own use of the resources available. He had very little opportunity to acquire income through predation. . . .The absence of organized authority and the scantiness of contact with established institutions (including the market) revealed to the frontiersman that institutional structures are subject to human will and design. He became distrustful of institutions the instrumental functions of which were not apparent to him. Institutions with heavy accent on invidious functions and distinctions the frontiersman disdained. He even tried specifically to forbid invidious distinctions in his Declaration of Independence and in his Constitution [Foster (n.d.) 1981, 983].

The outcome:

> The frontiersman worked his way across most of this continent in hardly more than one century. And through his efforts and the efforts of those in his wake the essential structure of the U.S. economy was developed. This structure included an amazing provision of physical capital by persons who were mostly poor in pecuniary terms. A large portion of that capital was not provided through money transactions, but by those who used it, and they did not

> account it in pecuniary terms. They accounted it in terms of the requirements for carrying on the productive process (983).

Perhaps most importantly, for purposes of economic analysis, the frontier tradition was a major conditioning influence in the generation and emergence of an indigenous democratic ethic—a credible and applicable theory of social value. In Foster's words:

> The frontier experience forced the mountain men and pioneers to construct a problem-solving theory of value. They had a plethora of skills, and demanded the right to be different as long as these characteristics did not hinder the effort to live. Freedom in the American experience means the enlargement of the area of genuine choice, whereas freedom in the European sense means an absence of prescription. The pioneer developed rules to aid in living better. An individual must do whatever he can according to his skills, and the community will help in those activities beyond his skills. . . .The instrumental theory of value involves enlarging the area of genuine discretion through prescriptions to develop society [Foster 1974 (CN) AmCont. 1].

Foster adds:

> The frontier has been the physical fact in U.S. history that has given functional reality to that peculiar complex of ideas and attitudes that are called the *American* when he is spoken of as a type. The frontier gave validity in a real sense to the fundamental ideal of human equality without reference to economic status. In short, the frontier furnished the most basic elements in American conceptuology, including its moral sense [(1942) 1981, 989-90 (emphasis in original)].

But what was the impact of the closing of the frontier in the late 19th century? Were the attributes, attributed to the presence of the frontier, abandoned? Foster draws on Walter Prescott Webb in posing these questions:

> The historians have not yet seemed to realize that if the frontier *was* a dominant factor until 1890 the *absence* of the frontier has been just as dominant *since* 1890. They have accepted the thesis that the frontier shaped American life, but they have not so readily accepted the corollary that the absence of the frontier must change the shape. They have told us that it promoted individualism, stimulated self-reliance, fostered equality and political democracy; they have not told us. . .that the absence of the frontier tends as surely through undernourishment to destroy those things that its existence stimulated [Webb 1937, 157-58; quoted by Foster (1942) 1981, 990 (emphasis in original)].

Foster shares the view that the disappearance of the frontier created problematic conditions for many. For some, it was, in some measure, "closed by ownership and land speculation in advance of population" [Commons 1950, 95). In some areas, ownership preemption produced a shrinkage in options available to latter day settlers. The government, itself, abandoned its policy of conferring title to public lands on "anyone who contemplated any enterprise calculated to be of ultimate public benefit." The government was compelled, more generally, to modify its land use policies. Increased attention had to be paid to soil types, potential and competing uses, private vs. public purposes to be served, et cetera [(1942) 1981, 990-91]. But Foster believes that the cultural conditioning of the frontier provided a social, behavioral, and conceptual legacy that continues to be reflected in American attitudes toward, and success in, social and economic problem solving.

One can gain an additional pervasive sense of the significance which Foster attributes to this emergent American economic experience with and on the frontier by noting his recourse to the frontier thesis, and its accompanying elements, in challenging the generality and relevance of the classical tradition in economics particularly in its late 18th and 19th century formulations. Foster suggests several different areas of conflict or incompatibility between English classical thought and American institutional experience:

In the classical tradition, abstention from consumption to generate savings was the determinant source of capital formation and economic growth. But for Foster, "the frontier experience did not indicate the necessity for previous savings to enable one to create capital." Indeed, the contrary is more likely the case. "Often the creation of capital was performed by self-employed individuals concurrently with the consumption of their entire consumable income and irrespective of whether the individual's income was increasing or decreasing. The provision of tool-like assets seemed to be specified more by the 'state of the industrial arts,' by the pattern of know-how, than by any previous or concurrent abstention from consumption" [Foster (1969) 1981, 863].

The extended frontier experience "inclined Americans toward means other than the market for a proper assignment of labor." Early in frontier history, "almost all labor there was self-directed. The market was for commodities, and it was far away. The market process was not a constant part of everyday life, and even its intermittent conscious impact was on commodities, not labor. The self-direction of workers became interwoven in a basic sense into most American folkways and mores (864).

The frontier experience did not particularly reinforce the classical advantages of specialization. As noted above, the frontiersman was perforce compelled to become a practitioner of multiple skills. Skills in several areas seemed not "to diminish his proficiency in any one of them." He did not see a need to reduce his own consumption when he fashioned so-called capital goods. "When he fashioned a chair or built a fence, he did not sense any previous or concurrent abstention from consumption; rather, he thought of such activities as integral parts of his capacity to solve problems as he encountered them" (864).

"The frontier did not permit the niceties of distinction among persons that were involved in the classical distinctions among rentiers, entrepreneurs, and workers. Americans in particular developed a vigorous disrespect for formalities that connote any invidious distinctions among persons" (864). The frontier experience also resulted in a rejection of received ideas about lineage, social class, hierarchy, authority, manners and mores, etc.

"The frontier experience and the attitudes and realizations arising from it disinclined Americans not only toward invidious distinctions, but also toward the acceptance of any particular institutional structure as perpetual." They saw institutional structures "as devices or means of carrying on the various functions of the social process, including the economic function. . . .Functions became the continuing factors, and all institutional structures became subject to adjustment"

(864). In the classical tradition, the structure of the economy is a continuing given; it is not the object of adjustment. It is called capitalism.

"Both the peculiarly American critique of the economic classicism and the positive analysis growing out of the peculiarities of the American experience began to emerge in a separate and formal way early in the twentieth century. That intellectual movement came to be called *institutional economics.*" Institutionalists demonstrate that "all answers to all economic problems necessarily take the form of institutional adjustments. . . .[T]he requisite institutional adjustments are specified by the problems at hand rather than by any arbitrary presupposition that limits adjustments to particular institutions such as price. The fundamental principles of economics then must take the form of the principles of institutional adjustment" (865, emphasis in original). The substance of these principles (technological determination, recognized interdependence, minimal dislocation), one will recall, was introduced in Chapter Four above.

Compulsions Toward Problem Solving

We contend here that a pervasive legacy of the American experience with an extended frontier over such a long period is that the community-at-large develops and continues to reflect a compulsion toward problem solving. While this quest is necessarily universal, the frontier experience provided for increased options and stratagems for such problem solving. Foster's theory of the economic process equips us to understand both the character and significance of this urgency. This acquired and conditioned compulsion may be characterized as activist, experimentalist, non-invidious and instrumentalist.

While our common experience is to acknowledge that most of our behavior necessarily becomes and remains habitual, Americans remain as a community unwilling simply to endure the habitual status quo in substantively problematic areas. They become *activists* when they recognize that problems exist and that the consequences need not be tacitly accepted, that the direction of attention, analysis and political initiatives can bring the problem into focus and raise conscious awareness of its particulars. Americans become *experimentalists* when they participate in the drawing up of alternative institutional prescriptions the purpose of which is to enhance basic social functions threatened by flawed judgments and/or inaction. They exhibit *non-invidiousness* in precluding recourse to discriminatory attributes that impose demeaning conditions in defining a resolution. They become *instrumentalists* in problem solving when they draft proposed adjustments in institutions that incorporate warranted knowledge about institutional means to employ in generating restorative structural changes supporting the continuing functions of the economic process.

What we learn from the frontier experience is that basic functions comprising the process of provision of the means of life—e.g., production of food and fiber, design and construction of enclosed space, determination of income shares, transport of goods and persons, provision of medical care, education of the young and others, et cetera—must be carried on at whatever level of efficiency our warranted knowledge and commitment permits. The frontier confrontation of new conditions, new constraints, new conceptions of purpose and progress, new ways of organizing conduct, prompted the appearance of pragmatic, real world responses. Those responses took non-conventional forms. Somewhat uniquely, American social, political, and economic reforms became a habitual pursuit in a post-frontier social order.

"The American Revolution" argues Foster, "goes on. By its very nature it can have no end; it is open-ended. It specifies no particular structure; it specifies only the process through which that structure is determined. And that process is founded on the idea that those who receive the incidence of policy and who live within the institutional structure should determine both the policy and the structure" [Foster (n.d.) 1981, 984].

Institutional Inventions and Innovations

A most significant implication of the foregoing is the continuing recognition that the primary continuing bodies than can act in, and on behalf of, the community-at-large are responsive democratic governments at national and sub-national levels. Governments that continuously provide for the popular determination of public policies are the inclusive community's primary instruments through which to fashion and pursue instrumentally efficient institutional adjustments in seeking restoration, enhancement and equitable distribution of the flow of real income.

To demonstrate something of the significance of Foster's perception of the roles of democratic governments in creating and implementing social and economic reform measures, we offer the following examples, from the decades of the Foster era, to illustrate and to emphasize the significance of institutional invention and adaptation undertaken by and through governmental bodies, in pursuit of instrumental ends and purposes:

Public Utililties

Foster considers the public utility concept and the structural character of its implementation to be an American institutional innovation of historic and contemporary significance. In the language of the Munn case, "when private property is devoted to a public use, it is subject to public regulation" (Commager 1948, Vol. II, 93). A legislatively constituted governmental public utility commission is charged with the regulation of prices set and of the quality and availability of commodity provided or service performed by specified corporate enterprises. The need for social control of that power, especially when exercised over the distribution of an essential service, would therefore be continuing. That the means of that control might, indeed almost certainly would, change is not an indication that the need for control has lessened. Such commissions have necessary and legally established discretionary authority to regulate private enterprise within specified limits.

Harry Trebing, a public utility institutionalist, characterizes its emergence and form:

> For more than a century the public utility concept has been synonymous with the regulation of prices and earnings of privately owned firms supplying electricity, gas, telecommunications, water, and to a lesser degree, air and surface transport. This largely American concept was the product of individual actions by courts and legislatures as they sought to constrain the behavior of firms that provided essential services, possessed market power and required

> grants of privilege. . .to operate. These firms were deemed to be affected by the public interest and were required to provide adequate service at just and reasonable rates. The institution of control was to be the independent regulatory commission, which would implement a broad mandate to regulate in a fashion that would promote the public interest. Hence the term "public interest regulation" (Trebing 1994, 200-01).

The independent regulatory commission is itself an interesting institutional invention. Its novelty arises in large part from the fact that it has tripartite responsibilities—legislative, executive, and judicial—all within a specified universe of discretion set in its legislative creation. For example, it sets rates of return allowable, implements these stipulations, and rules on the adequacy of compliance thereto.

From its inception, public utility regulation has been a stormy, power-driven tussle between private and public interests. There have been adjustments in structure both from the public legislative bodies seeking to secure more effective regulation and from the regulated corporations seeking to defuse or destroy effective constraints on their economic judgments and conduct. Additional observations by Trebing explain the turmoil:

> Since the 1960s, public interest regulation has come under increasing attack from historical revisionists, proponents of the interest group theory of governmental intervention, large buyers seeking to exercise monopsony power, and neoclassical economists who believe that unfettered markets provide a superior option for promoting efficiency. The result of these attacks has been to accelerate economic deregulation of air and surface transport, significantly diminish regulation in energy and telecommunications and raise questions about the legitimacy of public control of enterprise (201).

The New Deal.

Whatever the causal antecedents of the Great Depression in the 1930s, the New Deal was intended in myriad ways to salvage the substance of the existing system, however captioned, in the face of massive and continuing unemployment, agricultural crises, banks failures, labor unrest, et cetera. Differing theoretical explanations or accounts regarding such causal antecedents were legion, e.g., neoclassicist, Marxist, Keynesian, under-consumptionist. But the magnitude of the breakdown in the provisioning process generated major political incentives to experiment with various policy "remedies." How does one address the fact of concurrent deficient aggregate demand, encompassing unemployment, financial hysteria, and widespread desperation? It was recognized, by virtually all centers of economic influence, that major institutional adjustments would be required. What is distinctive is that it was a period of major and continuous experimentation reflecting differing, often conflicting, conceptions of what should be done. Accordingly, the Depression Decade was an inadvertent economic laboratory where a variety of responses to problematic conditions could be fashioned and experimentally introduced. The "alphabet soup" of the NRA (National Recovery Administration) to introduce price and production controls, the WPA (Works Progress Administration) to generate employment, the AAA (Agricultural

Adjustment Administration) to reduce production and raise farm prices, et al., were major components of the overall effort to cope with the depression. While the restoration of full employment was not obtained until the war economy emerged beginning in 1939, the New Deal reflected the American tradition of pluralism. activism and experimentalism. In words of Broadus Mitchell,

> [T]he New Deal took full advantage of the President's promise, early given, that efforts were experimental, that if one expedient proved faulty, another would be tried. The New Deal was grandly opportunist. The term might be used as a condemnation, but is here employed as a description. The administration did not stop at change of emphasis, but resorted to reversal of plans. Attempted inflation was abandoned for policing of prices. Profuse governmental spending was followed by restriction and spending again. Business collusion was at first promoted, later prosecuted. Economic nationalism was embraced, then rejected. These were the conspicuous about-faces. (Mitchell 1947, 368).

The legacy of the New Deal is still reflected in the significant institutional structures of the Social Security system, national labor legislation, federal lending programs to agriculture, et al. Demand management, job creation, financial stability, and micro economic planning were all enhanced by the New Deal experience.

Price Control in World War II

The American community, prior to the second World War, had never attempted, in an inclusive fashion, to use central governmental authority to institute and enforce comprehensive controls over prices and wages in a continuing effort concurrently to address the problems of economic stabilization, inflationary pressures, and resource mobilization for war. Orthodox and libertarian economists, of course argued that such an effort was both unwise and impossible [Galbraith (1952) 1980, 2]. It was unwise because it corrupted the markets' allocative functions and did not address the determinants of excessive aggregate demand. It was impossible because all earlier attempts of such draconian magnitude were deemed to have been failures; allegedly, there was no prior constructive experience on which to draw .

John Kenneth Galbraith, a renown institutionalist, in reflecting on his role as chief administrator of such controls, observes however, that "it can hardly be argued that price control led to the kind of debacle that prewar theory would have foretold. During the critical war years prices remained comparatively stable in face of a large and continuing excess of aggregate demand over supply. Moreover this stability was achieved. . .as the result of price-fixing *qua* price-fixing. . . .Governments during these years, came to look upon price control as an important instrument of stabilization policy" (1980, 8). Indeed, observes Galbraith "it is relatively easy to fix prices that are already fixed" [as corporate administered prices] (1980, iv). In sum, World War II wage and price controls constituted an institutional invention-adaptation that achieved the instrumental functions for which they were invoked. This institutional innovation succeeded in resolving the problem of constraining inflationary price increases in a condition of excess aggregate demand and without impeding enhancement of production.

The G.I. Bill.

This legislation to finance education and training was passed shortly after the close of World War II. Its purpose was to provide financial access to higher education and/or skill acquisition for American veterans of that war. It represents what Dale Bush, a student of Foster, characterizes as "progressive" institutional change. It "was a productivity-increasing investment in human capital that contributed significantly to post World War II economic growth" (Bush, 1986, 38). Estimates suggest that as many as eleven million men and women took advantage of one or more options provided by the Bill.

But the significance of the Bill extends well beyond the provision of extended access to learn and train; it reflects a change in value perceptions of its promoters. As Bush explains:

> The enactment of the G.I. Bill signified major institutional changes in American life. While the manifest function of this public policy was rationalized by the ceremonially adequate notion that we were "rewarding our returning veterans for the sacrifices they made for our country," the instrumentally significant changes that it entailed were changes in the standards of judgment by which the society went about allocating educational resources. The [often] invidious criterion of the "ability to pay" was displaced by an instrumentally warranted criterion of entitlement based on the "ability to learn". . . .[T]he G.I. Bill substantially reduced the importance of such invidious criteria as social and economic status in the allocation of educational opportunities" (Bush 1986, 37-38).

There has not been a more dramatic example in the U.S. of the enormous contribution that publicly supported education and training can make to the overall efficiency of the economic process. It seems fair to say that the American economy, in the last four decades or so, has derived a significant part of its growth in technological and institutional innovation, in productive capacity, and in its distributive benefits from this extraordinary investment in human capital.

In sum, one must reflect on the underlying sense of *purposiveness* that undergirds the emergence of regulation of private corporations via public utility regulation, the introduction of experimental measures to generate employment and maintain income flows through the New Deal, the direct public recourse to price controls throughout the economy during World War II, the GI Bill that set aside the "ability to pay" for the "ability to learn" in funding the education/training of millions of veterans. This commitment to purposive reform is also reflected in the quest for equity through Affirmative Action and Feminist equality measures, and, more recently, the *concurrent* reduction in rates of increases in prices and in levels of unemployment. Instrumental value theory, accordingly, provides the underlying criterion the use of which embeds substantive meaning in policy changes. These examples of institutional adjustments reflect the significance of instrumental "purposiveness" and demonstrate again the policy guiding significance of Foster's theory of instrumental value.

AMERICAN CONTRIBUTORS TO INSTITUTIONAL THOUGHT

In the foregoing sections of this Chapter, we have, for the most part, explored Foster's views and contributions in his analysis of, and reflections and commentary upon, the American historical *experience* and its characterizing attributes that are reflective of, or correlate with, heterodox American institutional economics. Now we turn to a consideration of Foster's views of specific *contributors* to this distinctively American theory of the economic process. A distinctive characteristic of all such contributors is that, in differing ways, they all accede to the dictum that the American contribution to economic analysis is in every case an avoidance of, or an abandonment of, any ismatic conception or characterization (feudalist, socialist, communist, capitalist, fascist) of the American economy. The U.S. is not an ism system comprised of a fixedly given array of institutional forms "validated" by some anterior nonscientific theoretical model.

In reference to Veblen, Dewey and Ayres, we will be extending earlier evaluative discussions; in the case of other contributors (Thomas Jefferson, Ben Franklin, Transcendentalists, John R. Commons, Wesley Claire Mitchell, and John Maurice Clark) we will be offering introductory and exploratory comments. Since source material (Foster's lectures and papers) is at times quite limited, consideration of contributed ideas will sometimes be necessarily terse.

Thomas Jefferson

Clearly, Jefferson was Foster's favorite "founding father." Jefferson's dictum from the Declaration that "All men are created equal" says Foster, "asserts that all invidious distinctions among men are figments of the imagination; it does not mean equal opportunity" [Foster 1974 (LN) AmCont. 1]. Jefferson understood, says Foster, that "the continuing factors lie in the continuity of economic development." The critical realities, the "actualities, are non-institutional in nature." [Functional applications of knowledge are required in the choosing of structure.] "The classical and utilitarian theories could not be used to solve problems. No markets existed on the frontier to correlate the factors of production. Laws and theories are not fundamental data, not continuing factors." Jefferson, early on, had a conception of "the distinction between ceremonial behavior and instrumental, problem-solving behavior. (Foster 1974,1).

Jefferson, with other Americans, did not accept major arguments of Smith's *Wealth of Nations*. "Jefferson held that the marketplace could not develop the wealth of nations; [the] market assignment of labor and wealth is fatal." Productivity times labor employed equals the wealth of the nation, "but not through savings and wages fund as Smith held. [A] worker should have discretion over his own effort and the tools he works with. For Smith, saving—what is not consumed and is assigned to workers as wages—determines productivity and [the] level of employment. From [the] frontier, Jefferson saw that work creates the wealth of nations, that investment generates savings (anticipating Keynes), and that money has nothing to do with capital formation" (Foster 1974, 1).

Benjamin Franklin

"Franklin applied instrumental theory in [his efforts in support of] public education. He insisted on referential checking of the validity of theory; theories must be applied outside of colleges to determine validity of their patterns of ideas. Private colleges had to change from training clergy and lawyers [in a religious setting] to produce 'leaders'" in a laic setting. "Frontiersmen were quasi-atheistic or against [a religious] institutional idea of a Supreme Being. They were religious in identifying the instrumental concept of problem solving" (Foster 1974,1).

Ralph Waldo Emerson, Henry David Thoreau

"The [T]ranscendentalists" Emerson and Thoreau among others, "attempted to articulate the distinctive American experience of the frontier that created our intellectual heritage. When national problems became conscious, especially slavery . . .[they] attempted to explain the instrumental character of honor, integrity, love, contract, and property. The American intelligentsia are those who work with ideas. They are held to the same instrumental task as the workers; [they are] never granted invidious distinctions common in other cultures. Every one has the same prescriptive responsibilities; no invidious differentiation. There should be universal formal education to introduce everyone directly to the arts and sciences and their application" (Foster 1974, 2).

Thorstein Bunde Veblen

Veblen's role in the development of the American contribution to Economic thought is, in Foster's view, twofold: First, he offered, as we noted in Chapter 3 above, an inclusive and incisive critique of the received doctrines of the traditional classical explanation of the economic process. Second, he began the reconstruction of the most basic tenets of economic analysis that were reflected in part in his understanding of the American experience as a political economy. He is commonly conceded to be the founding theorist of institutional economics in America. We comment on each aspect briefly.

Foster reaffirms four major assessments of orthodoxy in Veblen's contribution: Classical theory, for Veblen, is *tautological:* "You have to make assumptions which guarantee your conclusions before you can make the analysis by which you arrive at your conclusions" [Foster 1950 (LN) CompEconSyst, 35]. Classical theory is *teleological:* "The economy has direction in the sense of an ultimate end (a consciously built structure) at which it is to arrive. . .If you don't interfere with the process, it goes on of its own accord toward its established end [specific institutional structure](35). Classical theory is *hedonistic:* The associational psychology of the hedonistic calculus in its later version has man directing economic behavior in pursuit of utilitous desires. "If you take wants as given data, you are in the position of judging what man likes by what he likes" (36). Classical theory is *taxonomic:* It is more concerned with definition and classification than with causal analysis in real terms of process and growth.

Foster characterizes and comments upon Veblen's contribution to the development of institutional thought. Veblen's major concern seems to have been an effort to generate theory that would explain the economic emergence of America, and in so doing help develop a general and scientific mode of analysis of the social and economic processes.

> [Veblen decided that] the kind of theory we have had won't solve our problems. The reason is that we don't understand the difference between technology and institutions. [The] physical means of life determine the character of experience, and it becomes institutionalized through gradual, cumulative, and unconscious habituation. Persons act habitually; 'economic man' does not exist. Man acts a certain way because he learned to act that way, not because of his reason.
>
> What we mean by the Veblenian distinction is his distinction between technology and institutions. He confused the constitution of an institution (a pattern of habits) with the determination of an institution. They are not the same thing. . . .
>
> Veblen thought that institutions and technology are independently progressive. Neither depends upon the other. Institutions come into being through habituation, and they change with something of a consistent sequence. He did not know just what this sequence was. . .[but] thought it was economic in character. Men don't act very rationally when confronted with a problem they have to solve, but proceed more or less by trial and error. . . .Veblen found no direction in the development of institutions. All we can do is identify direction in terms of process. It is in terms not of an approach to a particular institutional pattern, but direction in terms of greater economy and efficiency. He was thinking of instrumental efficiency but didn't know it because he didn't know about the significance of science. He thought that scientific investigation was due to idle curiosity and he couldn't validate it (Foster 1950 (LN) CompEconSyst, 37).
>
> What Veblen was setting up is what the American people have been doing. They have always had a suspicion of the Veblenian distinction. But they never knew how to talk about it. The American system is what Veblen was talking about (38).

John Dewey

In Chapter 2, we briefly explored Dewey's contribution of instrumental logic, scientific reasoning and attributes of social inquiry on which Foster draws in framing his comprehensive theory of the economic process and the social value theory which gives it both pertinence and significance. It remains here, to address Dewey's contribution of democratic theory and practice on which Foster draws in his analysis of substantive problem solving.

Few would dispute that Dewey was the preeminent philosopher of democracy in America. His articulation of the distinguishing characteristics and compelling importance of the democratic form has no rival. Foster drew heavily on this contribution. We sample Dewey's characterization of "the democratic form":

> The keynote of democracy as a way of life may be expressed. . .as the necessity for the participation of every mature human being in formation of the values that regulate the living of men together. . . .Democratic political forms . . .rest back upon the idea that no man or limited set of men is wise enough or good enough to rule others without their consent; the positive meaning of this statement is that all those who are affected by social institutions must have a share in producing and managing them. . . .The individuals of the submerged mass may not be very wise. But there is one thing they are wiser about than anybody else can be, and that is where the shoe pinches, the troubles they suffer from (Dewey 1939, 400-02).

Foster's principles of recognized interdependence and of minimal dislocation, function most efficiently and creatively where democratic participation, as perceived by Dewey, is both available and genuine. Foster attributes such success as America has had in social and economic problem solving to the presence of democratic means to pursue democratically derived ends-in-view. Dewey continues:

> The foundation of democracy is faith in the capacities of human nature; faith in human intelligence and in the power of pooled and cooperative enterprise. . . . [I]f given a . . .[chance] they will grow and be able to generate progressively the knowledge and wisdom needed to guide collective action. Every autocratic and authoritarian scheme of social action rests on a belief that the needed intelligence is confined to a superior few, who because of inherent natural gifts are endowed with the ability and the right to control the conduct of others (402).

Foster's principles of institutional adjustment affirm the superiority of democratic over nondemocratic means of introducing institutional changes. The community at large can grasp the significant implications of technological determination in assessing the disjunction between what is going on and what could be going on in a knowledge based judgment. Those with concentrated powers and authoritarian controls corrupt a community's capacity to comprehend the existential realities of recognized interdependence. No autocrat is substantively concerned with minimal dislocation. Autocratic power may indeed permit intimidation and exploitation of those adversely affected with an existing institutional problem. Dewey continues:

> Belief in equality is an element of the democratic credo. It is not, however, belief in equality of natural endowments. Those who proclaimed the idea of equality did not suppose they were enunciating a psychological doctrine, but a legal and political one. All individuals are entitled to equality of treatment by law and in its administration (Dewey 1939, 403).

For "equality" read "noninvidiousness." Foster's concept of equality does not presume a sameness or equivalence of capacity. He argues that in social participation, no one should be denied the option to contribute because of one or another distinction judged invidious, i.e. discrimination involving the use of skin color, age, gender, wealth, position, ancestry, et cetera, as measures or indicators of relative worth of human beings and therewith the determination of who may, and who may not, participate substantively in institutional adjustments for problem solving. The democratic ethic in Foster's institutional economics is contributed in large measure by John Dewey.

Clarence E. Ayres

The contributions of Clarence E. Ayres to institutional thought are already largely reflected in the contributions herein of his student, Fagg Foster. Ayres was, as noted above, Foster's mentor and professional confidant for over two decades. Not only did Foster write many of his graduate papers under Ayres's supervision, including his doctoral dissertation, they were, in their mature years, engaging and persistent correspondents and discussants of each other's professional writing and career developments. Ayres was a sometime participant in seminars at the University of Denver. Foster designed and proposed a doctoral program in social science at U.D. incorporating the tradition and substance of Ayres's contribution (Foster 1948c "Prospectus Ph.D.")

There can be little doubt that Foster considers Ayres's most significant contribution to institutional thought to be his early on recognition and exploration of the correlativity of Dewey's instrumental theory of scientific inquiry and Veblen's dichotomous theory of the economic process. In the hands of Ayres, the former informed and extended the latter; the latter informed and extended the former. Dewey's method of scientific social analysis became the conceptual instrument, the analytical vehicle, for inquiry into the fundamental determinants of economic well-being and the ceremonial impediments thereto confronted in every social order. In the hands of Foster, this conjoining was intellectually absorbed and extended significantly, but not solely, in the theory of institutional adjustment, as discussed in Chapter 5.

Consideration above of Ayres's contribution is extended herein by addressing his aggregative perception of causal determinants and impediments of the economic process, and his most recent (1962) instrumental formulation of a theory of economic development. We consider each briefly:

Determinants and Impediments

For Ayres: "Two forces seem to be present in all human behavior in all ages: one progressive, dynamic, productive of cumulative change; the other counter-progressive, static, inhibitory of change" [(1944) 1962, xiv]. The former, drawing on Veblen, is designated "technology," the latter is "ceremonialism." Technology "includes all human activities involving the use of tools—all sorts of tools." Included are stone tools and atom-splitters, sign language and modern books, et cetera. But Ayres insists that "human skills and the tools by which and on which they are exercised are logically inseparable. Skills *always* employ tools, and tools are such *always* by virtue of being employed in acts of skill by human beings" (xv, emphasis in original).

Ceremonialism is the "curb" on technology that is reflected in social stratification, in mores that define and sustain conventions that "delimit and prescribe the behavior that is proper." Status and mores are further sustained by ideology or tribal beliefs "which purport to explain the magic potency" of those in higher ranks; community members are indoctrinated and conditioned to acceptance of such beliefs, mores, and caste lines; finally, "all these patterns of behavior are defined, codified, and intensified in mystic rites and ceremonies" that establish "ceremonial adequacy" [(1942) 1962, xvi]. This system of behavior is static and inhibitory of change. . . .[T]he ceremonial system is past-binding" (xvi-xvii). "Thus what happens to any society is determined jointly by the forward urging of its technology and the backward pressure of its ceremonial system" (xvii).

Theory of Economic Development

In seeking to contribute to the interest in recent decades in fostering and promoting economic development in less developed countries, Ayres presents elements of his basic analytical framework in offering and recommending recourse to four basic institutionalist principles of economic development:

"The process of economic development is indivisible and irresistible." The compelling force of the industrial revolution that began in Western Europe involved not only technological inventions (in agriculture and industry) but also institutional detachment. "The manifest break-through occurred during the fifteenth century. What was broken through was feudalism, the manorial-agricultural economy, the medieval world view, the absolute spiritual authority of the Roman Catholic Church and European isolation" (xxvi). Technological breakthroughs included "the germs of powered machinery." invention of movable type printing, gunpowder, navigation instruments, and the introduction of Arabic numerals ([(1944) 1962, xxvii, emphasis in original].

"The technological revolution spreads in inverse proportion to institutional resistance." The technological revolutions in Europe were resisted but with a somewhat diminishing force. The technological revolution made it possible for Europeans to penetrate to all parts of the world. Wherever they have gone, they "have taken their tools and know-how with them. Where they have encountered no effective resistance from alien cultures, technological development has continued and has even spurted ahead faster than in the mother countries" (xxvii). Encountered resistance has been both active and passive: "passive in the sense that illiteracy is more difficult to cope with in large masses than in small ones; active in the sense that teaching people to read and write almost inevitably involves interfering with their traditional way of life [(1944) 1962, xxviii].

"The creation of human capital is critical." For Ayres, "technology is human skills and know-how and the complement of tools and equipment in which such skills and know-how are embodied and through which they are exercised. The equipment is useless without the know-how. But given the skills and know-how, equipment can be reproduced. . .the most important factor in the economic life of any people is the educational level. . .of the community. . . .An ignorant and unskilled community cannot advance except by acquiring knowledge and skills" [(1944) 1962,xxix].

"Values which are engendered in the technological process are universal values." Science, the intellectual aspect of technology assumes and requires a commitment to the discovery of truth, and science prescribes its own conception of truth. It is a processual, or operational, or instrumental—tool-defined—conception of truth. This conception of truth and of human values generally is at variance with all tribal legends and all tribal authority; and since the technological

revolution is itself irresistible, the arbitrary authority and irrational values of pre-scientific, pre-industrial cultures are doomed" (xxxii).

"Three alternatives confront the partisans of tribal values and beliefs," argues Ayres. "Resistence, if sufficiently effective, though it cannot save the tribal values, can bring total revolution. Or ineffective resistence may lead to sequestration like that of the American Indians. The only remaining alternative is that of intelligent, voluntary acceptance of the industrial way of life and all the values that go with it. . . .For all who achieve economic development profound cultural change is inevitable. But the rewards are considerable." [(1944) 1972, xxxii-xxxiii].

John R. Commons

Certainly no institutional economist in the 20th century has had a greater impact on the actual structure of the American economy than has John R. Commons. In his position as Professor of Economics at the University of Wisconsin, Commons worked with doctoral students, elected officials and governmental administrators to promote structural change at the campus, state, and federal levels over a long career. The faculty (Commons and colleagues) at Wisconsin were the source of many of the specific innovations of the New Deal in dealing with the fact and impact of the Great Depression. It evidently was not uncommon for doctoral candidates to write dissertations on one or another aspect of the federal government's quest to relieve unemployment, generate income security, regulate private enterprise, and expand productive capacity. His approach was purposive (addressed real impairments in the economic process); pragmatic, (in his concern to ground all analysis in factual evidence) and pertinent (confronted difficult areas of private control of economic processes) et cetera. He acceded to Veblen's critique of orthodox neoclassicism, rejected its policy postures, and sought to avoid its utility value theory. He attempted instead to generate an alternate and more credible theoretical framework of analysis. Foster acknowledges and applauds Commons' many contributions. He has reservations, however, about two aspects of Commons' theoretical structure.

First, one of Commons's key constructs is the *principle of agreed compromise*. Foster is unable to accede to its character and concur in its significance. Observes Foster,

> Commons' principle of agreed compromise—what people think rather than what criterion of judgment is in fact true—led him to view the administrative commission as the American answer to the major economic problems which have arisen out of the new technology in combination with corporate organization. His view was that the traditional separation of legislative, judicial, and executive functions rendered our economy helpless when confronted with such problems as monopoly, public utilities, labor organizations, currency control, investment banking, taxation, etc. Problems of this sort require, he thought, agencies which combine the three functions because we must have a practical method of "correlating law, economics, and ethics". . . .And his concept of the "correlating" function is embodied in his theory of "due process of law" which, again, is an application of his principle of agreed compromise which, in another of its applications, constitutes what judicial institutions identify as "reasonable". . . .According to agreed compromise, findings of commissions may be held reasonable when all parties

> affected by the findings are given full opportunity to present their opinions and intentions and the reasons for them. Findings of agreed facts are then held "reasonable" and the courts may judge "interpretations" [Foster 1974 (LN) AmerCont, 5]

However, Foster is unable to find a scientifically applicable, therefore acceptable, criterion of judgment in the "principle of agreed compromise." Commons, as with many others, has no "rational value theory." How then can one judge among structural alternatives? The fact of agreement as compromise may well be a constructive aspect of negotiations in the sense of easing or eroding conflictual postures and proposals. But it does not speak to the *character* of the compromise or to the *kinds of consequences* resulting therefrom. How then does one distinguish between a *good* or acceptable compromise and a *bad* or unacceptable compromise? The normative implications are existentially present; their evasion or avoidance leaves the fundamental determinants of the problem inadequately addressed.

Second, Commons' develops five principles of explanation, he calls them "transactions," to attempt to explain how economies operate. Their captions are efficiency, scarcity, working rules, sovereignty and futurity. Foster reviews their content [Foster 1974 (LN) AmerCont, 5-6].

Efficiency. Concern is with managerial decisions (transactions), the rate of output per unit of input. Addresses the technological aspects of management in terms of use value. Labor and materials go into the process; commodities come out. It is a man-to-nature relation. But no unit of measurement is offered (5).

Scarcity. In bargaining transactions, "the rate of proprietary income from other persons relative to the rate of proprietary outgo [is] measured by the dollar." Commons sees this as a relation of man to man. "Without the instrumental-ceremonial distinction between the functions of institutions this is about as well as he could do—with the added explicit recognition that the sets of relations are inseparable aspects of the economic process" (6).

Working rules. "Custom compels the individual. Contract is not 'freedom from custom': rather, it is another custom. It is not rational choices as indicated by the classicists, but plain custom that determines choices in the market." Commons leaves unaddressed the question of how these customs come to be (6).

Futurity. This is the dynamic in the economic process. "Transactions are determined by expectations. . . .But [Foster argues] transactions are not repetitive reciprocations with a given pattern—there is no 'closed' economy; rather there is an on-going process, constantly changing. And therefore the indeterminacy of expectation permits continuity of the process because it results in different appraisals and therefore transactions which constitute the process. Economic institutions could not exist otherwise (6).

Sovereignty. This is "the changing process of authorizing, prohibiting, regulating the use of physical force in human affairs." Foster calls this function "mandamus and injunction." "[I]t affects rationing of factors and commodities in the economic process. The 'rationing transactions', at bottom, determine the pattern of economic power. Commons gets coordination of law and economics since both have a common effect in terms of rationing" (6). Commons was perceptive here in recognizing that capital formation, a determination of the character of production, is a consequence of sovereignty and its exercise. Power is held and power is used. "Wall Street didn't like Commons very well" [Foster 1950 (LN) CompEconSyst, 42].

For Commons, argues Foster, compromise was the most important principle. "People must learn to compromise. But the idea of compromise is fuzzy. He said that everybody gives up something, and by doing so you solve the problem. In the absence of a criterion of judgment this worked pretty well. Group judgments are better than individual judgment"(42). But the referent for "better" for Foster is, of course, greater instrumental efficiency.

Wesley Clair Mitchell

By common consent, Mitchell is viewed as the leading quantitative analyst among institutionalists in the first half of the 20th century. As a student of Veblen, he came early to a recognition that getting the facts involves systematic empirical analysis. He sought a "systematic account of what is being inductively investigated." In his inquiry on business cycles "he studies the actual events rather than orthodox speculations" [Foster 1949 (LN) CompEconSyst, 150]. Mitchell perceives the role of theory to be that of creating "order amidst the confused facts of observation." This can be accomplished through statistical analysis, using statistical norms, arithmetic means, modal averages, geometric means, and the like. "Economics will be less concerned with puzzles about economic motives and more concerned with objective validity of the account it gives" of the economic process (150).

But Foster asks:

> How can you give an objective account of something without considering motives, when motives determine the thing you're trying to give an account of? If economics is not a social but a physical science, if human beings do not use discretion, if economics is not an institutional science, then Mitchell's distinction is valid. But if economics is a social science. . .his distinction blocks his entire analysis. His confusion is that which is prevalent in our thinking [namely] that social "science" is an art. Mitchell thought that economics is a science, but that its analysis had to be restricted to an analytical description of the run of the facts, not to motives. But what is this explanation, this analytical description, this theory, if it excludes motives? [In fact] his business cycle theory "describes human motives" (151)!

Foster pursues the point: "Are not 'motives' a fact in the sequence of events we call the economic process?. . .[I]f motives are in fact a determinant, can we say that we shall explain the economic process but that we shall not consider its determinants? Can we scientifically explain anything without identifying its determinants?" [Foster 1974 (LN) AmerCont, 7].

Mitchell was seemingly turning to normative economics, but Mitchell's norm is "welfare", "positive or objective economics is something else." Foster asks: What is this something else? (8). At issue, of course, is the recognition that inquiry is and must be purposive. And the nature of the purposiveness is a central concern in the inquiry; it poses the question that directs inquiry; it identifies what is problematic; it injects the inevitable normative element in all inquiry. It appears that Mitchell was not able to escape his the dependence upon the normative-positive dichotomy.

Mitchell, in his empirical pursuits, attempted to recast the pertinent methodology for his study of business cycles: He proposed: A "new theory of causation, 'analytical descriptions' instead of 'causal theory'," reflecting and "applying his distinction between evolutionary and systematic theory." "Instead of 'the cause' he substituted 'the conditions' which result in fluctuations. But his 'conditions' which constituted the description are 'selective' and 'typical.'" Foster asks, "Are they not then causal?" The distinction is analytically flawed.

Mitchell sought to create "new statistical techniques to handle the 'conditions' at a level of inclusiveness which would permit their concurrent handling" [Foster 1974 (LN) AmerCont, 8]. Foster observes that:

> Mitchell's general theory of the cycle is that each phase contains the "conditions" which eventuate into the succeeding phase (depression, recovery, prosperity, recession) without outside-the-market-economy influences. The sequence runs as follows: Depression evolves into recovery because *(a)* stocks of goods are depleted, *(b)* population continues to increase, *(c)* new tastes and styles and commodities are developed, and *(d)* investment demand revives. . . .Recovery merges into prosperity, in the self-generating sense, until costs and growing tension in the investment market become obstructive. Recession evolves into depression, and depression proceeds until goods are depleted, etc.(8).

Mitchell's contributions consist of the development of theoretical and empirical tools with which to appraise and assess economic instability in the U.S. economy. His development of new statistical techniques and measures of economic performance remain significant for subsequent scholarship. He seems, however, to be unable successfully to work through the philosophical and methodological conflicts that his empirical inquiries disclose. For Foster, these limitations were significant.

John Maurice Clark

In Foster's judgment, John Maurice Clark "gets closer to a comprehension of the theory of value, as subsequently expressed by Ayres, than any of his predecessors" [Foster 1974 (LN) AmerCont, 9]. Why and how this is so, merits our attention in pursuing the American Contribution.

It is of interest at the outset that J.M. Clark was the son of one of the most able neoclassical economists of this century, John Bates Clark. He was therefore "imbued with received doctrines." As he matured, however, he became critical of neoclassical theory as being inadequate and incomplete. In the Preface to his definitive study on overhead costs, he says "it is an experiment in a type of economic theory which is largely inductive, which comes to grips with the dynamic movements and the resistances to movement, and the organic interrelations of parts, which make our economic world a dynamic social organism rather than a static mechanism with an endless uniformity of perpetual motion (Clark 1923, ix).

Foster presents some of his contributions:

J. M. Clark challenged the neoclassical concept of the immortality and mobility of capital. i.e., that capital is non-material; it changes form but is not destroyed. Foster says "the American contribution retained this neoclassical recognition that there is accretion of the means of providing the means of life, but rejected the classical market explanation in favor of explanation in terms of the technological continuum" [Foster 1974 (LN) AmerCont, 8].

Clark thought "it strange to consider wages a cost, since labor is the embodiment of a large part of human experience itself." Clark did get beyond prime costs (profits, rents, wages, etc.) to some notion of residual costs to the community but he did not anticipate what Keynes would later characterize as user costs. "Clark recognized that labor is not a cost in the economic sense. Inefficient use of labor costs the community, but efficient labor is one of the rewards of life" (9).

"Clark struggled with the issue of 'social values', vaguely recognizing that 'values' (things we hold dear) are never continuing factors; they refer to temporary situations rather than to continuing conditions and thus cannot serve as ground for judging what is good and what is bad economically. 'Social values' are created by non-market institutions; they may be intangible assets such as a patent created by legislation. Market (exchange) values cannot be determined by alternative utility of the marginal unit because it would destroy the economic process" (9).

"Clark is saying that the whole concept of exchange value is not a consideration of natural order at all, but rather a consideration of institutional adjustment. He says what ought to determine exchange value is contribution to the social process. We need, therefore, a new accounting system to indicate social values as a parallel check against the business accounting. We need an accounting system to show the actual contributions of any and every economic enterprise" (9).

"What Clark is getting at under the caption of 'variable costs' is identifiable specifically in terms of institutional inefficiency and only there. It is identifiable only in the ceremonial functions of institutions. What he calls 'overhead costs' don't exist. But what he is getting at are the real costs that Keynes conceived as user costs, costs that are experienced anyway"(10).

For Clark, "the determinants of the economic process are beyond price theory. The determinants lie in the operations that eventuate into decisions regarding good and bad wants and the institutional devices for the satisfaction of those wants. When Clark says that each generation must 'discover anew the essence of economic truth,' he is carrying along the neo-classical dichotomy between individual and social problems in trying to apply the Veblenian distinction" (10). "Conditions change; therefore human behavior changes; therefore economic operations change; therefore there are no continuing factors and each generation has to learn it over again" says Clark. "'But Clark made clear that the continuing factors cannot be stated in terms of conditions or situations. And their correct identification permits resolution of the seeming paradox of continuing change in the presence of continuity. Resolving that paradox constitutes the American contribution in economics"(10).

The American Contribution: Foster's Attestation

The following affirmations briefly characterize Foster's formulation and understanding of institutional economics.They represent something of a summary of crucial elements of his own "American contribution:"

The function of scientific inquiry in the realm of economics is to comprehend and facilitate the resolution of problems as institutional impairments in the creation and distribution of real income.

To be relevant, social and economic inquiry must incorporate scientific methodologies.

Economic inquiry and institutional adjustments are perpetually processual. Arrivals at understandings and solutions are provisional and temporal.

The criterion of judgment that identifies problems and directs their resolution is instrumental efficiency of the social process.

Problem solving requires application of the theory of institutional adjustment.

Democratic modes of problem solving are more instrumentally efficient in problem solving than are undemocratic modes.

The dominion of orthodox neoclassicists over the mode and practice of economic inquiry must continuously be challenged and, as feasible, displaced.

These tenets will be manifest in the following Chapter that considers Foster's substantive critique of Ism-Ideologies.

REFERENCES

Bush, Paul Dale. 1986. On the concept of ceremonial encapsulation. *The Review of Institutional Thought;* III: 25-45.

Clark, John Maurice. 1923. *Studies in the Economics of Overhead Costs.* Chicago: University of Chicago Press.

Commager, Henry Steele, ed. 1948. Munn v. Illinois. *Documents of American History, Vol II.* New York: Appleton-Century-Croft.

Commons, John R. *The Economics of Collective Action.* New York: Macmillan

Dewey, John .1939. "The Democratic Form." In *Intelligence in the Modern World: John Dewey's Philosophy.* Joseph Ratner, ed. New York: The Modern Library.

Foster, J. Fagg. 1942 . Effects of the frontier on the American labor movement. Unpublished.

———. 1949. Lecture Notes (LN). Comparative Economic Systems.

———. 1950. Lecture Notes (LN). Comparative Economic Systems.

———. (1966) 1981. Freedom and license in higher education. *Journal of Economic Issues;* 15:969-73.

———. (1974). Lecture Notes (LN). American Contributions to Economic Thought.

———. (1969) 1981. Economics. *Journal of Economic Issues;* 15:857-69.

———. (n.d.) 1981. The American economy. *Journal of Economic Issues;* 15: 981-84.

Galbraith, John Kenneth. (1952) 1980. *A Theory of Price Control: The Classic Account.* Cambridge: Harvard University Press.

Mitchell, Broadus. (1947) 1969. *Depression Decade: From New Era through New Deal.* New York: Harper & Row.

Trebing, Harry M. 1994. "Public Utility Regulation, Institutionalist Contribution to." In *The Elgar Companion to Institutional and Evolutionary Economics , L-Z* , G.M. Hodgson , W.J. Samuels, & M.R. Tool, eds. Aldershot: Edward Elgar.

7 A CRITIQUE OF ISM-IDEOLOGIES

Science is not an ism; it is a method, a process. Democracy likewise. J. Fagg Foster

INTRODUCTION

Foster's theoretical characterizations and assessments, of feudalism, utopian socialism, Marxism, Fabian socialism, capitalism and fascism presented in this Chapter may, in some preliminary sense, be somewhat familiar. But they are in many respects both unique and significant. They are unique in their reflection of institutional economic analysis and instrumental value theory. They are significant in the sense that they equip us with fresh understandings and insights for contemporary analysis of problems and their determinants.

Isms often serve as popular characterizations of contemporary economic systems. Ism-based constructs continue to be used to define problems and to propose solutions for flawed economic performance. Solutions of problems are assumed to be realized if greater conformity to the preferred ism model is achieved. For uncritical Americans, then, "proper" policy is to move in the direction of capitalism and away from all other isms. Much of our consideration of public issues continues to be shaped, tainted or colored by apriori ismatic commitments and derivative public policies.

Indeed, for some individuals, being committed to a specific ism represents the singular most defining and important form of self-identification. Where this is the case, ideological preconceptions, behavioral responses, emotive defenses in service of the received ism may well forestall or corrupt any contribution by the individual to the identification and actual resolution of economic problems. When ism-oriented persons have significant discretion over the terms and conditions of institutional adjustment, such ism-based adjustments will be inadequate, if not stillborn. Ism advocacy of a priori universal solutions can contribute very little to the resolution of social, economic and political problems through institutional adjustments.

Our purpose here is briefly to consider these historically significant and conventional ismatic models in *this* institutionalist context in order to demonstrate, by comparison and contrast, the character and extent of Foster's evidentially based alternative to these conventional ismatic systems and explanations. He demonstrates that all politico-economic isms create more problems than they resolve; they reflect mistaken conceptions of the nature of the social process and of the human beings who participate in them. Their criteria of judgment are time and experience bound.

No ismatic account can demonstrate scientific credibility, although efforts are made in that direction. Claims to alleged achievement are commonplace. Isms remain as reservoirs of pre-scientific, or insufficiently scientific, historical models of economic organization. Retrospectively, they include major misconceptions that erode, if not destroy, their contemporary significance.

In contrast, Foster's theory of institutional adjustment, as explored above, reflects his non-ismatic institutionalist and instrumentalist perspective. This theory has an analytical and philosophical claim to significance as a scientific explanation and clarification of how economies may be rationally constituted and sensibly managed to achieve institutional adjustments that actually do solve problems. Such solutions, by removing institutional impediments and distortions, provide for the production and distribution of real income as efficiently as our comprehension of technological resources, economic substance and political feasibility permit.

Conceptions of problems and their purported resolution through social change specified by conventional isms, Foster argues, do not demonstrably enhance the community's ability to understand and direct change. In differing ways ism-oriented advocates approve economic change supportive of their ism model but they preclude the continuing adjustment of institutions. The sometimes coercive imposition of ismatic structural "solutions" prevents instrumental problem solving from being undertaken through democratically generated and controlled institutional adjustments.

For Foster, then, "an ism is a systematized body of theory which validates a particular institutional structure" [1950 (LN) CompEconSyst, 24]. Accordingly, Scholastic doctrine validates feudalism, a system in which function and status are based on birth and family; the Medieval Church is the dominant institution. Utopian socialists validate self-sustaining communitarian villages as models for adoption. Marxian theory validates, via a particular version of dialectical history, a post-capitalist communism. Fabian socialists validate through public education the merits of a sizable governmental ownership sector. Classical and neo-classical theories validate free-market capitalist systems that inherently defer to market allocations of both products and incomes. German and Italian fascisms reflect moderately different "theoretical" ancestry, but in each the overriding structure is an authoritarian dictatorship. Contemporary systems in quest of "ethnic cleansing" indicate that fascism is still present though in somewhat different forms.

Ism-ideologists, those trapped in ismatic thought, are engaged either in pursuit of the particular structure of the ism that is not yet attained, or in the defense of the ism presumed to be presently in force. In either case, the ism is given the role of serving as the criterion of judgment in defining, pursuing and assessing current problems. What conforms to the ism, *ought* to be adopted; what does not, *ought* to be rejected or suppressed. Converting an ismatic structure into a dominant or determinative criterion of judgment makes it impossible to choose from *among* instrumentally conceived and normatively validated institutional structures.

For ism-ideologists, their specified institutional arrangements are perceived as both an ideal goal and a prescriptive design. They claim and affirm, implicitly or explicitly, control over social structure; they publicly embrace their ismatic aims; they ridicule or otherwise discredit opposition. For those advocating each of the respective "isms," their particular set of institutions is presumed to be inherently "superior" to all others. But the referent for *superior* cannot be established instrumentally. Control over the social and economic processes is sought and held by the most "worthy," a particular invidiously validated segment of the community who seek to ensure their retention, and extend their range, of that discretionary control. Most ism-ideologists as advocates understand, whether acknowledged or not, that "to gain control of government, you get [and retain] *de facto* control of the means of life" [Foster 1950 (LN) CompEconSyst, 24, emphasis in original]. The creation and modification of economic structure can only be accomplished through political decision making. An implication is that social inquiry, then, must address the *politico-economic* system. The guiding tenet for ism-ideologists is that institutional adjustments must reflect a shift from what is *not* convergent or compatible with the particular ism and its assignment of discretion to what *is* consistent with that ism. For ism-ideologists, modifications of institutional structure, then, are not designed to solve problems by enhancing instrumental functions but rather to achieve, and/or perpetuate, and/or extend the invidious structure that assures the continuity of control and retention of status for invidiously privileged individuals and fragments of the community.

At bottom, ismatic models are inherently teleological. They are presumed to culminate in a final term. That is, there is to be no structural adjustment beyond realization of the institutional structure prescribed by the ism. For Foster and institutional economists, in contrast, there is no "final term." As was suggested in Chapter 5, Foster's theory of institutional adjustment demonstrates the continuing process of problem resolution. A continuing *process* of instrumentally warranted institutional adjustments is *sine qua non* of problem solving.

We consider now these ideological models of feudalism, utopian socialism, Marxism, Fabian socialism, capitalism, and fascism from Foster's critical instrumentalist perspective. In each case, with an exception or two, brief mention will be made of: *(a)* claimed philosophic or theoretic underpinnings *(b)* structural elements of the ismatic model, *(c)* invidious/ceremonial criteria reflected in or employed by ism-ideologists, and *(d)* fundamental inadequacies for problem solving. We conclude *(e)* with some behavioral and theoretical observations on isms vs. democracy.

FEUDALISM

Introduction

"European feudalism was the result of technological innovation and social adjustments" [Foster 1968 (LN) HistEconThou, 5]. Technological innovations included mortar architecture; weapons that enhanced defense measures and permitted "impact combat;" improved agricultural instruments (e.g. plow) and practices (e.g. crop rotation); commerce (e.g. double entry booking); innovations in ships (e.g. capacity, navigation), among others. The Roman Empire was dismembered in large part because of its difficulties in sustaining military rule over extended and increasingly hostile areas, financing its hegemony through the collection of taxes, covering the cost of conquering, and extending and enhancing invidious display (slave owning). "The economy of predation overextended itself" (4-5).

The major social adjustment was the emergence and dominion of the Medieval Church. It became the dominant institutional structure over most of Europe. Priests became central figures because of their literacy (oral and written) and their willingness to serve as arbitrators of disputes. They held a monopoly on learning; early universities were established to train priests. The Church acquired encompassing discretion over social, economic, and political processes and structures. "The Bishop of Rome was the central decision maker." But the Church was without any physical means to enforce decisions. Its exercise of discretion was "enforced by religious conviction." It held a monopoly on salvation. And salvation had become the preoccupation, if not obsession, of an increasing segment of the community. Feudal thought developed to justify the existing system [Foster 1968 (LN) HistEconThou, 4-5].

Theoretical Underpinnings

Aquinas was perhaps the most mature expositor of the feudal system. "He joined Church dicta and Greek philosophic principles" [Foster 1968 (LN) HistEconThou, 7]. The basic theological datum was God's will. "The feudal system was the result of God's will." Given this dictum, the Church provides itself with a universal accounting for whatever occurs. God's will is omnipresent and determinative. Aberrations from established practice must also be a reflection of God's will. Consequently, one has then a universal explication that in fact explains nothing. The theory is tautological in its repetition of the omnipresence of a supernatural determinant. It is teleological in its presumption of divine guidance to a presumed end-in-view. God's will is perceived as the "final cause" in all matters of substance. It was an "anthropomorphic concept of the deity. . .God [is just] like us" (7). Diseases, for example, are God's punishments for "straying" humans.

Institutional Structure

The conjoined monopoly on learning and monopoly on salvation held by the clergy of the Church provided the continuing de facto instruments of social control available to the Church. Sustaining such control over a largely illiterate laic community was accomplished by controls over the disposition of property, tithing requirements, laical dispute settlements, et cetera. The establishment of immense and awesome cathedrals with their interior Biblical frescos (paid for by tithings and contributions) promoted deference and subservience in ordinary illiterate folk. The Church established order and predictability. Its clergy controlled the religious ceremonies and festivals throughout the year. The Church leaders, in effect, exercised the powers of mandamus and injunction; they provided legislative and judicial functions, but with no formal accountability. There was no appeal or recourse beyond the Church. It was the de facto site of political authority and governance.

The economic structure was most typically manorial. The Church did not formally "own" manorial property because to do so would appear selfish and un-Godly. But it did exercise significant discretion over property. Manors were the dominant agricultural production unit. In everyday affairs the manor was sovereign; the "body social, body politic, body economic" (Foster 1968 (LN) HistEconThou, 5). The manor was largely a self-contained agricultural unit. Land use was typically provided as a fiefdom. Oaths and pledges were made in order to have access to manorial lands for agricultural production. The structure within the manor was heavily traditional. Land access passed through the eldest male heir only. Serfdom prevailed. Men and women were bound to the soil; roles were defined and retained. Manors were largely, but not elaborately, hierarchical in pattern. The economic process was in large part a system of self-provision within the manor augmented by trading some goods for other goods within and between manors. Money was little used. Monetary exchange "was improper to mankind." Only with the long-drawn out enclosure movement did agricultural lands pass into private ownership, per se (6).

Invidious Criteria Employed

The feudal system under Church dominion was profoundly invidious in at least three respects:

Use of birth order and family identities: The agnatic status roles associated with the birth of the first male son were substantial. He alone could inherit discretionary control of the land and therewith continue the family's identity and status. Later born sons could join the church, seek control over other manors, become soldiers, or work in the "cracks and crevices" of the feudal order, e.g., signing on as apprentices in emerging urban communities [Foster 1968 (LN) HistEconThou, 6].

Gender discrimination: For women, there was "no way to participate in the [social, political and economic] process except through father, brother or husband" (6). Women could not participate in most of the discretionary functions of the Church; they could not own property in their own names. Marriages, including those of the nobility, were often "arranged" for family, political and/or military reasons. The assignment of status for males precluded comparable acceptance for females.

Religious discrimination: The "feudal system at first was enforced by religious conviction" (6). Jews and Zorasters, being non-Christian, had no authorized access to any of the social, political and economic facets of the feudal order under control of the Medieval Church. They were not Christian; the shift to characterizations of *anti*-Christian was a modest further step. They, and others similarly judged, were outside the purview, and the control of, the Church. Their souls did not matter. As "comprehensive outsiders" they could not accept the Sacraments of the Church, or even be buried in a Christian cemetery. That many, experiencing these exclusions, would turn to commerce to secure an income could have been anticipated. Indeed, since engaging in commerce was a continuing threat to the soul of the Christian, it was preferable for non-Christians, rather than Christians to be so engaged.

Fundamental Inadequacies

In the "cracks and crevices" of the feudal order, the technological progression of evidential knowledge continued. Institutional innovations eroded and ultimately displaced the institutional hegemony of the Medieval Church for the following reasons:

The Church was unable to maintain its monopoly on salvation with the emergence of the Protestant Reformation in which man's relation to God became a matter of personal commitment. It was unable to maintain its monopoly on learning with the emerging scientific inquiry originating outside the Church. The printing press, the Copernican demonstration, and the spread of literacy were indicative of this scientific awakening. It was unable to retain its monopoly on public policy making with the rise of the earliest non-Church nobility, the raising of personal armies, the invention of gunpowder. Recall the symbolic image from Twain's *Connecticut Yankee* in which a bullet pierced the breast-plate of an armored soldier implying the end of feudal military prowess.

The Church could not escape the horrendous consequences of the advent of the Black Death (bubonic plague) in killing from one-third to one-half of the population in most areas of Europe. It literally destroyed much of the existent labor force—urban and rural. Wage labor gradually replaced manorial labor. Wage payments for work done became increasingly the institutional pattern. Manorial arrangements of crop sharing, et cetera, became less significant.

Finally, the Church was unable to forestall the rising level of commerce outside the structure and aegis of the Church. Medieval fairs were an early large-scale institutional innovation that provided extensive, but periodic, markets promoting the exchange of goods for money in what would now be characterized as wholesale and retail commerce. The hegemony of the Medieval Church shrank as laic commercial groups organized (e.g. Hanseatic League) to create trading structures beyond the purview and control of the Medieval Church.

Foster offers a concluding observation:

> Feudalism. . .is characterized by a specification of function and position in the economy on the basis of birth (on the basis of family). Its importance is due not to the fact that any important economies are based upon it, but rather to the fact that it still pervades other isms. It is very apparent in our own economy, for example, as in the family. We inherit wealth and in some sense [we] inherit occupation. Education is left in large measure to the parents. [We] inherit the [family] name [Foster 1950 (LN) CompEconSyst, 34].

We easily recognize these non-trivial remnants of feudalism. More generally we must acknowledge that recourse to Church dicta and Feudalism as an economic system obviously does not contribute to Foster's functional model for inquiry or an instrumentalist approach for problem solving. They are not compatible with an instrumental theory of value or a credible theory of institutional adjustment. But the early juxtaposition of emerging warranted knowledge and its application in technology confronting institutional rigidities, in this case of the Medieval Church, pose questions of compatibility and relevance that are still reflected in contemporary economies.

UTOPIAN SOCIALISM

Introduction

The utopian socialists, herein limited to Charles Fourier (French) and Robert Owen (English), were early 19th century reformers who were products of the age of reason. They were advocates of institutional change of a demonstrational character. Their approach was to create the model community as an example incorporating and exhibiting their beliefs and recommended behaviors. That example, then, would be mimicked by others seeking similar social goals. Their contributions, as they perceived them, were to foster reform at the micro level, then expand it to the macro level. The caption "utopian" was attached by some who wished to discredit their doctrines.

They shared a conviction that man had rational capabilities more developed than other species. This man can "learn vicariously. He is a theory-creating and theory-applying animal. He can conceptually project what he knows" [Foster 1950 (LN) CompEconSyst, 2]. Accordingly, the utopians were reformers; they wished to change institutional structure in particular ways to achieve greater amounts, and better distribution of real income; they wished to teach what they thought they knew. They were realists in the sense that men and women can take responsibility for their current conditions and can modify structure and conduct to enhance their own well-being. Fourier proposed a singular shift from "what is" to "what ought to be," a particular model of a community with elaborately stipulated detail captioned the "Phalanstère." Robert Owen's initial venture (there were others that came after) was a model textile factory town, a communitarian village called "New Lanark."

Theoretical Underpinnings

Fourier

Charles Fourier had an elaborate theory of human nature. A dozen different instincts caused people naturally to act in particular ways. He wanted to reorganize the institutional structure so that these basic instincts could operate without interference. In that way the obvious inefficiencies of the economic process could be corrected. For example: People were starving in Paris when quantities of food were wasted because they could not be sold for profit. "Eating was a natural process and the institutions interfered."

Fourier was not concerned with the abandonment of private property or the equality of income. He thought everyone should have a minimum income to meet basic needs. Income left over should be distributed 1/3 to labor, 1/4 to management and 5/12 to property owners [Foster 1950 (LN) CompEconSyst, 4]. It was Fourier's policy to "transmute the divergent interests of capitalists, workers, and consumers by giving to each individual a share in these conflicting interests. Under existing conditions they are in conflict with one another simply because they are focused in different individuals. Were they to be united in the same person, the conflict would cease, or at any rate the battleground would be shifted to the conscience of each individual" (Gide & Rist 1947, 260). He was sometimes characterized as a bourgeois socialist.

Owen

Owen viewed human nature somewhat differently. He characterized it using the "clay-tablet" concept. People are born as clay-tablets on which "experience writes character and personality." Humans are basically rational; "what is wrong is the institutions." Man is naturally reasonable. Given the capacity to reason he can assess his own condition, takes steps to revise it, and create a substantially different, and more effective and humane, environment.

Owen's conception of economic theory undergirds several of his proposals for economic reform: For him:

> "All value comes from labor.
> Labor receives only part of the money value of what it creates.
> Therefore, it is impossible to recover the goods from the market.
> Therefore, the defect lies in the money system, because there is no correspondence between [the supply of] money (founded on gold) and money's worth (founded on labor).
> If workers received the money's worth of what they produced, all goods could be sold" [Foster 1950 (LN) CompEconSyst, 6].

Institutional Structure

Fourier

Fourier's model of a self-sustaining community resembled a very large and grand hotel involving extensive living quarters, surrounded by several hundred acres of agricultural land. Workers could work in any aspect of the operation. Rivalry in work was permitted. Working groups were organized with specialized functions. Income above the minimum was based on how hard one worked. Work was to be regarded as play. All opprobrium attached to it was to be suppressed. The "dirty work" that remains would be performed by children as apprentices to encourage discipline [Foster (LN) CompEconSyst, 5]. Differentiation of function required some 1500 people in the phalanx. Everybody participated in decisions; no regulations required; no "anti-social" behavior would occur; no coercion would be required; no courts were needed. Some forty Phalanxes were set up in the United States. Most failed because of insufficient capital, too few members, and deviant participants who did not fully enough share Fourier's vision.

Owen

Owen's experience with communitarian models is much more extensive; it covers some four different institutional designs and structure:

Philanthropic capitalism: As an early apprentice, sometime inventor, and exceedingly ambitious young Welsh man, Owen built a water-powered textile mill at New Larnark in southern Scotland. At the New Larnark mill, he introduced, astonishing for the day, many reforms in industrial organization: He limited child labor, abolished the pauper apprentice system, reduced the length of the working day, paid reasonable wages, provided a company store with comparatively modest prices, established schools for children of workers, introduced a program of adult education, brought in guest artists to entertain workers, provided decent living quarters for all of his workers, and absolutely forbade the introduction of organized religion. This last mentioned move later armed his critics. In any case, he became a very wealthy and leading industrialist. His subsequent approaches to economic reform were financed out of revenues from the New Larnark mill. (The mill itself remained in operation until the 1950s).

Villages of Cooperation: In the United States, Owen sank much of his fortune in a communitarian village at New Harmony in Indiana. It failed in three years from dissension, disorganization and disenchantment.

Co-op exchanges: Back in England, poorer and wiser, Owen set up a worker co-op. Since real values reflect labor content, "each man should be paid according to the amount of his labor." Then there would be no depression. But "workers used the coop exchanges to dispose of goods they couldn't sell in the regular market;" salable goods went to the regular market.

Trade unions: Owen wanted to organize workers as a vehicle for the achievement of socialism. But against his directions, they struck for higher pay. Owen's socialist goals were not realized.

Foster's Assessment of Utopian Socialists

Shortcomings

Foster explains that the Utopians "overlooked the degree of interdependence of the economic world." They did not understand that "people *believe* in class interests, even though they correctly pointed out the harmony of interests in fact. They failed to understand the significance and function of habits of thought and action." Moreover, " they failed to think of ways and means of arriving at the Utopia." They thought that a community could comprehensively "stop and start over. They assumed that people would do what they understand without understanding its relationship to all the rest of their experience." They believed that "institutional change must have an institutional structure in view as the end" toward which the society must move. They offered "rigid forms and perfect plans;" their inquiry did not envision a continuing need for institutional adjustment.[Foster 1950 (LN) CompEconSyst, 7].

Contributions

Foster recognizes several constructive insights of the utopians: They contended "that reason is the driving force of history." They believed in the "the possibility of social progress." They revolted "against [economics as] the dismal science" and served as "effective critics of the society in which they lived" by reminding "the community that the community might be wrong. They kept before the community the idea that institutions influence in a very important way the behavior of individuals." Moreover, "they emphasized the fact that institutions are man-made" and "even made a large part of the community conscious of that fact" [Foster 1950 (LN) CompEconSyst, 7].

Utopians distinguished "between personal and social problems [on the one hand] and well-being [on the other]. They made the wrong distinctions, but they brought to the attention of the community that there are such distinctions." They recognized "the potentialities in technological development and its service to human beings." Utopians sought to enhance "human well-being and, in some sense or other, happiness. . . .Divine decree was not to contravene human happiness."

Significantly for their day, they "placed emphasis on the matter of the inequality of income" and acknowledged it as a disruptive "source of our difficulties." To their credit, they showed the necessary relationship between education and economic welfare. . . .Utopians held to [the] idea of education as free inquiry" (7).

MARXISM

Introduction

Foster thinks that the work of Karl Marx should be taken very seriously. "He produced something which fired the imagination of a large part of the world. He is perhaps the most important man of the 19th century—that is, he has influenced, is influencing, and will influence the lives of more people than any other man" [Foster 1948 (LN) HistEconThou, 25].

Marx was an astute observer in that century of the industrial revolution in Europe. He acknowledged its accomplishments, but he had a profound conviction that something was fundamentally wrong with the nature and impact of its development. He spent a decade in the British Museum (library) working out an alternate explanation of how a capitalist system operates and what its consequences were. Although no engraved brass plate identifies his worksite in the library (to the lament of Russian visitors), his *Das Capital* I, written there, opened a whole new field of inquiry and advocacy in political economy.

Theoretical Underpinnings

Marx draws on two main sources for his philosophical and theoretical insights: Hegelian philosophical method and Ricardian classical economics. The Hegelian dialectics posited a fundamental triad of thesis, antithesis, and synthesis. "The thesis is the formulation of the concept of dynamics in the form of positive development, the antithesis is the opposing elements," and from the resulting conflict a new synthesis emerges, "which then becomes a new thesis." "The whole of human affairs is presumed to travel in this way. It is something of an equilibrium analysis, but it is a moving equilibrium." But Marx inverts the Hegelian concept of reality: "Hegel says that reality is the human mind and things are a projection of that mind. Hegel [moves] from God to clod. Marx starts from observable facts and bases his formulations thereon; he perceives his approach to be scientific. Marx [moves] from clod to God" [Foster 1948 (LN) HistEconThou, 25.] Historical inquiry, then, is materialistic not idealistic.

In his economic analyses, Marx borrows heavily from Ricardo. They "essentially agreed on theories of price, labor, rent, profits, value, and capital formation" (25). Marx's unique contribution was to formulate an economic theory of history, imaginatively drawing on these two sources for insights. He emerges with a theory of the development of capitalism which, he believes, explains the inclusive social process.

His historical assessment is based on two foundational constructs: The "forces of production" and the "relations of production" which jointly constitute the *mode* of production. The forces of production are "patterns of human relationships, not technology." They shape the physical aspects of the productive process." They are by nature dynamic and processual. "The forces change as the technology changes." Human relationships are rooted in the physical aspects of the productive process; "such relationships and productive processes" are part of the social process. "The physical situation dictates the forces, the pattern of human relationships, in all its complexity" [Foster 1948 (LN) HistEconThou, 25] The proletariat class is commonly and inherently identified with the forces of production.

The relations of production are "patterns of human relationships determined not by physical character of the productive process but by power arrangements. They are inherited, substantiated by force, enforced by human beings." They specify the relative position and power, that is, the property relations, of the classes, the proletariat and the bourgeoisie, in the economic and social hierarchy. "They are arrangements that empower individuals to exercise discretion over the economic process. Relations are by nature static; power begets power, it will seek to maintain itself" (25).

In sum, the "forces develop as specified by technology, [the] relations develop as specified by inherited patterns of power." These two, "working together and in conflict, [constitute] the mode, which is the whole of the productive process and which determines the whole of institutional structure and therefore the whole of human experience" [Foster 1948 (LN) HistEconThou, 26]. "Forces are inherently changeable; relations are inherently static." The changes wrought by dynamic technology cannot subsist within the bounds of prevailing property relations. "The unpropertied proletariat with naught but their labor to sell, and the bourgeoisie, who own the means of production and thereby control the processes of production and employment, are in essential and inevitable conflict. Conflict develops between the two patterns of human relationships; but it is not a conflict between institutions and technology" (25-26). Technological change, the struggle between the classes and the conflict between the forces and relations of production are the causal and dynamic element in economic and social changes. These conflicts drive the process to its final and necessary conclusion. Class struggle continues until there is a revolutionary displacement of capitalist by Marxist relations of production. A synthesis ultimately emerges that, after time, constitutes the relations of production. Given the theory of history employed, the synthesis comes into conflict with new "forces" which sets the stage for renewed conflict between the two patterns of relationships (26).

Marx's driving concern is to use the foregoing historical theory to explain the character of the capitalist mode and to explicate why it *must* collapse. The class struggle continues until there is a revolutionary displacement of capitalism with communism.

Institutional Structure

The institutional structure that Marx does recommend for communism is comprised of inclusions and exclusions of prescribed and proscribed patterns of behavior, all in contrast with capitalism. As Foster puts it:

> Marx's institutional structure [for communism] is as follows: The disappearance of private property or state property or any other kind; the disappearance of the need for the state; distribution according to need as

> determined by the community at large; elimination of classes; the separation of means and ends in the recognition of the final purpose. A political state is an instrument the sole function of which is to maintain a pattern of production. In the Utopia [of communism] the state would have no ceremonial function. There would be community distribution of production, with everything commonly available in accordance with need. There would be no need for money, there would be no price [Foster 1948 (LN) HistEconThou, 26].

Again, these are the structures Marx expects to appear and those he perceives and recommends as continuing. There would be no need for further institutional adjustment.

Invidious Criteria Employed.

It is not just a recitation of the obvious to suggest that Marx and Marxists make invidious use of class distinctions and membership. Anyone who can be identified with the capitalist class (through ownership of private property, for example) is perceived of as an enemy of society, without reference to any other attribute or capability. Conduct, behavior, commitments, and/or contributions of individuals are without merit *if* the individual is a member of the bourgeois class. The fact of ownership is sufficient to warrant invidious classification. Class distinctions then are routinely used to discriminate without reference to conduct. In contrast, Marx's proletariat class are presumed to exhibit only what institutionalists would characterize as instrumental behavior. They do not abuse their possession of power; they are, allegedly, indifferent e.g., about divergent ancestry, gender, race, color or financial status.

Fundamental Inadequacies

History abandoned: Marx contributes little, in this context, to a warrantable theory of social and economic change. He has no continuing or warrantable theory of institutional adjustment. His theory of dialectical change itself is discontinuous. A singular shift through revolution from capitalist to Marxist institutions does not change further. His identification of economic agents by economic classes truncates the perception of human motivation as the pursuit of change. Purposiveness is defined a priori by class interests. His extended historical and analytical explanation of the decline of capitalism (the five laws of capitalist decline) envisions an increasing deterioration, and an ultimate comprehensive abandonment, of capitalist institutional structure. After a transitional stage of socialism, imposed by the dictatorship of the proletariat, communist structure (the prevailing forces of production) will necessarily appear; no other structures are admissible. Historical perception, for Marx, has a deterministic character. But the "determiner" disappears with the establishment of communism; his general perception and construct of the conflictual "forces" and "relations" of production, must disappear following the necessarily successful communist revolution. The establishment of the communist economy will require no further changes in structure.

Foster argues that Marx's historical theory is both invalid and contradictory: His " theory is invalid because there is no permanent structure which can be arrived at. Marxian theory is as tautological as any that has ever been constructed." [[(1949) 1981 (LN) HistEconThou. 27].The Marxist defined "forces" will prevail: capitalist identified "relations" will be abandoned. His historical theory is contradictory; it is "both inevitable and necessary of attainment. Marx must formulate his theory so that those who must revolt will understand it and act. [I]t is going to happen anyhow but won't [occur] unless those who are to make it happen know [what they must do]." (28).

Utopia proposed: Marx argues that the capitalist *dominion* will not erode without coercive displacement; it must be overturned by force. Only an overthrow of the capitalist power system will permit the induction of a new system, an economic transformation to a Marxist designed communism. Marx's analytical error, however, is that his ism, once established, is presumed to continue indefinitely. His theory does not permit or provide for a post-communist political-economy. No more Hegelian thesis-antithesis-synthesis explanation; no more class conflict; no more use and abuse of economic power. Communism allegedly will continue because conflictual forces vs. relations and conflictual owner vs. non-owner classes are forever abandoned. "His communism is to be a sort of Utopia which continues ad infinitum because there are no problems and no conflicts" [Foster 1948 (LN) HistEconThou, 26].

Democracy denied: Foster observes that: "Marxian analysis encompasses a theory of history which may be. . .applied as a guide for policy and action. . . .That application involves the idea that the transition to the truly democratic society can be accomplished only through what they speak of as a dictatorship of the proletariat. The dictatorship itself is conceived as the instrument for making the transition to ideal democracy. That dictatorship is thought to be different than others by virtue of the character of the dictator" [Foster (1949) 1981, 977]. To which Foster responds: "If history has disclosed anything with certainty, it is that arbitrary power begets arbitrary power. It is that dictatorship, under whatever name and to whatever degree, never willingly adjusts toward democracy" (977).

The Marxist model is, then, fundamentally undemocratic, claims to the contrary notwithstanding. The recommended structure for the communist mode of production does not provide for the continuing popular determination of public policy. It is characteristic of Marxists, having achieved some measure of discretion over the behavior of others, to use that power to perpetuate their own positions of discretion. Marxists are quite willing to impose their ism on others in the confident insistence that their scientific communism is an unchallengable truth warranting coercive implementation where necessary. Communist regimes around the globe have typically been and remain authoritarian systems. [See also Tool 1986, 135-178].

FABIAN SOCIALISM

Introduction

Fabian socialism is largely a product of the early 20th century. It is primarily a British perspective although its theorists draw heavily on the writings (and lectures) of Henry George, an American. The Fabians were advocates of gradualism in the making of social and economic policy. Named for a Roman General admired for his holding tactics—the "delayer"—the Fabians were a group of persons who "organized themselves to educate the people of Britain for socialism" [Foster 1950 (LN) CompEconSyst, 28]. One motto, "step by step," echoes the Fabian caption, and the need for research and persuasion. "They are evolutionary socialists." They were committed to pursue strategic, but democratic, means to achieve fundamental change in the economic structure of Britain. The Fabian society, as such, was a comparatively small group but had illustrious members including Sidney and Beatrice Webb, H. G. Wells, and George Bernard Shaw, all of whom were internationally acclaimed writers. It was "an educational institution not a political party" (28). The significance of the group's impact is indicated by the fact that some of their proposals have been implemented not only in Britain, but also in Australia, New Zealand, and Canada. In Britain, the Fabians have been associated, in the post WW II period, with the Labour Party, whose nationalization program, prior to Thatcherism, accounted for perhaps twenty percent of the economy's output.

Theoretical Underpinnings

Fabian socialism is based especially upon the Ricardian theory of rent and the marginal utility theory of value. Ricardian rent theory comes to Fabianism through the writings and lectures in England of Henry George (especially his *Progress and Poverty*). Interestingly, "Henry George was an individualist, not a socialist. He wanted to facilitate free private enterprise, to further the accumulation of capital equipment" [Foster 1950 (LN) CompEconSyst, 29]. He wished to assist both capital and labor.

Foster presents his rent theory:

> As population increases, the market's worth of product decreases as more and more capital and labor are applied to land. . . .[R]ent is proportionate to richness of land. Speculators purchase land and cut off the return to labor of higher production. Wages and profits then are reduced; wages are reduced to what can be produced on marginal land, and the margin is extended by speculation. Like Ricardo, he points out that income coming from product of land other than at the margin becomes rent. [It] becomes a payment for non-productive "participation" in the economic process. So, since land is limited and differs in fertility, wages must be forced down as poorer land is brought into use because wages are the product of the poorest land use [Foster 1950 (LN) CompEconSyst, 28).

Foster continues:

> Again, like Ricardo, George says that if all the product of land went to labor and capital, society would be richer. So George proposes to destroy rent, through the single tax on land. [He wishes to] tax the entire differential.
>
> This would help labor and capital formation by taking away the burden of their tax liabilities; and by increasing productivity by the use of more productive land, it would increase the wealth of the nation in Adam Smith's terms. The unearned increment that is rent is the product of the community and should not go to individuals [Foster 1950 (LN) CompEconSyst, 29].

> Ricardo did not propose the single tax, but he made it possible for George to do so by developing the differential rent theory. . . .Then the Fabians took off from George and extended the theory to capital as well as land. Income from capital [is] also unearned (29).

Since the Fabian's case for socialization of major components and sectors of the national economy, as their primary institutional adjustment (see below), hinges on the denial of this distinction that Ricardo and George make between land and capital, we pursue the distinction further through Foster's commentary:

> The Fabians extended this differential rent theory to all assets, and thus extended George into Socialism. They maintained that George and Ricardo were in error in thinking that capital was productive. Proof of this required a shift to the marginal utility theory of value. Here there are two alternatives: neoclassical position, and Fabian position. If you use the marginal utility theory of value (price theory), there is no distinction between land and capital. Money's worth is all you have. So the Fabians by shifting to marginal utility theory shifted from capitalism to socialism, by taking the only other alternative—unearned income is that going to *other* than labor [Foster 1950 (LN) CompEconSyst, 29, emphasis added].

This Fabian shift from capitalism to socialism rests on the repudiation of the distinctions Ricardo and George make between land and capital: *(a)* Ricardo & George: "land is a gift of God; capital is created by man." Fabians reply: "capital and land produce nothing alone; usefulness of both is a result of application of labor." *(b)* Ricardo & George: "land is limited in geographical sense." Fabians deny: "land area is a function of know-how. . .economic significance of land is not its lineal measurement. . .but economic use. Thus there is no such thing as marginal land [in general]. There is marginal land for particular uses. The Fabians are right about that." *(c)* Ricardo & George: "there is no cost of production in land [whereas] capital involves real cost." Fabians disagree: "both have price, so they are the same thing as far as economic price is concerned." Accordingly, for the Fabians, "The Ricardian theory of rent is quite as applicable to capital as land" [Foster 1950 (LN) CompEconSyst, 29-30].

Institutional Structure

The Fabian socialists' recommendations of institutional structures to carry on the social process consist primarily of two major areas of institutional adjustments: democratic processes in determining public policy and the socialization (nationalization) of major institutions providing the means of life and experience.

(a) The Fabians are genuine democrats, although predictably there are some differences among members as to just what democratization means and how it is to be implemented and sustained. They seem to agree that both political and economic policy must be democratically generated. They recognize that the political function, popular determination of policy, is "inextricably bound" up with the economic function, the production and distribution of real income. "You cannot have one without the other" [Foster 1950 (LN) CompEconSyst, 30].

> Classical theory holds that effective demand operates in markets in terms of income. "Dollars vote." Fabians say that's right except it is the dollar, not the man, that chooses. A man with a million dollars has a million more votes than a person with one dollar. It should not be that way. Each man should have equal voice in the determination of the character of production. Capitalism doesn't accomplish this; only socialism does. So representation, in both the economic and the political sense, should be functional rather than geographical. Persons have interests not tied to geography (30).

Fabians identify three major groups in any political economy whose interests must be identified and addressed through democratic processes: consumers, producers and citizens. Accordingly, provision must be made for each of these three groups. "Moreover, their economic interests are far from being identical." The proposed solution is to return to a distinction between political and economic functions. "Have a political government for government of people, for defense, justice etc. Have a second government for the government of things, to take care of economic [matters]. The "political legislature would be based upon territorial representation, as now. But the economic or social legislature would have discretion over health, education, taxation, art, recreation, public services, etc." Representatives, then, "should be chosen in part territorially, insofar as territory identifies an interest, such a ship building, and in part according to industries [communal functions]" (30). Consumers and producers interests would be cared for through socialization.

(b) Socialization is to be accomplished "step by step." The Fabians do not wish to "disrupt the flow of consumer goods." And when socialization does occur, it need not encompass the whole of an industry. They recommend socialization for industries at the national level and socialization of local industry on a community scale. Most would retain private management of one-man operations, such as farming. Indeed, "most Fabians oppose complete socialization."

> Another way that consumer's interests are taken care of is through the compulsory establishment of consumer coops. Advantages: they have been successful as owners of means of production; [provided] more equitable distribution of gains; [are] more adaptable to changes in the state of the industrial arts, [i.e.] permit use of new inventions; allow greater choice and freedom in occupation, etc.; allow greater choice in the character of consumption. [But] consumer coops cannot be allowed full power. . .in dealing with comparative costs vs. comparative wants. [They] propose to control this matter by setting up trade unions and professional organizations . . .to set limits on [coop discretion over pricing and product policy.] [T]hese unions. . .will [improve] conditions of work, improve the dignity and character of workers, provide a very ready institutional device for securing cooperation, and improve the rate of invention and development by permitting interchange of ideas and ready access to improvements [Foster 1950 (LN) CompEconSyst, 30].

Fundamental Inadequacies

Although Foster does not provide a comprehensive assessment of Fabian Socialism, he does offer comments that suggest something of his interest and concerns. The following brief observations on Fabianian thought are intended to represent derivative, implied and consistent comments reflecting Foster's views on Fabian political economy. We intend only to stimulate some continuing reflection on the role of Fabians in pursuing social and economic change especially in Britain. We believe that Foster would concur:

(a) Although Fosterian instrumentalists applaud Fabians for their commitment to democratic processes in reaching public judgments, there seems to be something of a running conflict between their commitment to the democratic determination of policy on the one hand, and their advocacy of nationalization and/or socialization of a significant segment of the "private sector" on the other. The conflict appears in the presumption that a genuinely democratic community *will* choose to nationalize their basic industrial structure, if given the chance. Fabian socialism presumes to offer specific and allegedly pertinent structural institutions before the actual determinants of problems of mal- or non-performance are comprehensively identified. Would a Fabian emerge unequivocally with a nationalization solution for *any* breakdown in megacorps or the economy at large? The fundamental concern is the enhancement of instrumental functions through institutional adjustments. Can we assume at the *outset* of inquiry, that it is necessarily the instrumentally warranted adjustment? We think not. Certainly nationalization is a possible option, but there are other options (regulation, shared ownership, et cetera). The experience of most developed countries is that in each, a culturally specific set of connections are established involving public and private discretion at differing levels of control in the economy. Sometimes that discretion can be held continuously accountable, sometimes not. Socialism does not guarantee the former. The democratic process is the vehicle for the latter.

(b) There remains in Fabian socialism a remnant of orthodoxy which impairs analysis of problem solving in a contemporary economy. Recall the discussion introduced above, but not resolved, in the concern over "earned" versus "unearned" income. George saw rent as unearned; the Fabians perceive rent and returns to capital as unearned. The presumption is that the recipient of rent, the owner or the capitalist, did not incur disutility in consequence of his ownership. There was no pain, discomfort, or disutility as that for which his rent is a payment. Receipt of rent is unearned. Receipt of capital, similarly, is unearned. Equational justice is not served. There is no establishment of equivalence that would constitute equational justice. But as we saw above, an instrumentalist rejects the equational justice tenet because it is analytically and substantively irrelevant.

(c) We must moderate our conception of "Fabian inadequacies" in one respect: Do we not all become "bale-out socialists" when, as is typical in the United States and abroad, we conceive government as the "owner of last resort" and/or government as the "employer of last resort"? The answer, we believe, is affirmative. If we can not, for whatever substantive reasons, pursue other options, in a democratic community we turn necessarily to government for institutional adjustments. There is no other authoritative structure available for the community as a community with which to pursue the issue and attempt to resolve the problem.. An example is the history of the British coal mines over the last century. During war time or in an energy crunch, the economy needs augmented energy and if no other options are

feasible and made available, the national government *must* act instrumentally to "keep the machines running," using Ayres phrase. And in the United States, in the 1990s, many are recommending an institutional adjustment to make the government the "employer of last resort" for those involuntarily unemployed.

(d) Finally, to close with questions, consider the Fabian socialist analysis in light of Foster's theory of institutional adjustment. Does the Fabian literature take account of the principle of technological determination? Does the universe of technological determinants figure prominently in their deliberations on structural change? Perhaps in a small way in their efforts to keep industrial structure technologically current. Does their analysis consider the principle of recognized interdependence? Perhaps in a small way in discussions of the role and significance of coops and unions. Does their analysis acknowledge the principle of minimal dislocation. Perhaps in a small way, in their political quest for democratic authorization for socialized industrial structure.

CAPITALISM

Introduction

The term "capitalism" is almost universally used to identify and characterize the kind of economic systems that prevail in the United States, most of Western Europe and the Asian "tiger" economies. Most thoughtful observers agree that these ismatically identified economies do not "fit the model" in a variety of significant ways, but the caption continues to serve in the role assigned. Those guiding economies, especially in eastern Europe and central Asia, are encouraged to identify their emerging economies as capitalist and to move as rapidly as possiblc to implement that model (e.g. Sachs 1993*)*. The model of a capitalist economy, in the normative sense of what ought to be, constitutes the economic "common sense" of many developed and developing countries.

Moreover, this view is continuously reinforced by formal university level instruction in the discipline of economics, from the introductory Principles course through to the completion of a Doctorate in Economics at conventional schools. With rare exceptions, as in the United States, this instruction begins and ends with "capitalism" as the caption defining the universe of their respective areas and foci of economic inquiry. To characterize this mode of inquiry and its capitalist model of an economy as ismatic, then, with the infirmities implied, is to challenge the substance and overwhelming dominion of neoclassical orthodoxy in economic inquiry. It is a formidable challenge in every sense of the term.

In brief, then, the ismatic model of capitalism has become the criterion of judgment in deciding which direction is forward for most Western and emerging Eastern economies. Whatever moves toward a fuller implementation of the model is "good policy'. Whatever adjustments move away from or contradict the capitalist model are "bad policy." The content of the criterion then is a particular array of institutional forms.

Theoretical Underpinnings

For Foster, classical and neoclassical economic theory purport to validate the economic ism of capitalism. It is this extensive body of theory that culminates in the unwavering advocacy of capitalism as the only economic system that is naturally emergent, consistent with human nature, efficient in performance, and highly productive. While the American economy, in particular, reflects this advocacy and incorporates some of its structure (see below), this economy, as with all others, is a mixed system. Accordingly, the orthodox theory, at best, explains only a modest part of the actual functioning of the US economy, strident assertions to the contrary notwithstanding. The theory's descriptive relevance is quite limited; its appeal as an ism-ideology somewhat tarnished. Yet given its wide acceptance, we must acknowledge and briefly explore this long tradition of scholarly inquiry that claims capitalism as the most credible, most adaptive, most natural economic system. Since problems are only resolved through institutional adjustment, one must be wary here, as with other isms, of claims that sustain that ideological conviction that a particular set of institutions is universally and timelessly legitimate.

This body of formal theory has been derived largely through what is usually characterized as deductivist modes of inquiry, deducing inferences from assumptions that appear plausible but are not necessarily credible. Deductive inferences can, in a scientific context, be useful but they can never be sufficient. The assumptions from which the inferences are drawn may have little or no evidential grounding. The attribution of a "profit motive," peculiar to capitalism, sees all persons as motivated to "get as much as they can for as little as they can." And the "much" and "little" refer to magnitudes of "utility" that as "feelings of the human heart" are hardly measurable even in the more or less context; they are not warrantable in any demonstrable sense. Simply alleging that *price* is a measure of utility value, is interesting but at bottom wholly conjectural.

Similarly, the underlying contention in orthodoxy that presumes the existence of a natural economic order, that struggles constantly to sustain its character, is largely a conjectural posture. Allegedly a natural order exists: "In capitalism that which is natural is what would exist if you didn't do anything about it" [Foster 1949 (LN) CompEconSyst, 11]. The advocates for capitalism allege naturalness: the motivations exhibited in buying and selling in markets are natural; the behavior of entrepreneurs in maximizing profits and of laborers constantly seeking higher wages are natural. Markets naturally clear; the market is never at rest. Presumptions of a natural economic order are remnants of earlier classical doctrine.

A corollary of these natural order presumptions embedded in the ismatic construct of capitalism is the presumption of the omnipresence of equilibrating tendencies in all capitalist market behavior. Allowing alleged natural market forces to operate without intrusion or hindrance results in the emergence of equilibrium conditions. With equilibrium, there is no further movement, unless and until previously established conditions change. Thus markets have inherent tendencies for supply to equal demand. It is a process involving disruption from outside markets that naturally moves toward restoration within markets. Equilibrating price movements and their stabilizations then may be presumed to provide for the equivalencies of utility and disutility, of pleasure and pain. Equational justice, as assessed in Chapter 3, is presumed to be accomplished with the operation of price competitive markets in all areas of the economy.

Institutional Structure

To set a context, we begin by identifying some structures and patterns of economic conduct that are *not* peculiarly or uniquely identified with capitalism [Foster 1949 (LN) CompEconSyst, 8]: Machine technology is not particularly capitalistic. All economic systems make more or less extensive use of productive and distributive technologies in generating their aggregate product and service. Similarly, the accumulation of capital goods is accomplished in all economies in some considerable degree given their prevailing level of technological competence. The achievement of mass production is not peculiar to capitalist systems. Although patently obvious, neither the getting and spending of money, nor the selling to another what one produces is peculiarly capitalistic.

What then are the particular and distinguishing features and structures of capitalism? Ism-ideologists committed to the capitalist model perceive economic change to be a continuing consequence of the operations of "free" unfettered markets. The free-market price system is the only acknowledged and theoretically warranted institutional vehicle of economic change. The causal elements prompting changes are the inherent, insatiable, and unexamined wants, tastes and preferences of persons engaged in market participation as buyers and /or sellers.

The recommended institutional structure of a capitalist system is presumed to adapt to and facilitate this market participation. The institution of private ownership provides exclusive and legally protected possession of and discretion over items owned, and of revenue derived therefrom. Its presence is *sine qua non* for capitalists. Markets exist in consequence of individuals' inherent propensity to "truck, barter, and exchange" to satisfy their unsatiated hedonistic desires. Self-serving and self-regarding individuals, with given tastes and preferences, engage in market exchange through institutional structures that are inherently natural and given. These structures are: private ownership, as noted, unfettered markets; a passive government that, even so, protects and sustains capitalist structure; competition in which no one has power to affect price by his/her own efforts; and utilitous desires that activate and direct each participant.

Property ownership alludes to the formal acquisition of a legally established title to the item owned. As owner, one has a legally enforceable claim to pecuniary returns from its economic use. It follows then that most of the processes of production and distribution are controlled by owners of property. In the capitalist model the market is the central structure; indeed buying and selling in markets is the only means of establishing accountability. [Foster 1949 (LN) CompEconSyst, 9-12].

From a capitalist perspective, discretion over the institutional structure of the economy allegedly is held by no one; markets govern. Economic agents must adjust *to* the market; they do not control the market. Individuals exercising choice in competitive markets are characterized as utility-maximizing, egoistic, individualistic, "globules of desire." (Veblen) seeking through exchange to reflect their profit motive by getting as much as they can for as little as they can. Such individuals participate in markets as exchange arenas; their conjoint participation comprises economic behavior. The price system, then, is the central focus and concern of the economy; significant economic change, in consequence, is accomplished primarily by the impact of price and wage changes on individuals.

Individuals' private choices, in the aggregate, direct the economy. Whatever intrudes on individuals in their market conduct, affects the character and extent of institutional change in the larger economy. Social change is thought to be mainly a product of manifest economic change via markets.

In the model of capitalist economic systems, then, the free competitive price system is thought to be the primary locus and vehicle of economic change. Free markets are envisioned as an ideal goal and a potential realization. Individual conduct is directed to personal accommodation to a largely autonomous price system. The price system and its determinants are assumed a priori. Economic judgments are left to the market; the market decides.

But markets must be competitive! Language usage, and meaning intended, require clarification. Historically, competition, as a necessary structural condition in capitalism, meant that there were so many firms participating in a market that no one of them could affect price by its own efforts. None could administer price. Participants are price takers, not price makers. Prices were set by the supply of and demand for goods in an open market with many buyers, many sellers; prices moved with market activity. More recently, with the advent of large scale, corporate enterprise, the referential content of the term competition has changed to a struggle for market share through the exercise of market power, control over prices, control over needed imports, control over advertising products, control over delivery options, influence on government policies, et cetera.

Competition has come to mean the *exercise* of market power, not its absence. The corporate pushers of the capitalist ideology use the zero-power referent for competition to direct attention away from the market-share referent. However, the alleged "price takers" have quite obviously become "price makers." The struggle for market share among oligopolistic national and international corporate conglomerates is an exercise of encompassing discretion that, to function in a democratic polity, must be held accountable by governmental bodies of commensurate size. We must continue to reflect on control problems of this magnitude.

Invidious Criteria Employed

As we noted above, Foster uses the expression "invidious distinction" in the Veblenian sense: "The term is used . . .as describing a comparison of persons with a view of rating and grading them in respect of relative worth or value" (Veblen 1899, 34).

In the ism-ideology of capitalism, the unfettered market is presumed to be bias free. Participation in market exchange is supposedly governed wholly by pecuniary exchange in which "worthness," other than the money price paid for the utility of the product received, does not appear. But the moral equivalencies assumed to be generated by market exchange, are textbook fantasies, not descriptive realities. As casual observation confirms, the "markets" for credit and money, wage labor, managerial direction, real property, and the like, are not the "purely competitive" institutions the ideology sanctifies. Actual markets, unless instrumentally structured by policy stipulations, often, if not usually, reflect invidious judgments.

Ownership is sometimes invidiously tainted. Ownership of properties confers upon the possessor the right generally to sell or not sell based upon any number of considerations including the invidious use of wealth possession, family ties, Mafia protection, et cetera. The widely acknowledged denial to sell homes in some white residential areas to blacks, Asians, Mexicans, et al,. finally led to policy denials of much such discrimination. Ownership *means* possessing an area of discretion over the item owned; that ownership conveys to the owner discretion over other peoples' choices and behavior. Those areas of discretion, of course, have never been infinite. But in defining, through public policy, which discretionary judgments may be made with the item owned, invidious criteria may be required or denied, depending on the loci of more inclusive discretion over the political life of the community.

The hiring of people is sometimes invidiously tainted. Capitalist owner-managers typically assume that their discretion to hire is an exclusive prerogative based on their own judgments of the probable capabilities of the candidates for employment and the wage or salary payments warranted for the hired person. That this discretion cannot be exclusively held reflects the community's decision, through public policy, that denials based on ancestry, race, gender, et cetera. may not be used invidiously in the acquisition of a labor force.

Access to credit (loans) is sometimes invidiously tainted. All are aware that the creation and retirement of debt is an essential and major aspect of the operation of any so-called capitalist economy. Consumers generally are dependent upon access to credit as a critical and essential option in their acquisition of any "large ticket" item (home, auto etc.). Owner-mangers often require access to debt creation for most routine acquisitions of inventory, plant, equipment, and the like. Yet, here again, access to the needed credit line may be denied altogether or delimited by invidious denials of varying forms that go well beyond the reasoned expectation of the ability of the borrower to repay, as directed, the debt instrument as drawn.

In sum, it seems clear that the self-declared positivist (value free) claims of capitalist participants provide no more than a thin film of obscurantism in making normative assessments of the criteria of judgment actually employed in making economic decisions.

Fundamental Inadequacies

First, even a casual reflection upon the existing structure of any contemporary "capitalist" economy suggests that any actual "free market participation" is a function of access, pecuniary discretion and tacit or overt governmental tolerance or concurrence. Market *power* is the quest: power to administer prices, power to manipulate consumer activity through advertising, power to create technologies and specify their roles, power to define and enforce conditions of employment, power to extend international presence and control. Actually, free market ideologists notwithstanding, no viable community can ever (or has ever) organize and sustain the economic process merely or even primarily through the actions of economic agents seeking to maximize utility through the unchallenged institutions of capitalism and with impersonal price determinations therein. Perceiving the task of institutional change, then, as a shift from what is *not* capitalist to what *is* capitalist is a recipe for economic disaster as the post-Communist Russian experience demonstrates (Tool 1995, 171-236).

Second, as will become clear in Chapter 8 where we explore Foster's perception of Keynes' institutionalist contribution, the ism-ideology of capitalism was and is incapable of providing a credible theory of the determination of the level of employment in a quasi-capitalist system. The capitalist model provides no guidance for public policy to address the catastrophic impact of The Great Depression on the American community. Pursuing the "non-intervention" dicta of orthodoxy in the late 1920s and early 1930s contributed to the greatest peacetime economic disaster in American history. Yet nearly all efforts to initiate make-work programs, address agricultural gluts, restore purchasing power, salvage the banking system, and generate employment were met with capitalist ideological resistance. The "alphabet soup" generated (NRA, WPA, AAA, et al.) was no panacea, but it did restore enough stability and income flow to give people incentives to experiment further.

As a matter of fact, capitalist ideology is without instruction on the character of production as well. Capitalist ideologists envision large numbers of players, all price takers, consensually negotiating, transacting and engaging in free market exchange. They do not foresee a small number of well positioned players who themselves are able disproportionately to influence the direction of the market; that is, of production, pricing, distribution, etc. That is to say, the modern oligopolistic organization of the economy is not a constructural component of the original capitalist ideology, nor of the orthodox thought that purports to describe the workings of capitalism. Modern corporations do not just respond to demand, through multi-media advertising they create demand. Neither prices nor wages are established solely or primarily by market forces, but rather significantly are administered, that is, directed.

Third, capitalism's defenders fail to provide a credible theory of capital formation. Voluntary savings, as abstention from consumption, has long been presumed to be the primary source of funds for investment. It is alleged that abstaining from consumption generates savings that then fund acquisition of capital goods. This savings theory of economic progress, then, justifies and validates substantial inequality of income distribution. The rich, via abstention from consumer expenditure, must forgo indulgence if there are to be funds for economic expansion. The community must depend upon their sacrificial forbearance of expenditure in order to purchase investment goods, new plants and equipment, et cetera. But since Keynes, we have understood that the abstinence theory is untenable; it has no explanatory credibility. The debt creation theory of capital formation has replaced the savings-centered theory (Ranson 1988, 315-28; Junker 1967, 25-43).

As Foster makes very clear, virtually all investment expenditure is financed through debt creation somewhere in the economy. Banks and other lending agencies create debt and therewith create money. The money to repay the debt is drawn from the income produced by making goods. Making goods creates income. Voluntary savings is not the source of capital formation. As Foster observes, "Anything that is technologically possible is financially possible" [Foster 1949 (LN) CompEconSyst, 13]. Before Keynes, this saving theory of progress was generally accepted as warranted explanation. Regrettably this abstinence theory of capital formation has not yet been wholly abandoned. (We return to this matter in Chapter 8 below).

Fourth, capitalist ideology has no theory of public governance vis a vis the economy and accordingly has no constructive contributions to make for the continuing problem of sustaining performance. It is a distinguishing element of the democratic form of governance that those who determine public policy, economic and political, must continuously perform adequately and instrumentally as judged by those experiencing the consequences of their judgments. Accountability is critical. Otherwise, impairments and impediments in the production and distribution of real income can never be resolved through institutional adjustments.

For illustrative purposes, we consider Foster's approach to the performance question, *vis a vis* capitalism, in his doctoral dissertation entitled *Theoretical Foundations of Government Ownership in a Capitalist Economy* (1946). Foster examines the historical circumstances that led the United States to introduce government ownership in various sectors of the economy. Those sectors are: streets and highways, harbors and waterways, waterworks and sewage disposal, schools, forestry, and housing. His research leads him to conclude that "the economic enterprises which have become government-owned. . .cannot be characterized in terms of a particular type of physical process or equipment or organizational structure; and they cannot be explained in terms of rates of profit or loss to private owners or by ratios between operating and capital costs or by a dearth of private capital funds" (177).

> The only general pattern of explanation which corresponded with the evidences examined included the following three characterizations: *(a)* a problematic situation arises in relation to an economic enterprise. What constitutes the problematic situation in each instance is divergence between the possible contributions of the enterprise to the economic process and the actual performance in that regard under non-governmental ownership. *(b)* Government ownership of the enterprise in question becomes recognized as a possible alternative control device. *(c)* In establishing government ownership of an enterprise, institutional adjustments are held to the minimum. In no instance do the adjustments exceed those which are necessary in order to resolve the problem (178-9).

This explanation of the emergence of selective governmental enterprise by Foster reflects application of his theory of institutional adjustment (Chapter 5).Technological determination is recognized in the evidences of inadequate performances of significant productive functions by existing institutional structure and by evidential expectations that government enterprise would utilize existing knowledge in assuming responsibility for efficient performance of its designated function. Recognized interdependence is acknowledged in the realization and demonstration that new government enterprise would be instrumentally incorporated and integrated into the remainder of the economy with the establishment of connections and interdependencies with other relevant sectors of the economy. Minimal dislocation is recognized in the fashioning of limited adjustments to reflect evidential understanding of the explicit need for, and the solution of, the problem which prompted the introduction of governmental ownership. These adjustments do not disrupt adjacent or corollary structure and behavior.

FASCISM

Introduction

Fascism poses a dilemma in discourse.

First, there is general agreement among scholars that the core of fascist ideology is expressly anti-rational. How then can a theory that purportedly *explains* be based upon a denial of the relevance of theoretical *explanation*? The analytical dilemma remains. However, fascist doctrine has sufficient coherence that it has become a basis for action. "It has influenced behavior. Its repudiation of rational theory does not disallow specification in the theoretical sense [Foster 1949 (LN) CompEconSyst, 43]

Second, there is at issue the nature and validation of legitimacy of political rule. As Baldwin Ranson explains: "In every politico-economic system, *except for fascism*, discretion over policy is assigned on what are regarded as socially desirable criteria that distinguish legitimate from illegitimate exercises of discretion." The referents for legitimacy, of course, differ among advocates of the economic *isms*; in the main they are unsupported by warranted inquiry or instrumentally validated norms: "European feudalism is legitimated by God's Will, as known and understood by the clergy of the Medieval Church. Socialisms are legitimated by rational plans to eliminate inefficiency and exploitation, as known and understood by the planners. Marxism is legitimated by identifying the public interest with the proletarian class interest, as known and understood by the Communist Party. Capitalism is legitimated by the natural workings of utilitarianism, as known and understood by market participants. Foster's instrumental analysis and democratic processes [non-ismatic], are legitimated by the continuum of evidence as it comes to be known by participants in the continuum of inquiry and understood by the community at large" (Ranson 1999, emphasis in original).

In each of these cases, whatever the source of credibility, a distinction is drawn between legitimate and illegitimate validations of the possession and use of discretion. These "sources" in the isms range from the conjectural to the theologic. But, except for fascists, there is a normative implication of preference or oughtness that undergirds these assertions of legitimacy or illegitimacy. Fascists, however make no such distinction on *any* grounds, scientific or nonscientific.

As we noted in Chapter 5 above, Foster distinguishes between the exercise of power and the exercise of authority. *Power* is simply the imposition of discretion over other people's behavior. Unless that exercise can be held democratically accountable, it is *illegitimate*. *Authority* is the exercise of discretion over others *with responsibility*, that is, guided by the non-invidious interests of the recipient. There is attendant legitimacy validated by accountability.

Fascists do not recognize the distinction between power and authority. Power is coercively acquired; authority is invidiously proclaimed. As noted, fascism is the only ideology the proponents of which deny any distinction between legitimate and illegitimate discretion. Indeed, the issue is never raised by them. Power is imposed; accountability is nonexistent. "Fascists alone make *irresponsible discretion* the standard or criterion" of political rule. Legitimacy does not arise. (Ranson 1999, empshasis in original).

Theoretical Underpinnings

Given the fascists' basic contention that people inherently are either "at your throat or at your feet," power over others' behavior is alleged to be the only significant determinant of human relations. "[F]ascists claim that the attainment of power is a fundamental motivation and natural function in human beings" [Foster 1949 (LN)

CompEconSystems, 46].

The fascist "initiation and use of force [is]. . .an effort to determine institutional structure" [Foster 1948 (LN) Value, 312]. The decision to use force reflects achieved power by fascist leaders to impose institutional change at will. Social change for fascists can only be perceived as the exercising of power, not authority, as coercive control in a manner to assure the sustainability of that power (Foster 1949 CompEconSyst, 38-40). This is a version of the "great man theory of history" (Neitzche). Social change is nothing but the "lengthening shadow of great men." Accordingly, "the exercise of power is a cultural emanation of a much more fundamental characteristic of man. Power is associated with honor and prestige" (48).

The exercise of power over others, defines one's own identity and significance. The possession and exercise of power is its own justification. Purposiveness is limited to retention and expansion of discretion over others' behavior. Public accountability and responsibility do not arise. Democracy as self-rule, then, is an illusion; it is neither achievable nor desirable "because of lack of ability of [the] average person. He has not demonstrated his ability to attain power. Democracy is a government by the least able as demonstrated by action." [Foster 1949 (LN) CompEconSyst, 40]

Accordingly, for fascists, truth is a matter of party affirmation and coercive imposition, not of causal demonstration. Truth is an affirmation of power.[Foster 1949 (LN) CompEconSyst, 45]. "Things can be made true by an . . .exercise of power. They solve problems by simply stating an answer. . . .Kings can do no wrong, nor can the dictator. They have demonstrated rightness by attaining power" (40). Fascist leaders say that the adjustment of institutions cannot be achieved by recourse to deliberation and rational appraisal. They use force to deny discretion and participation to non-fascist persons; they reserve for themselves the right by force to determine who will have the opportunity to address problems and formulate and enforce institutional adjustments as social policy. Fascism itself is the heart of the problem; it is not an analytical instrument for problem solving that provides for the rational determination of social change.

Institutional Structure

Fascism differs from other ism-ideologies in that it does not have a slate of particular institutional forms which together constitute the fascist model of a political economy. It exhibits, rather, a singular tenet and purpose that has been accomplished in a variety of different sorts of institutional arrangements, as indeed the differences between the historical fascist states of Nazism in Germany and Fascism in Italy demonstrate. As Foster, argues, the criterion of judgment in fascism is power. "Power means [unaccountable] discretion over behavior of other persons. . .it means making them behave like you want them to behave. And that means kicking them around. . . .[F]ascism is a. . .[validation] of kicking people around, with impunity" [Foster 1948 (LN) Value, 55].

Accordingly "you will find in fascism no particular structure other than the necessary culmination [of power] in one person, the leader, the great man. . . .That's the only thing common to all patterns of fascism" (55, emphasis added). Then the actual institutional structures established are those that function as effectively as possible to establish and sustain coercive control by the fascist leader.

Invidious Criteria Employed

Fascism clearly is the most invidious ideology conceivable. Since the only admissible criterion of merit is the achieved possession of coercive control, any one without such discretion, standing and status, clearly is "worth" less and may (indeed must) be discriminated against in a quest to sustain the power of those already possessing encompassing unilateral discretion.

This translates, illustratively, into a recognition that fascists, as suits their purposes, whims and insecurities regarding the retention and extension of their control, invidiously and continuously discriminate among persons based on human differences of power held, gender, ancestry, national origin, race, skin color, age, appearance, and the like. German fascists, for example, imbedded racial discrimination in their legal codes. Concentration camps were an obvious implementation of their invidious mind-set. All who are not in the elite cadre of power are "degraded" by these and comparable invidious characterizations. Continuity of power is the fascist constant in politico-economic structure.

Fundamental Inadequacies

For the fascists, then, people generally are perceived as incapable of making basic decisions; they are incompetent. The fact of their powerlessness is indicative of their ineptness. Fascist structures of social and political control permit only the self-proclaimed power elite to exercise discretion over other peoples' behavior. Propaganda replaces education; public lies replace warranted public information. Media of communication are converted into instruments of psychological and emotional repression. Therewith, one can allegedly demonstrate superior status and standing. A community's continuing need for institutional adjustments to restructure significant processes and functions of its economy can not be achieved by the application of coercive power employed, accredited and sustained by invidious judgments of fascists.

To whatever degree the coercive violence of fascists is successfully imposed on a community, denies those communities the option of making institutional changes that would resolve their own problems. The continuing functions of the economy cannot not be carried on rationally and successfully where power sustaining coercion is substituted for substantive inquiry into the causal determinants of structural breakdowns. The question is not whether a fascist system will ultimately collapse from failures to promote rational, scientific institutional adjustments, but when it will collapse from politico-economic malfunctions that undercut the claims to pre-eminent power of the elite. Tragically, there are still fascist power systems engaged in "ethnic cleansing," tribal warfare, intimidative international impositions, and elitist status discriminations.

AMERICAN INSTITUTIONALIST THEORY (A REPRISE)

Isms and Democracy

Foster argues that ismatic ideological systems are unable to resolve continuing problems; democratic systems are able to solve institutional problems. An ism specifies particular institutions. Democracy does not; it utilizes all sorts of institutions. "The democratic process is not an ism. It prescribes no particular institutional pattern; [for example] voting may be the least democratic thing there is. An examination is better than voting for determining who should build a dam. It is more efficient. But voting is the best device we have found for determining fundamental public policy" [Foster 1950 (LN) CompEconSyst, 47].

All economies necessarily tap the general fund of warranted knowledge in some measure; they could not survive otherwise. Teaching the young to think critically and coherently is pursued by most developed economies. Making steel auto bodies in Germany is much like making steel auto bodies in Japan. The quest for warranted knowledge to enhance capabilities of providing modern health care is global. The facilitating institutions do well or poorly depending on a range of instrumentally supportive and enabling institutions available. But where the isms direct, even coercively demand, the presence of particular institutional structures, especially those that establish and sustain coercive control over the economy, preserving and/or extending the power structure takes precedence over the creation and/or adjustment of institutions in developing and applying warranted knowledge. As we have seen, the adjustment of structure to enhance instrumental functions, to more fully incorporate and utilize warranted instrumental knowledge, is the only route to follow that will significantly enhance the economic well-being of an inclusive community. All economies confront this reality but ism-defined and undemocratically managed economies constrain such use where it threatens the continuity of control by an unaccountable fragment over the community.

All economies are of necessity mixed in some sense, but in undemocratic systems the nature of the institutional mixture is typically defined by the ism that leaders attempt to implement. In democratic systems the institutional structure is amenable to revision when inquiry generates warranted knowledge that discloses a more instrumentally efficient revision or replacement. In the development and use of technology, however, there is only one admissible criterion of judgment—the instrumental criterion. Some institutions incorporate this knowledge in determining the character and quantity of real income; some do not. In democracies, the nature of the mixed structure is always amenable to examination and potential revision. In isms the structure is ideologically given; the processes must be adapted to accommodate the approved apriori institutional arrangements.

In sum, we have seen, then, that if a body of social theory contains an affirmation of a particular and enduring set of organizing institutions that invidiously rationalize power-conferring structure, as the above isms do, such theory cannot be relevant to actual problem solving. Problem solving is not a matter of deferring to markets, pursuing the class struggle, or imposing continuing coercive and invidious control over the political economy. Problem solving requires a continuing adjustment of institutions as problems of malfunction and disjunction appear and are acknowledged. Indeed, problems tend to intensify where those with discretion, out of ignorance and/or ismatic commitments, fail to see the analytical significance of the connection between prescriptive organizing patterns identified instrumentally, and those identified invidiously.

Not only must the "actual character of answers to social problems. . .take the form of institutional adjustments"; such answers must be generated by instrumental reasoning and proposing. As Foster observes: "what we mean by a social problem is that an institutional structure is not performing its instrumental functions as well as it might." [Foster (n.d.) 1981, 910]. "[I]f we are to solve problems we must look toward institutional adjustment that will increase instrumental efficiency of the institutions in question (912).

Concluding Observations of Foster

The American economy is a mixed economy but not a mixture of ism models. The experience with a land frontier over an extended period, as noted, largely forestalled the application of a preconceived slate of institutional forms that were developed in other cultures at other times with differing perceptions of public purpose and social value.

> Americans have talked like other peoples, ismatically, because that was all that was available. But they haven't acted that way. [They are the] least legalistic minded people in the world. That is because they have confronted problems that couldn't be solved in terms of an ism; problems have been continuously such that survival depended upon application of other than ismatic theory. In other communities it was not quite so serious—application of ismatic theory did not so frequently mean failure to survive, although it did mean a low standard of living [Foster 1950, (LN) CompEconSyst, 35].

Foster acknowledges, of course, that capitalism originated largely in Europe and that the American heritage is dominantly European. Predictably, the immigrants then brought some knowledge of capitalist institutions. But they discovered that, in important respects, the actual circumstances confronted forced modifications in ism-applications. Market dominion rooted in ownership was not everywhere an accepted goal. The individualism of capitalism was undercut by compulsions to cooperation and mutual responsibility that were most visible on the frontier. Natural resources outside the market process were available for settlement in new lands to the West. "Rugged individualism is not a characteristic of the frontiersman"(34). Where circumstances permitted, Americans kept the economy ceremonially adequate in the capitalistic sense; when problems arose with respect to which such deference to the ism did not result in a restoration of the function at issue, the structure was abandoned and new structure invoked. "Americans have insisted upon institutional adjustments where it was necessary to solve a problem, irrespective of the ism. . .not because we're wiser but because of our experience. We are peculiarly unbound." The "American people have created all kinds of institutions that have no relationship to the ism that is being applied. We have been forced to act instrumentally" to resolve problems (35). That means establishing institutions that are certainly non-capitalist but not necessarily by design, anti-capitalist. Says Foster, this non-ism peculiarity of American experience probably [is] best summed up in the presence of the frontier. That, plus the fact that we are still close to it [in historical time], plus the change in the industrial arts, distinguishes us as Americans—[it] makes us what we are. We [have] had to solve problems instrumentally instead of ceremonially, not that we did not try the latter. . . .[W]e have developed a 'mixed" economy more than others. Our mixed economy is not a mixture of isms. . . .[W]e have invented a bunch of institutions. We have found that the isms won't solve problems [1950 (LN) CompEconSyst, 37].

In conclusion, Foster observes:

> All economies are of necessity mixed. The economic process can be conceived of as a mixture only by virtue of isms; in terms of technology there is only one criterion of judgment [the instrumental efficiency criterion]. In this sense no economy is mixed; there are economies which are more or less efficient. Sooner or later almost every institutional device comes to be associated with a particular ism, but when you get down to its economic functions, it is no more one ism than another. Some institutions are identifiable in terms of ism[s]; others are not. When. . .economics [replicates] . . . the chemistry stage of chemistry, the isms will disappear; there will be no schools of economics just as there are no schools of chemistry. Chemistry is the same in Germany as in. . .[America]; economics (in the scientific sense) is also [the same] [Foster 1950 (LN) CompEconSyst, 46].

Foster contends that: "We have *never* seen the [consistent] application of an ism. There has always been institutional change. New institutions coming, old institutions changing, and completely new additional institutions arising. None of them ever constituted an ism or structure" [Foster 1948 (LN) Value, 201 (emphasis in original)]. People formulate isms; they attempt to apply isms; but always non-ism-generated changes in institutional structure are required to sustain the social process and the production of the means of life and experience.

REFERENCES

Foster, J. Fagg. 1946. *Theoretical Foundations of Government Ownership in a Capitalist Economy*. Ph.D. Dissertation. University of Texas, Austin.

———. 1948. Lecture Notes (LN). Value and Its Determinants.

———. 1948. Lecture Notes (LN). History of Economic Thought.

———. (1949) 1981. The United States, Russia, and democracy. *Journal of Economic Issues;* 15: 975-980.

———. 1949. Lecture Notes (LN). Comparative Economic Systems.

———. 1950. Lecture Notes (LN). Comparative Economic Systems.

———. 1968. Lecture Notes (LN). History of Economic Thought.

———. (n.d.) 1981. The effect of technology on oinstitutions. *Journal of Economic Issues;* 15:907-913.

Gide, Charles and Rist, Charles. (1907) 1947. *A History of Economic Doctrines*. Boston: D.C. Heath.

Junker, Louis J. (1967). Capital accumulation, savings-centered theory and economic development. *Journal of Economic Issues;* 1: 25-43.

Ranson, T. Baldwin. 1988. The institutionalist theory of capital formation. *Journal of Economic Issues;* 21: 1265-78.

———. 1999. Personal correspondence.

Sachs, Jeffrey. 1993. *Poland's Jump to the Market Economy*. Cambridge: MIT Press.

Tool. Marc R. 1995. *Pricing, Valuation and Systems*. Aldershot: Edward Elgar.

———. "Social Value Theory of Marxists: an Instrumentalist Review and Critique." In M. R. Tool, ed. *Essays in Social Value Theory*. Armonk NY: M.E. Sharpe.

Veblen, Thorstein B. (1899) 1934. *The Theory of the Leisure Class*. NY: Modern Library.

8 FOSTER AND KEYNES

It is ideas, not vested interests, which are dangerous for good or evil.
J. M. Keynes

INTRODUCTION

The twentieth century was for many, if not most, economists "The Age of Keynes." Clearly no professional economist had a greater impact on the way the economies of the West were perceived and explained than did John Maynard Keynes. His *The General Theory of Employment, Interest and Money* (1936), published during the Great Depression, addressed the then most crucial problematic conditions that Western economies were confronting. He critiqued and displaced many of the foundational tenets and policies of orthodoxy, especially those relating to the determinants of employment, national income, investment, and growth.

The text of *The General Theory* opens with what has become a familiar declaration: "I shall argue that the postulates of the classical theory [includes neoclassicism] are applicable to a special case only and not to the general case, the situation which it assumes being a limiting point of the possible positions of equilibrium. Moreover, the characteristics of the special case assumed by the classical theory happen not to be those of the economic society in which we actually live, with the result that its teaching is misleading and disastrous if we attempt to apply it to the facts of experience" (Keynes 1936, 3).

Keynes's *General Theory* had a substantial impact both on the substance of economic theorizing and also, if somewhat tardily, on economic policy making. It was uniquely relevant to the major issue of the day—pervasive unemployment. It became a most influential work although its critical implications for orthodoxy were resisted; some were acknowledged only gradually and begrudgingly. But Keynes's work could not be ignored. He had already established a distinguished and compelling record as a theoretical economist in England. His prior work was published and well known. His substantial experience as advisor to the British government was exemplary. His heterodoxy could not be casually dismissed as that of a crank or heretic. The frontier in aggregate analysis and policy applications became distinctively Keynesian in Britain and shortly thereafter in the United States. What would later be characterized as macroeconomics drew importantly on the contributions of Keynes.

At the outset, a clarification of referential content and usage is required:The term "Keynesian" is used in this Chapter to refer *exclusively* to the contributions of John Maynard Keynes especially as developed and presented in his *General Theory*. It is *this* referent that is consistently incorporated by Foster in his comments on Keynes. "Keynesian," as used herein, then, does *not* refer to the work of any subsequent interpreters of Keynes (neo-Keynesians, new Keynesians et al.), some of whom, for example, purport to synthesize Keynes's thought and neoclassical theory. Post Keynesians more frequently approach Foster's usage, but their analyses are not pursued in this Chapter.

Foster acknowledges the extraordinary impact of the Keynesian contribution on economic inquiry:

> The evidences [of Keynesian influence] are everywhere: the popular familiarity with the name, the almost universal use of the Keynesian symbols and the constructs for which they stand, the extensive use of the Keynesian taxonomy, and the widespread suggestions of policy along with overt applications of policy under the Keynesian banner. All of these, and more, bespeak an enormous impact. There probably has been no instance in history in which a pattern of ideas has had so much effect on the everyday life of everyone in so short a time. [Foster (1966a) 1981, 949].

The Keynesian contributions to economic analysis were explored and appraised in Foster's courses over three decades. He began his extensive consideration of Keynesian theory in his doctoral dissertation on the *Theoretical Foundations of Government Ownership in a Capitalist Society* (1946) in which he addresses Keynes's willingness to see governments, if necessary, stabilize economies. Extensive treatment of the Keynesian contributions, especially in comparative contrast with one or another orthodox position, were incisively presented in his courses on Business Cycles, History of Economic Thought, Contemporary Economic Theory (Chamberlin, Hicks, Keynes) and Comparative Economic Theories (Marshall & Keynes).

We must acknowledge an anomaly, however. With but few exceptions, including Foster and his students (Gladys Foster, Baldwin Ranson, Dale Bush, Louis Junker, et al.) and macro-institutionalists (Dudley Dillard, Wallace Peterson, Clarence Ayres and Philip Klein), institutionalists have not sought out analytical linkages between Keynesian and institutionalist theory (Klein 1998, 44-65). Foster adds, many "institutionalists have not even contemplated the possibility of any generic relationship between the Keynesian theory and their own" [Foster (1966a) 1981, 954].

So far as is known, Keynes never identified himself as an institutionalist although he evidently read works of Commons (Keynes 1932, 134-36). Indeed, in a letter to Commons he said: "Judging from limited evidence and at great distance, there seems to be no other economist with whose general way of thinking I find myself in such genuine accord." [1] Keynes also discussed administered prices and their import with Gardner Means (Blair 1959, 431-50). But Foster obviously would not object to being identified as a vigorous supporter of Keynes. Among Foster's many contributions to economic analysis is his recognition and demonstration of the commonalities and compatibilities between American institutional thought and the tenets of Keynesian theory. The joining of these two analytic approaches to economic inquiry is something of a radical departure for the conventional readers of either Foster and/or Keynes. But, for Foster, it is both essential and productive to recognize these commonalities and to continue to build on both contributions.

Clarence E. Ayres (Foster's mentor), in a late essay, suggests convergence:

> In a very basic sense. . .what we now call macroeconomics is Veblenian economics, notwithstanding the fact that Keynes did more than anyone else to establish macroeconomics as a distinct discipline. . . .Macroeconomics is Veblenian in precisely the sense that it turns away from the sterilities of price equilibrium theories to the realities of the community's efforts to feed and clothe and house itself. This is what Keynes prevailed upon us to do, pointing out that in such an affluent society as ours people go hungry not because of any inexorable laws but only because we choose to do as we do in respects that are quite amenable to alteration (Ayres 1964, 61; quoted in Klein 1998, 49).

The primary focus of this Chapter, then, is limited to a search for commonalities and convergencies between Keynesians and Institutionalists in their respective approaches to inquiry and the importance thereof as Foster perceives them. To present and develop Foster's perception of Keynes's work and its significance, we consider the following topics: *(a)* the core of the Keynesian contribution; *(b)* the merging of institutionalist and Keynesian theory; *(c)* the convergence of Foster and Keynes on value theory *(d)* some clarifications of Keynesian theory; *(e)* concluding affirmations.

THE CORE OF THE KENYESIAN CONTRIBUTION

Keynes and Foster share a sense of purposiveness regarding economics. In a draft of economic material for a text in social science, Foster affirms that economics fundamentally is concerned with "the character and level of real income. . .with the provision of the *means* of live and experience. . . .The rate of provision of and the character of the means of human experience determine in a very significant way the quality and level of life itself. . . .Economics [is the] rational analysis of the determination of real income" [Foster (1969) 1981, 857-58, emphasis in original]. Keynes, in effect, agrees and argues, in contrast to orthodoxy, that he too is concerned not only with the "distribution of a *given* volume of employed resources" but with the determinants of "the *actual employment* of the available resources (Keynes 1936, 4, emphasis in original). For Foster, the Keynesian contribution is "[t]he most notable application of the institutional approach to [the]. . .fundamental economic problem of determining the level of real income [(1969) 1981, 865].

In sum, Foster contends that,

> The Keynesian thesis is an explanation of the proximate relationships among the determinants of real income. Except for the rate of interest, which is one of those determinants, Keynes does not pursue the explanation of each of them beyond pointing out that they are institutionally determined. His analysis is restricted to the pattern of simultaneous and immediate relationships among the independent variables in the specification of real income. And many of these relationships are sufficiently simple to be stated mathematically [(1969) 1981, 865-66].

Foster offers the following outline sketch of the Keynesian explanation of the determination of real income:

> The "propensity to consume" and the level of income vary in opposite directions. That is to say, the *ratio* between the rate of consumption and income goes down as income goes up, and *vice versa.* Another way of saying the same thing is that high income persons and communities consume a smaller fraction or proportion of their incomes than do lower income persons and communities.
>
> But the *rate* of consumption varies in the *same* direction as income. That is, high income persons and communities consume absolutely more than do lower income persons and communities.
>
> Therefore, given the schedule of the propensity to consume, the level of income depends on the rate of investment (the rate of production in excess of the rate of consumption).
>
> But the rate of investment is determined by what the purchaser thinks he can gain by purchasing an additional asset as compared to what he can gain by purchasing a debt. The ratio between what one expects to gain through the use of an additional unit of an asset and what one surrenders for the asset is the "marginal efficiency of capital" of that kind of asset; and the ratio between what the purchaser expects to gain from the purchase of a debt and what he surrenders to obtain the debt is the rate of interest. So long as the marginal efficiency of capital is greater than the rate of interest, those in a position to surrender money for something else purchase additional capital rather than debts.
>
> Therefore, the level of income is determined by the relationships among the propensity to consume, the marginal efficiency of capital, and the rate of interest [Foster (1969) 1981, 866, emphasis in original].

Foster explains that each of these three variables "is determined independently of the others" and that "each is determined by the mores and folkways and the institutional structure of the community. That is why the Keynesian theory appears as an application of the more general institutional theory of the economic process" [Foster (1969) 1981, 866]. Keynes treats institutional structures as patterns of behavior that can be modified or adjusted. For Keynes, as for Foster, institutions are not presumed to be given data; they are prescriptive structures that can be transformed or even abandoned. "If the Keynesian thesis be correct, then substantively obscure 'laws' of supply and demand need not restrict a community's activities below its technical capacities. Within the technical know-how of the community, the question of whether an economic activity is to be carried on could no longer be framed in terms of 'can'; it must be framed in terms of 'should'" [Foster (1969) 1981, 866-67].

The *level* of real income is determined in the manner Keynes explains. The *character* of real income is an equivalent concern; ought we to produce guns or butter, or both? Keynes makes passing references to the character of real income but offers no systematic analysis. Institutionalists, through inquiry, take on the question and provide theoretical analysis for raising and responding to normative concerns about the *kinds* of goods and services generated and distributed in the economy.

MERGING INSTITUTIONALIST AND KEYNESIAN THEORY

As Foster observes, "Institutional economics and. . .Keynesian economics conjoin in relation to the questions asked, the philosophical foundations of economic theory, and the identification of the dynamic factors in the economic process. But the integration of these two bodies of theory still requires integration in the professional literature" [(1966a) 1981, 949]. We explore these conjoining relations.

Questions Asked

The posing of the six following illustrative queries apply to both Keynesian and institutionalist inquirers. They suggest the substance and characteristics of what is perceived of as significant and meaningful inquiry. Responses to these queries from the institutionalist perspective have already been introduced in the preceding Chapters. It suffices here to suggest illustrative responses of Keynes, from his *General Theory,* that confirm the merging of the two approaches:

(a) How are economic "problems" identified? Each would respond that the concern of inquiry is with institutional impairments in the production and distribution of real income. Keynes says: "The outstanding faults of the economic society in which we live are its failure to provide for full employment and its arbitrary and inequitable distribution of wealth and incomes" (Keynes 1936, 372).

(b) How are solutions to economic problems perceived? Each would agree that all problem resolutions take the form of changes/alterations/adjustments in the problematic institutional structure of economies. Keynes says: "Whilst. . .the enlargement of the functions of government, involved in the task of adjusting to one another the propensity to consume and the inducement to invest, would seem. . .to be a terrific encroachment on individualism, I defend it. . .both as the only practicable means of avoiding the destruction of existing economic forms in their entirety and as the condition of the successful functioning of individual initiative" (380).

(c) How do technological and informational innovations and enhancements generate and exhibit institutional inadequacies? Institutionalists and Keynes share the view that both theory and institutions previously thought to be adequate have become unacceptable with the growth of warranted knowledge, and of consequential institutional outcomes. Keynes says: "the postulates of the classical [and neoclassical] theory are applicable to a special case only and not to the general case, the situation which it assumes being a limiting point of the possible positions of equilibrium. Moreover, the characteristics of the special case assumed by the classical theory happen not to be those of the economic society in which we actually live, with the result that its teaching is misleading and disastrous if we attempt to apply it to the facts of experience (Keynes 1936, 3).

(d) What are the determinants of the level of real income? Institutionalists concur with Keynes that the determinants are the relationships among the propensity to consume, the marginal efficiency of capital and the rate of interest, each of which is determined independently of the others. [Foster (1969) 1981, 866]. "[E]ach is determined by the mores and folkways and the institutional structure of the community." Each relates to and is constituted as institutional structure.

"That is why the Keynesian theory appears as an application of the more general institutional theory of the economic process [Foster 1981, 866].

(e) Where should discretion over institutional adjustments reside? Explicitly with institutionalists, and implicitly with Keynes, ultimate discretion over aggregate income and employment policy should reside with a democratic government. Keynes does see the need for an extension of governmental responsibilities for stabilizing the economy. There is a

> [V]ital importance of establishing certain central controls in matters which are now left in the main to individual initiative. . . .The State will have to exercise a guiding influence on the propensity to consume partly through its scheme of taxation, partly by fixing the rate of interest, and partly, perhaps in other ways. . . .I conceive [that] a somewhat comprehensive socialization of investment will prove the only means of securing an approximation to full employment" (Keynes 1936, 378). . . .The central controls necessary to ensure full employment will. . .involve a large extension of the traditional functions of government. . . .But there will still remain a wide field for exercise of private initiative and responsibility (380).

(f) Do politico-economic "isms" offer relevant problem solving approaches to, and resolutions of, economic problems? Institutionalists have comprehensively rejected ismatic analyses and accompanying policy recommendations, as explored in Chapter 7 above. Keynes recognizes the capitalist remnants in neoclassical analysis, and acknowledges his "long struggle of escape" from earlier support thereof. But in *The General Theory,* he does not use capitalism as a criterion of what ought to be. He is seeking institutional adjustments to recast public responsibilities for the maintenance of aggregate demand and employment.

Philosophic Foundations

Foster provides an illustrative commentary that introduces one of the philosophical commonalities between institutionalists and Keynes. Each accepts Veblen's demonstration of the tautological character of neoclassical general theory, and each agrees that economic inquiry should be "open ended", nontautological, and scientific. Observes Foster:

> The Keynesian theory is clearly open-ended. Its assumptions and its fundamental determinants, as well as the pattern of causation which it sets forth, are subject to evidential verification and correction. And its conclusions are not simply the . . .[validation] of its assumptions. Its assumptions, aside from the scientific principle of consistency, are that the independent variables within the system of the analysis are in fact independently variable. The conclusions identify the level of income and the direction and rate of variation of income—far different matters than the assumptions. These assumptions are not arbitrary, nor are they merely predetermined predilections the validity of which is to be established in the conclusions. These assumptions are subject to observation and to evidential verification or refutation. The [Keynesian] theory is, at least in this respect, subject to indefinite development [(1966a) 1981, 955].

How does Keynesian theory pass muster with reference to Veblen's other three fundamental neoclassical infirmities: taxonomy, teleology, and hedonism (see Chapter 3 above)? Keynes grew up in, and taught, neoclassical economics early in his career, as he acknowledges. But in formulating his *General Theory*, he largely abandons neoclassical limitations. Do his "Concluding Comments" in the *General Theory*, for example, reflect an attribute of inquiry in which "the theoretical aim is taxonomy—definition and classification—with the purpose of subsuming its data under a rational scheme of categories which are presumed to make up the Order of Nature" [Veblen (1919) 1961, 190-91]. Not at all. An example, is Keynes abandonment of the savings theory of progress. In neoclassicism, given its overall classificatory structure and design, high rates of interest are needed to generate savings to provide capital formation required by the economy. Keynes rejects this derivative taxonomic, savings-centered theory in favor of his debt creation theory of capital formation. The latter, drawn from the realities of evidential inquiry, requires a low rate of interest to stimulate debt creation, investment and economic growth (1936, 375). This shift means "the euthanasia of the rentier. . .and the euthanasia of the cumulative oppressive power of the capitalist to exploit the scarcity-value of capital" (376). Keynes does deal non-taxonomically with the "phenomenon of growth", that is, with the need for institutional change to better insure the expansion and more equitable distribution of real income.

Is Keynes's *General Theory* teleological in the sense that it is based on what Veblen describes as "the great law of the order of nature [that] is of the character of a propensity working to an end, to the accomplishment of a purpose. . .the process of nature?" [Veblen (1919) 1961, 188]. For Keynes there is no basic hidden force, purpose or phenomenon that is moving the economy toward full employment. Rather, he suggests institutional policy options that will be overtly contributive to the achievement of that goal. Finally, Keynes does not exhibit the basic hedonistic tenet of neoclassicism in which "the human material with which the inquiry is concerned is conceived in hedonistic terms, that is. . .in terms of a passive and substantially inert and immutably given human nature."[Veblen (1919) 1961, 73-4]. On the contrary, Keynes, unlike most of his neoclassical contemporaries, speaks openly about the aspects and impact of psychological influences on economic participation. He does not employ utilitarian dicta alleging the "painfulness" of work and the "pleasure" of not working. He acknowledges that in some contexts, pecuniary outcomes of conditioned judgment and habitual conduct are central and often important.

The methodological commonalities between Keynes and the institutionalists are illustrated in a preliminary way by Keynes's own characterization of his mode of inquiry. Institutionalists support Keynes in his effort to set off his own instrumentalist methodological position from that of orthodox mechanistic model builders. Keynes observes:

> The object of our analysis is not to provide a machine or method of blind manipulation which will furnish an infallible answer, but to provide ourselves with an organized and orderly method of thinking out particular problems; and, after we have reached a provisional conclusion by isolating the complicating factors one by one, we then have to go back on ourselves and allow as well as we can, for the probable interactions of the factors amongst themselves. This is the nature of economic thinking. Any other way

> of applying our formal principles of thought. . .will lead us into error. (Keynes 1936, 297).

As noted in Chapter 2 above, Foster offers a comparable characterization of his own methodological vision: "Science is the building of generalizations and their constant verification and/or negation through. . .applications of those generalizations as working hypotheses. Neither is. . .separately operative, although they are separately identifiable. In fact, [the former] is accomplished through the operation of. . .[the latter]. Neither can exist without the other, and the kinds of mental operations in each are generic with those in the other" [Foster (n.d.) Philosophy and Science, 1].

Keynes offers a caveat with which Foster would agree: "Too large a proportion of recent 'mathematical' economics are mere concoctions, as imprecise as the initial assumptions they rest on, which allow the author to lose sight of the complexities and interdependencies of the real world in a maze of pretentious and unhelpful symbols" (1936, 298). But behind the rhetoric are some profound, if implicit, implications all of which undercut the efforts of orthodox economists productively to inquire primarily with mathematical constructs. As Baldwin Ranson reminds us: "'utility,' the neoclassical meaning of value, is impossible to measure mathematically. In consequence, efforts to use price as an indicator or evidence of utility is impossible. In contrast, Keynes seeks to define measurable aggregates (non-utilitarian) to show instantaneous (not time period) determinants of income. Also, he refuses to adopt a strictly physical or natural unit of measurement for national income, e.g. labor content. Keynes's unit is institutionally determined." (Ranson 1999).

Dynamic Factors

Foster and Keynes concur in the identification of two dynamic factors prompting institutional adjustments. They are:

First, the growth of scientifically warranted knowledge—social and physical—has been, and remains, the chief dynamic factor in economic inquiry and in economic processes. Clearly the initiation, utilization, and expansion of continuously developing areas of warranted knowledge are *sine qua non* of the continuity of the human community. The pursuit of warranted knowledge is the central conceptual and behavioral concern of institutional economists and of Keynes.

As our earlier discussion of the Theory of Inquiry (Chapter 2) indicates, in the absence of intimidative and coercive resistance, it is unequivocal that the magnitude and *rate* of growth of warranted knowledge will continue to increase. Reflection on the current state of the physical and social sciences confirms the point. Witness the impact of the computer revolution in the last decade on the creation and management of information. The growth of knowledge is, as noted, cumulative. Each new contribution of warranted precept, tool, technique, insight, hypothesis and/or causal accounting expands the inquiry base. New questions are formed; new data become available; new theoretical models are fashioned and become the inclusive and expanding basis for further inquiry. Of such is the inherent developmental nature of scientific inquiry comprised.

Institutions, then, that were initially created to facilitate recourse to and utilization of what earlier was new knowledge, will be perceived over time, often by those adversely impacted, to have become inadequate, ineffectual, and/or less and less relevant to contemporary tasks of creating and distributing real income. A brief list of historic and contemporary impediments to this growth of warranted knowledge would include: coercive denial of information access, inadequate support of educational institutions, invidious discrimination in pursuit of inquiry, a captive or restricted press, political impositions of ism-ideologies that do not tolerate questioning nor admission of exceptions, deference to religious or other non-evidential belief systems (e.g., "creationism") that denigrate the growth of warranted knowledge, and the dominion of orthodox neoclassical economists (academic vested interests) over economic instruction and publication. Those identified with, or attached to, institutional structures that are faltering in the performance of their primary instrumental functions and therewith are becoming obsolete, will feel threatened and predictably so. Their resistance to change must be anticipated. Assistance in adapting to institutional adjustments should be forthcoming. Utilization of Foster's theory of institutional adjustment will guide the quest for intellectual creativity and social change. Affected individuals may well find it essential to prepare for and seek new connections (skills, employment, funding, services) to sustain their access to the flow of money and real income.

Second, another dynamic factor that institutionalists and Keynes share is the continuous prodding and prompting that new knowledge provokes and provides for the consideration of the adequacy and pertinence of existing institutional structures. While much of our behavior is indeed path-dependent, and largely habitual, new knowledge forces consideration of path-independent approaches to the organization of the economic, social and political processes. The growth of warranted knowledge, does not, per se, create new institutional forms. Problematic realities prompt policy makers to propose the creation of new structural arrangements that are able in new ways to incorporate and utilize the new knowledge that has become available. Institutional adjustments are prompted by cognition of discrepancies between what is and what ought to be, but the design of institutional adjustments must be addressed in the particular problematic context of its existential presence and character. In Chapter 5 above, we explore some of the theoretical details of the social implications of adapting to and incorporating new knowledge. The Keynesian contribution is a case in point.

Historically, in orthodox neoclassical economics, the act of saving (abstaining from present consumption) has long been thought to be the single most significant act in promoting investment. Ayres encapsulates the orthodox position as follows:

> The very existence of the community together with all the material progress which recent centuries have witnessed depends upon the existence and use of capital (meaning the physical tools and materials of industry, the knowledge and skills of the community); but it is only by "saving" that we are able to accumulate capital (meaning funds of money values capable of being "invested" in capital equipment); consequently it is upon the accumulation of capital (funds) that the whole of the life of the community depends.
>
> The expression "saving" used with reference to the accumulation of capital (funds) is such a travesty of the ordinary meaning of this word that it has become a cynosure of dissident opinion.(Ayres 1944, 50).

Prior saving, then, was thought to be essential for the expansion of private investments, and by extension, the expansion of the economy generally. Keynes refutes this "saving fallacy" contention, as follows:

> [A]n individual decision to save does not. . .involve the placing of any specific forward order for consumption, but merely the cancellation of a present order. Thus, since the expectation of consumption is the only *raison d'être* of employment, there should be nothing paradoxical in the conclusion that a diminished propensity to consume has *cet. par.* a depressing effect on employment. . . .The absurd, though almost universal, idea that an act of individual saving is just as good for effective demand as an act of individual consumption, has been fostered by the fallacy, much more specious than the conclusion derived from it, that an increased desire to hold wealth, being much the same thing as an increased desire to hold investments, must, by increasing the demand for investments, provide a stimulus to their production; so that current investment is promoted by individual saving to the same extent as present consumption is diminished.
>
> It is of this fallacy that it is most difficult to disabuse men's minds. It comes from believing that the owner of wealth desires a capital-asset *as such*, whereas what he really desires is its *prospective yield*. Now, prospective yield wholly depends on the expectation of future effective demand in relation to future conditions of supply. If therefore, an act of saving does nothing to improve prospective yield, it does nothing to stimulate investment. . . .Every act of saving involves a "forced" inevitable transfer of wealth to him who saves, though he in his turn may suffer from the saving of others. These transfers of wealth do not require the creation of new wealth—indeed. . .they may be actively inimical to it. The creation of new wealth wholly depends on the prospective yield of the new wealth reaching the standard set by the current rate of interest. The prospective yield of the marginal new investment is not increased by the fact that someone wishes to increase his wealth, since the prospective yield of the marginal new investment depends on the expectation of a demand for a specific article at a specific date (Keynes 1936, 211-12).

Moreover, as Ranson observes: "Investment cannot get returns that would be assigned to it on grounds of the equational theory of justice, that is, equating cost with reward. In classical theory, the return to capital has to be sufficient to pay for the disutility of abstaining from consumption in order to save in order to invest. Not so, says Keynes. Investment is not furthered by abstaining from consumption; savings cannot occur until investment occurs, since the community [as such] cannot save money" (Ranson 1999).

Savings, as a source of capital formation, and therewith presumed to be the prime vehicle for the expansion of an economy, is, with Keynes, converted from a promise to a threat. Since Keynes's *General Theory*, justifications for the inequality of income distribution can no longer be grounded in the alleged constructive role played by the wealthy whose personal savings are mistakenly alleged to be the source of the community's capital formation (See also Junker 1967, 25-43).

FOSTER AND KEYNES ON VALUE THEORY

In Chapter 4 above, we explore Foster's theory of instrumental value in some detail. Foster's referent for social value is there identified as "the continuity and instrumental efficiency of the social process." Moreover, it is perceived to be the criterion of judgment necessarily embedded in the process of scientific inquiry itself. The question we now confront is this: Although Keynes's *General Theory* does not specifically include consideration of criteria of judgment in economics as such, is it not the case that Keynes's theoretical formulations and their applications, including his theory of real income determination, are compatible with, indeed reflective of, Foster's value theory? We shall argue: that Keynes was a practicing normativist, not a positivist; that he refused to use and defer to certain value principles incompatible with his normative analysis; and that he actually employed the instrumental value premise without being aware of its identity *per se*.

Keynes as a Normativist:

Perhaps if economics had not long been mistakenly perceived by the neoclassicists as a positive, value-free science, Keynes's normative analysis would not appear so novel and threatening. On an earlier occasion, I wrote,

> That Keynes was a practicing normativist needs little defense or elaboration. Virtually all his academic and public life was devoted to the formulation and application of theory to permit or facilitate the resolution of real problems. Accordingly, he distinguished in scores of settings a difference between "what is" and "what ought to be." Of course, it is both logically and operationally *impossible* to distinguish between the two without applying a criterion of judgment—a social value principle. Since Keynes's career is replete with policy recommendations for substantive institutional adjustment—revision of the Versailles treaty, scaling down of reparations, abandonment of the gold standard, invocation of compensatory fiscal policy, introduction of a deferred income scheme during W.W.II, establishment of the World Bank and the International Monetary Fund—he is indeed a practicing, *de facto* normativist (Tool 1986, 188, emphasis in original).

Moreover, as Dudley Dillard suggests, there are normative implications in Keynes's work that resemble Veblen's basic dichotomy between industrial and pecuniary employments. Says Dillard, "Keynes's categories, Industry and Finance, are cognates of Veblen's Industrial and Pecuniary Employments" (1980, 267). For each, industrial activity is normatively approved; financial or pecuniary activity is normatively suspect. The former is concerned with the provision and distribution of real income; the latter is in large measure concerned with the acquisition of pecuniary power over others. "Throughout his career, Keynes remained critical of speculation, the gold standard, policies of the Bank of England, and rentiers, or absentee owners" (267).

Keynes, like Veblen, frequently exhibited his implicit instrumental value theory in his commentaries on what is, and is not, purposeful and constructive economic inquiry and activity, what is and is not instrumentally warranted. We note here three illustratively pertinent examples of Keynes's normative assessments from his *General Theory* (Ranson 1999).

(a) Keynes speculates on the reasons for Ricardo's victory over Malthus vis a vis the theory of the "aggregate demand function," the effects of which blocked interest in its relevance and significance for a century. Keynes speculates about the ceremonial suppression of this theory:

> The completeness of the Ricardian victory is something of a curiosity and a mystery. It must have been due to a complex of suitabilities in the doctrine to the environment into which it was projected. That it reached conclusions quite different from what the ordinary uninstructed person would expect, added. . .to its intellectual prestige. That its teaching translated into practice, was austere and often unpalatable, lent it virtue. That it was adapted to carry a vast and consistent logical superstructure, gave it beauty. That it could explain much social injustice and apparent cruelty as an inevitable incident in the scheme of progress, and the attempt to change such things as likely on the whole to do more harm than good, commended it to authority. That it afforded a measure of justification to the free activities of the individual capitalist, attracted to it the support of the dominant social force behind authority (Keynes 1936, 32-33).

This roster of apologetics on Ricardo's behalf contains no instrumental warrant or justification. Ricardo's victory served only to preclude inquiry into the actual causal determinants of flawed economic performance and to generate indifference to the devastating consequences of impaired production and inequitable distribution of real income. The rationale invoked in Ricardo's defense is wholly insidious and invidious. Keynes as a normative economist, cannot abide the flawed theory and the indifference to consequences reflected in the century of Ricardian dominion.

(b) Keynes's normative, although implicit, commitment to the instrumental efficiency criterion of economic judgment is perhaps nowhere better expressed than in his comments on the *character* of historic production:

> Ancient Egypt was doubly fortunate, and doubtless owed to this its fabled wealth, in that it possessed *two* activities, namely, pyramid-building as well as the search for precious metals, the fruits of which, since they could not serve the needs of man by being consumed, did not stale with abundance. The Middle Ages built cathedrals and sang dirges. Two pyramids, two masses for the dead, are twice as good as one [ceremonial function]; but not so two railways from London to York [instrumental function]. Thus we are so sensible, have schooled ourselves to so close a semblance of prudent financiers, taking careful thought before we add to the "financial" burdens of posterity by building them houses to live in, that we have no such easy escape from the sufferings of unemployment. We have to accept then as an inevitable result of applying to the conduct of the State the maxims which are best calculated to "enrich" an individual by enabling him to pile up claims to enjoyment which he does not intend to exercise at any definite time (1936, 131, emphasis in original).

(c) In a discussion of what is and is not wasteful (echoes of Veblen), Keynes observes that

> If the Treasury were to fill old bottles with banknotes, bury them at suitable depths in disused coal mines which are then filled up to the surface with town rubbish, and leave it to private enterprise on well-tried principles of *laissez-faire* to dig the notes up again. . .there need be no more unemployment and,with the help of the repercussions, the real income of the community, and its capital wealth also, would probably become a good deal greater than it actually is. It would, indeed, be more sensible to build houses and the like; but if there are political and practical difficulties in the way of this, the above would be better than nothing (1936, 129, emphasis in original).

Keynes's satirization of investment decision making as the counterpart of playing Old Maid (1936, 155-56) also implies normative assessment of economic behavior.

Obviously, Keynes is engaged, in these observations, in distinguishing between what is and what ought to be, actually and conjecturally. These "oughts" and "ought nots" exhibit, though without specific reference to instrumental social value analysis as such, Foster's distinction between what is an instrumental judgment and what is an invidious or ceremonial judgment.

Keynes's Non-Invidiousness

As reflected in his frequent advisories to members of the government and to his colleagues in economics, Keynes demonstrates his unwillingness to use or defer to non-instrumental, invidious or ceremonial criteria of judgment. The following are multiple indicators:

Keynes is no conservative; he does not use "what is" as a criterion of "what ought to be". In his roles as a member of the government, and as a sometime advisor of government, he was often involved in considerations of what changes in public policy should be supported and implemented.

Keynes does not make normative use of the competitive model. His willingness to recommend or allow for the continuance of some capitalist institutions (distributive arrangements, private property, etc.) is to be judged by his provisional acceptance of their then current performance, not on some a priori basis of their naturalness or inevitable efficiency. He does not presume that departures from the competitive market are "bad" per se or that closer approximations are necessarily "good."

Keynes seems not to use a *pecuniary* criterion in identifying "what ought to be." Profit maximization is not necessarily a success indicator. "There is no clear evidence from experience," he argues, "that investment policy which is socially advantageous coincides with that which is most profitable" (Keynes 1936, 157). Price, as such, is not a measure of economic worth.

Keynes emerges from what many might call an elitist social and economic background. Yet he seems not to use status, wealth, rank, gender, position, or ancestry as *invidious* criteria of appraisal. His observations of national or personal characteristics of those with whom he studied, worked, or negotiated were not demeaning or destructive. Although his membership in the Bloomsbury set of avant garde writers and intellectuals did evince some sentiments of exclusivity, his contests were mainly intellectual, not personal.

Keynes's frequent denigrative comments on authoritarian politics obviously imply his unwillingness to permit the achievement and use of coercive power as the meaning or measure of "what ought to be." Keynes was a democrat. (Tool, 1986, 188-89).

Keynes as de facto Instrumentalist

The fact that Keynes made no evident use of non-instrumental and anti-instrumental criteria in the above observations implies that he had some sense of that of which an instrumental criterion consists. Although Keynes does not routinely use the institutionalist's characterizations of "instrumental," "invidious" or "ceremonial" in his evaluative commentaries, his concern with the instrumental use of warranted knowledge is shared with Foster. Throughout his long career his quest was to contribute to an understanding of, and the generation of warranted solutions to, problems of flawed structures that threatened the continuity and efficiency of the economy. His agenda of pervasive threats "included extensive involuntary unemployment, economic determinants of warfare, the effect of domestic instability on international harmony, monetary determinants of economic instability, and the like" (Tool, 1986,189).

Although he did not use Foster's terminology, Keynes understood that the instrumental efficiency of the economy would be impaired if judgments were made on the basis of the discriminatory use of wealth, economic power, self-aggrandizement, or rentier status, in deciding whose economic interests matter or count. He had an astute sense of the absolute necessity of addressing problems with reference to their actual institutional determinants. He was in quest of evidential comprehension and policy options based thereon. He sought no scape goats. Can an economy be productive where policy is dictated by invidious or ceremonial judgments? Keynes, using different but incisive evaluative terms, did not think so. And of course he is correct.

Finally, Keynes's demonstrates instrumental reasoning and evaluation in his pursuit of a credible theory of real income determination. As I argue elsewhere:

> Keynes developed new knowledge and modified and adapted old knowledge in order to achieve more definitive understanding. He engaged in conceptual tool and idea combining activities in his area of interest, reflecting Ayres's view of the cumulative growth of knowledge. Keynes's theory building tacitly reflects the awareness that the term *instrumental* addresses the appropriateness, fitness, and relevance of the conceptual tool in its role and capacity of explaining phenomena. Instrumental use implies both functional pertinence and normative admissibility. . . .An illustration is the relevance and use of . . .the Keynesian theory of income determination for compensatory, economic stabilization measures. Keynes made instrumental use of warranted knowledge (Tool 1986, 190, emphasis added).

CLARIFICATIONS OF KEYNESIAN THEORY

As the foregoing commentary indicates, Foster perceives the main Keynesian theoretical contribution to be a comprehensive analysis of the determination of the level of real income. Because the theory's three independent variables are institutionally determined, it is compatible and conjoining with the basic institutional economics mode of inquiry, as noted. Moreover, given the substance of that convergence, it is to be expected that the Keynesian analysis would and did largely displace the explanation of aggregate income determination embedded in neoclassical orthodoxy.

But displacement of constructs of the status quo never comes easily as earlier comments herein suggest. Confusions and evasions have arisen, partly among neoclassicists and partly among neo-Keynesians, the implications of which, in Foster's view, threaten to dissipate the significance of the Keynesian theory of real income determination. In a short paper in 1966, Foster addresses some of these uncertainties in an effort to clarify and sustain Keynesian macroeconomics. At issue here are some fairly technical considerations of meanings of constructs,, of dependent and/or independent variables, of compatibility, and the like. The general concern is to demonstrate Foster's effort, in working with the Keynesian contribution, to be meticulous in the creation, ordering and assessment of constructs and the roles they play in the more inclusive causal explanations. Illustratively, four of these conceptual uncertainties or dilemmas are here briefly considered.

What is Referential Content of "Saving" and "Investment"?

Latter-day "neo-Keynesians" have, in some instances, modified definitions of key Keynesians concepts. In Foster's view, they at times disregard the original Keynesian content. He explains:

> The most common example of this disregard is the inclusion or exclusion, in their own definitions, of parts of what Keynes defines as investment. In this way a difference between saving and investment is established. By retaining the fairly universal definition of saving as the difference between income and consumption, and at the same time modifying the definition of investment, the instantaneous equation between saving and investment is changed to inequation. The analysis of variations in income then can proceed in terms of the forces of supply and demand brought into play by the divergencies between saving and investment. But thereby the Keynesian demonstration of saving as precisely the accounting of investment is lost. And the appearance of money savings in excess of investment in the aggregate specifies a positive account of the rate of proceeds in excess of the rate of expenditure, which is a palpable impossibility if the entire area of economic intercourse is taken into account. But the concomitant adjustment of the definition of saving and of other elements in the theory which are required in order to maintain consistency in the structure of the theory is not made. The fundamental Keynesian concept of constant and instantaneous equation is thus abandoned. [Foster (1966a) 1981, 950].

Is there Hoarding in the Aggregate?

Foster here poses the question of what is and is not Keynesian analysis with special reference to the concept of "hoarding." "The Keynesian definition of investment," Foster argues, "is not merely a taxonomic convenience":

> [Investment] is defined by Keynes so as to reveal the absence in the aggregate of unencumbered net money proceeds beyond factor costs. . . .[I]t reveals the absence of aggregate hoarding if that term be defined as money proceeds minus total expenditures, or as income minus the sum of consumption and investment, or as saving minus investment, all of which amount to the same thing. And hoarding is universally thus defined. Now, the magnitude of the time rate called hoarding is not something which can be changed simply by defining the other components of income so as to include or exclude part or all of what Keynes calls saving. Can money proceeds, in the aggregate be received in excess of concurrent expenditures? This question is identical to asking if the monetary accounting of purchases can be more or less than the monetary accounting of sales. Since these are simply two accountings of the very same transactions, the obvious answer is no. But if investment be defined otherwise than production in the present for use in the future, then investment, as a time rate, can be made to appear as greater or less than saving. And then by easy imputation, aggregate hoarding can be presented as greater than or less than zero. But this operation cannot change the actual fact as to whether aggregate money proceeds can be realized in excess of aggregate money expenditures. The Keynesian position on this question. . .is key to a large part of the Keynesian general theory of income. To change the definition of investment . . .leads easily away from the Keynesian general theory of income and employment [Foster (1966a) 1981, 952].

Are Saving and Investment Independent Variables?

In neo-Keynesian literature, it is sometimes the case that the saving function and the investment function are thought to be determined independently of each other, at least "in the short run." Similarly, each is presumed to be determined independently of the propensity to consume. Although such claims would seem to cast doubt on the credibility of the Keynesian analysis generally, no such claim appears to have been made. Interestingly, "nowhere in the neo-Keynesian literature is the independence of the determination of the schedule of the propensity to consume brought directly into question." But, argues Foster,

> if the schedule of the ratio between consumption and income be an independent variable in the proximate determination of income, then neither the investment function nor the saving function can be independently determined. For, if the ratio between consumption and income be an independent variable, the ratio between saving and income is a dependent variable since it is simply one minus the propensity to consume. Both ratios cannot be independent variables since their sum is a constant. . . .In the intrasystemic structure of the theory, either the propensity to consume must

be shown to be a dependent variable, or the treatment of the ratio between saving and income as an independent variable must be abandoned. To do neither. . .does not erase the inconsistency. [Foster (1996a) 1981, 952-53].

Is the Keynesian System Static and Restricted?

In brief, the answer is negative on both counts. Foster is adamant in his insistence that Keynesian theory is generally applicable to monetary exchange economies. Its relevance derives from its capacity to generate and direct causal inquiry into the determinants of real income, perhaps the most fundamental economic function of all human communities. Keynesian analysis is a contribution to the general developmental science of economics. This means that constructs and processes explained are themselves continuously the objects of further inquiry as the problem solving needs for augmented explanations and resolutions become evident. As was discussed in Chapter 2, instrumental inquiry is a continuing process; Keynesian analysis is characteristically instrumental. As Foster observes:

> The Keynesian theory is an explanation of the proximate determination of income—proximate in the sense that it does not include the determination of the independent variables (except the rate of interest), the relationship between which determines the level of income in the immediate sense. It is not proximate in the sense that it applies only to a given time or place or to a certain institutional and technological situation. Its structure and constructs exhibit generality and foundation.
>
> Generality is attained by identifying income as the instantaneous concomitant of *any* particular combination of the whole range of possible relationships between the three independent variables. Since the theory is equally applicable to any, it is applicable to all patterns of relationships between the propensity to consume, the marginal efficiency of capital and the rate of interest. This could hold even in the absence of one of the variables such as the rate of interest, which would be the case in a nonpecuniary economy. Even in the absence of money, judgments would have to be made about whether to add to inventory and what the components of the inventory should be. . . .
>
> The dynamic quality of the Keynesian theory is attained by considering the rate of change in income in terms of the concurrent rates of change in the components of income, which are in turn determined by constantly changing patterns of the mores and folkways and by institutional adjustments. The instantaneity of the relationships between concurrent variables set forth in the theory does not disallow application to dynamic processes. Rather, that very quality, together with the concept of instantaneous and constant equilibrium, permits the most facile and the simplest explanation of processional phenomena. [Foster (1966a) 1981, 953-54, emphasis in original].

FOSTER'S CONTINUING AFFIRMATIONS

In a public address in 1966, Foster sought to further integrate the Keynesian contributions and those of institutionalists by focusing on four "propositions which are warranted by the current stage of understanding in economics and the other social sciences" [(1966b) 1981, 963-64]. These affirmative propositions are presented here as a partial summary of major conjoining elements of the Keynesian and institutionist traditions. In addition, they invite attention to some significant implications of having recourse to these linked approaches to inquiry. These propositions address institutional adjustment, the level of economic activity, technical feasibility and funding, and the transfer of aggregate income.

All Answers to All Economic Problems Necessarily Take the Form of Institutional Adjustments.

Foster distinguishes between the technological aspects of the productive process, now largely industrialized, and the social aspects, now largely institutionalized. The former aspects rest on physical knowledge generated by scientists and engineers; the latter aspects rest on social and cultural knowledge generated by social scientists. The latter incorporates the former in carrying on functions that generate and sustain the flow of real income. That incorporation is accomplished through patterns of correlated behavior—prescribed and proscribed stipulations of how warranted knowledge is given effect in the production and distribution of real income. More particularly, "[t]he entrepreneurial function of decision making includes decisions regarding the use of technological processes, but that function is one of assent or veto; it is not one of design and operation. The entrepreneur as such serves as a permissive factor in the technological sphere; in the sphere of institutional structure and operation, he serves as designer and operator. It is in this sphere that he seeks answers to entrepreneurial problems through the application of social theory" [Foster (1966b) 1981, 964].

But to what social theory does the entrepreneur, as designer and operator, appeal in comprehending the need for and character of institutional adjustments that will assure continuity and sufficiency in the flow of real income? His recourse typically and habitually is to standard neoclassical theory that regards institutions as static and prices in markets as the only allocative instruments that adjust. The level and character of production are presumed to be determined through unfettered market forces. The only institutional adjustments incorporated are price changes. Foster asks: "[W]hat shall we say of theory which assumes the possibility of adjustment is restricted to price? Price is only one of an indefinite number of institutional structures, and so we must say that the significance of such theory is very limited—limited to applications in which solutions can be attained through changes in prices" [Foster (1966b), 1981 964].

Foster explains why economic problems of non- or malperformance of needed instrumental functions require institutional adjustments for their correction and resolution (see Chapter 5 above). Keynes demonstrates in myriad instances how the economic and financial problems on which his attention is focused require institutional adjustments to sustain or enhance the generation and distribution of real income, explicitly instrumentally and implicitly noninvidiously.

The Level of Economic Activity Cannot Remain Constant

The level of economic activity either increases or decreases. As Foster's explains:

> The level of income and employment either contracts or expands. The reason for this has to do with the fact that, with a fractional propensity to consume (C/Y), two conditions are inescapable. The first is that a positive level of investment would be necessary to maintain any level of income, and the second is that a positive level of investment increases both the aggregate productive capacity and the productivity per unit of the other factors employed. And it usually stimulates technological innovation, which in turn further increases production capacity and productivity per unit of all the factors, including capital. Thus, with the rate of investment specified for any given level of income by the schedule of the propensity to consume, the result is an increase in the level of income, not a constant income. And in case the rate of investment is reduced at any level of income, income itself is reduced at the commensurate rate, specified again by the schedule of the propensity to consume. Thus any rate of investment that is specified by any given level of income results in an increase in that level of income and therefore in that rate of investment, and any diminution in the rate of investment diminishes the capacity to maintain the reduced level of income and investment. Either way, the level of income cannot remain stable. In common parlance, what this means is that we must continue to progress or we decay. We cannot stand still. [Foster (1966b) 1981, 964-65].

The implications of this proposition are significant: First, this Keynes-Foster proposition would seem to erode, if not destroy, the orthodox assertions that a market economy, if unfettered, will naturally achieve and sustain a full employment equilibrium over time. Second, as Foster explains, "we have learned to use autonomous investment (mostly government purchases of public capital) to counteract any deficiency in ordinary induced investment" (965). The prospects, then, of our incurring another "prolonged recession" seem remote.

Aggregate Income Cannot be Transferred from One Period to Another

Given parsimonious upbringing, it is not uncommon for individuals to perceive of their own generation as being engaged, regrettably, in a spendthrift mode that necessarily culminates in the creation of destitution for subsequent generations. Our children, and our children's children, are alleged to be burdened, indeed imperiled, by the profligate conduct of any present generation that spends more than its means. The refutation, via Keynes and Foster, of this apprehension involves distinguishing between the circumstances and options of individuals in contrast with the circumstances and options of the community at large. Foster explains:

> [O]ne generation cannot implement or diminish the income of future generations by expending less or more than its own means. The traditional concern with this issue arises out of the palpable fact that individuals can

> hoard, and they can incur debts beyond their accumulation of assets. These opportunities to individuals arise out of the fact than an individual can, and often does, buy more than he sells or sell more than he buys.
>
> But this opportunity is not available to the entire economy. In the entire area of economic transactions, sales and purchases are necessarily equal. And this equation is an *instantaneous* one. There is no "time lag" here. The community at large cannot "save money"; it can save only by investing, and its savings are constituted by that investment. The instantaneity of the equation between aggregate sales and aggregate purchases forces the instantaneity of the equation between saving and investment. And the equation between saving and investment precludes the financing of investment out of previous hoarding. But since individuals can and sometimes do finance investment out of previous hoarding, other individuals or institutions are thereby forced to incur debts beyond their individual accumulations of real assets [Foster (1966b) 1981, 967-68].

Whatever is Technically Feasible is Financially Possible

From our habituated perceptions of the inflow and outflow of our individual money funds, the foregoing caption seems flawed, even bizarre. Keeping spending, in some continuing sense, below our levels of income receipt is thought to be not only prudent, but essential. And for individuals, this is plausible common sense. But what is true for an individual is not necessarily true for an economy as a whole. When we ask, "where is the money coming from" for the community at large, the individual case is no longer governing.

As Foster makes clear, writing in the Keynesian tradition, for the community at large, money "comes from the only two institutions we permit to create money funds: the treasury of the sovereign government and commercial banks. And the rate at which we permit either to create funds is [largely]. . . a matter of public policy" [Foster (1966b) 1981, 966]. To clarify: In the U.S. commercial banks operate in a fractional reserve system. The individual bank's ability to create credit (debt) is limited by its excess reserves. The limit for the banking system is some multiple of the system's actual reserves. The monetary authorities determine what the reserve requirements will be and therewith the extent of credit expansion. (Bush, 1999). Coins and currency, "non-interest bearing and nonterminal debt," are issued, as needed, to meet the *transaction* requirements of the economy. It thus is a discretionary responsibility of the monetary authorities. The history of governments that attempt to use this capacity for other purposes is a sorry one indeed. e.g., post W.W.I Germany.

Foster focuses especially on the creation of money funds through the banking system, which he regards as "the most effective system now in existence."

> For the financing of investment, we have come to rely on bank credit. . . .Through fractional banking there is no theoretical limit to the possible creation of funds. The question is no longer whether the funds can be made available; the only question is *should* they be made available. The banks stand ready to provide the funds if agreement can be reached between the banks and the borrower regarding the second question. We thus have a double check on the propriety of each investment financed through bank credit. And the

> propriety of each investment hinges on the security of repayment, that is, on the soundness of the investment. And the soundness depends, at bottom on whether additional real income is created through the investment commensurate with the face of the loan. Some conjugate correspondence is thus maintained between the rate of variation in money income and real income, with the beneficence of that correlation accruing to the community as a whole [Foster (1966b) 1981, 966-67, emphasis added].

Foster acknowledges that the banks' money creation function must be carefully regulated by governmental bodies. But, he argues, "the difficulties in the system are not in the *capacity* to create funds; they lie in maintaining correspondence between increments in money income and increments in real income [967, (emphasis in original); see also G. Foster, 1996].

A CONCLUDING COMMENT

The foregoing exploration of the commonalities and convergencies of Keynesian economics and institutional economics is intended to demonstrate that each inquiry approach has much to contribute to the extension, refinement and enhancement of the other. The shared commitment to the pursuit of explanatory theory and substantive reform is a convergent and guiding stimulus for current problem solving. We have noted commonalities in normative purposiveness, inquiry method, problem identification, and the need for institutional adjustments to restore and extend non-invidious participation for all members of communities. Each mode of inquiry, although from somewhat different cultural settings and inquiry traditions, demonstrates that each democratic community has substantial discretion over its own condition and well-being. Each intellectual tradition culminates in the public recommendation of social policies, proposals for structural change, that remove impediments in the provision of the means of life and experience, comprehensively and non-invidiously. Continuing recourse to the combined institutionalist and Keynesian theory will permit the community to sustain, enhance, and distribute a continuously developing flow of real income. Keynesian money management will assist in the pursuit of such endeavors.

ENDNOTES

[1] From a letter from Keynes to Commons, dated 26 April 1927 (John R. Commons Papers, State Historical Society of Wisconsin, 1982); quoted in Hodgson, Geoffrey M. 1999. *Evolution and Institutions.* Cheltenham UK: Edward Elgar, p. 154.

REFERENCES

Ayres, Clarence E. 1964. "The Legacy of Thorstein Veblen." In *Institutional Economics: Veblen, Commons, and Mitchell Reconsidered.* Joseph Dorfman, Clarence E. Ayres, Neil W. Chamberlain, Simon Kuznets and Robert A. Gordon, eds. Berkeley: University of California Press.

Blair, John M. 1959. Administered prices. *American Economic Review*; 49 (May): 431-50.

Bush, Paul Dale. 1999. Personal correspondence.

Dillard, Dudley 1980. A monetary theory of production: Keynes and the institutionalists. *Journal of Economic Issues*; 14: 255-273.

Foster, Gladys P. 1986. The endogeneity of money and Keynes's General Theory. *Journal of Economic Issues*; 20: 953-968.

———. 1991, The compatibility of Keynes's ideas with institutionalist philosophy. *Journal of Economic Issues;* 25: 561-568.

———. Institutional economics, Keynes's theories and finance. *Economies et Societes;* Serie MD 10:211-28.

Foster, J. Fagg. (n.d.) Philosophy and economics. 1-2.

———. (1966a) 1981. Understandings and misunderstandings of Keynesian economics. *Journal of Economic Issues;* 15: 949-957.

———. (1966b) 1981. The reality of the present and the challenge of the future. *Journal of Economic Issues;* 15:963-968.

———. (1969) 1981. Economics. *Journal of Economic Issues;* 15: 857-869.

Hodgson, Geoffrey M. 1999. *Evolution and Institutions*. Cheltenham UK: Edward Elgar.

Junker, Louis J. 1967. Capital accumulation, savings-centered theory and economic development. *Journal of Economic Issues;* 1:25-43.

Keynes, John Maynard. 1932. *Essays in Persuasion*. New York: Harcourt Brace.

———. 1936. *The General Theory of Employment Interest and Money.* New York: Harcourt Brace.

Klein, Philip A. 1998. "Normative Macroeconomics: Conjoining Keynes and Institutionalism." In *Institutional Theory and Applications,* Sasan Fayazmanesh & Marc R. Tool, eds. Cheltenham: Edward Elgar.

Ranson, T. Baldwin. 1980. Rival economic epistemologies: the logics of Marx, Marshall, and Keynes. *Journal of Economic Issues;* 14:77-98.

———. 1983. The unrecognized revolution in the theory of capital formation. *Journal of Economic Issues*; 17: 901-913.

———. 1999, Personal correspondence.

Tool, Marc R. 1986. *Essays in Social Value Theory.* Armonk, NY: M. E. Sharpe.

9 INSTRUMENTAL POLICY

Freedom is discretion, the right to choose among available alternatives.
J. Fagg Foster

INTRODUCTION

Fagg Foster was not, in the ordinary use of the term, a political activist. His operating "turf" was, in the main, his classroom. He was a masterful and compelling lecturer. Humor was one of his many vehicles of communication. His continuing audiences were, with only infrequent exceptions, his students in regular courses in economics and social science—undergraduate and graduate. He was an occasional lecturer or participant at public forums and seminars.[1] On campus, he was most active in designing curricula, and advising on and participating in collegial governance. He was a continuous and vigorous defender of intellectual freedom most conspicuously in the era of loyalty oaths and McCarthyite threats to academic freedom. He was occasionally involved in informal discussions on proposed or pending state and national politico-economic policies. But he was not affiliated with, nor did he write proposals for, any policy-generating "think tank" or pressure group.

Rather, as the preceding Chapters indicate, Foster conceived his primary role as a professional scholar to be a contributing formulator of an encompassing and applicable theory of the social process and social value. His tasks were to help identify problems as impediments in the production and distribution of real income and to propose provisional revisions of institutional structure to create or restore instrumentally efficient performances through democratic processes. He sought to "get the theory right" with which, then, one can identify and address socio-economic problems. "Getting the theory right" means developing a body of explanatory analysis that is scientifically warrantable, pertinent, and feasible. Obviously the determinants of such impairments—invidious and/or ceremonial judgments supporting inappropriate, inefficient, or irrelevant structure—vary over time and differ from one area to another. Making instrumental policy judgments then must be time, place, and subject specific.

Foster did, on occasion, assist with the implementation of public policies. He had significant participation in policy design and implementation in public agencies. In 1943 he was employed as an economist for the Federal Public Housing Authority in Cleveland, Ohio, seeking ways to reduce the numbers of people living in slums. He also worked briefly in the Office of Economic Warfare.[2] During the Korean war, he was an economic analyst in the Denver office of the Wage Stabilization Board.[3]

Foster's professional role was to assist his students—many of whom would become professional scholars, policy framers, political activists and/or participating public citizens—with the acquisition of analytical skills and normative knowledge so that they would be able to participate in the creation and implementation of timely and feasible policies as institutional adjustments in those areas where coercion, invidiousness and/or ceremonialities were corrupting the social process in any of its significant aspects. He sought to assist in providing explanations of the adverse impact of malfunctioning institutions and to indicate the direction and nature of genuine policy "solutions".

As the foregoing Chapters indicate, Foster's main concern is to conjoin pragmatic instrumental philosophy and analytical elements of institutional economics and therewith explain the reality of the economic process and the problems arising therein..

In an early work, John Maynard Keynes says: "Perhaps the chief task of Economists at this hour is to distinguish afresh the *Agenda* of Government from the *Non-Agenda*; and the companion task of Politics is to devise forms of Government within a Democracy which shall be capable of accomplishing the *Agenda*" (1926, 40-41, emphasis in original). Foster, we think would share this view. But any "Agenda of Government" must first past muster as an agenda for inquiry. In any fashioning of judgments herein on an agenda of social and economic policy, then, we are reminded that, for reasons already introduced, there will be no recourse to ethical absolutism (the "oughts" of which are given by sources anterior to, or outside of, scientific inquiry); no use will be made of ethical relativism (the "oughts" of which are merely matters of personal taste and preference as reflective of utility theory). Instead, we will employ ethically instrumental criteria, as developed especially in Chapter 4 above, (the "oughts" are products of warranted inquiry). In proposing institutional adjustments as policy shifts, then, the criteria must be realistically relevant, scientifically validated, and normatively restorative.

It is essential that we reiterate, in this context, that any serious attempt at social policy making consists of efforts to change the prevailing institutional structure from its present patterns of behavior to new and different instrumentally warranted patterns. When Foster explains and recommends his principles of institutional adjustment—technological determination, recognized interdependence, minimal dislocation—he is advising us concerning how we should go about the task of generating policy to alter existing prescriptive and proscriptive patterns of conduct so as to bring them into instrumental rapport with current levels and content of warranted knowledge.

Accordingly, in this concluding Chapter, we address instrumental policy making in two ways: First, we consider Foster's policy advisories that reflect his continuing concern with the significance of policy making by noting, illustratively, two areas in which he directly or indirectly addresses policy issues per se. These policy advisories concern *(a)* macro-management and economic growth, and *(b)* utilization and management of the environment. Second, we further explore Foster's approach to instrumental policy making by employing elements of his theory in two contemporary policy advisories: *(a)* reducing poverty through income generation and distribution, and *(b)* facilitating structural transition in developing economies. Our intent is to demonstrate something of the broad applicability of Foster's encompassing instrumental theory of value and its reflection in his theory of institutional adjustment, in comprehending earlier and contemporary policy issues in political economy. It should be clear at the outset, of course, that our primary concern here is to explore Foster's way of identifying and inquiring about substantive economic problems. We don't presume to be offering definitive solutions in the areas addressed. This volume is concluded with an Epilogue on aspects of Foster's analytical interests in his later years.

FOSTER'S POLICY ADVISORIES

Introduction

The significance of Foster's contribution of a body of instrumentalist theory for economic analysis resides not only in its fundamental critique and displacement of neoclassical theory and its policy compulsions, but, as noted, in its even more significant provision of an alternate institutionalist theory of the economic process grounded in the methodology of science. The foregoing Chapters have addressed both of these aspects and objectives. The significance of Foster's scholarly work resides as well in its implications for, and guidance of, the fashioning of economic policy at all levels of governance. Fashioning policy requires, as we have seen above, the careful identification of a problem, including a causal accounting of its origin, character and significance. Any such conception of a problem requires inquiry into the demonstrable determinants of breakdowns (flawed performance), mis-directions (inaccurate view of causality), or impairments (invidious discrimination, ceremonial blockages) in the production and distribution of real income. Substantive and pertinent inquiry, then, is concerned with what corrective or restorative policy options can be identified and implemented through recourse to Foster's theory of institutional adjustment.

Macro-Management and Economic Growth

The continuing difficulties of attempting to explain economic phenomena through recourse to standard neoclassical theory are illustrated in a brief article Foster wrote on policies concerning the increasing growth rates among developed economies and on related policy matters of oligopolistic pricing, autonomous investment, and financial feasibility. [(1960) 1981, 959-962].

Aggregate Growth Rates

As we noted earlier, for Foster, economic growth rates are heavily dependent upon development and use of warranted knowledge and its applications in technological advancement. Technology is the most obviously changing aspect of any modern economy. "The more advanced technology becomes, the more rapidly it advances." It follows, then that the concept of a "mature economy" is without substance or credibility. If maturity "connotes a cessation of the processes and forces which brought it to the stage," maturity is not realized. The greater the development and employment of evidential scientific analysis "the more compelling are the processes and forces which bring about change. The instrumental aspects of the economic process do not mature; they develop. They show no tendency toward finality; they in fact display the contrary tendency" [(1960) 1981, 960]. Foster continues: "Thus the more advanced economies find themselves advancing ever more rapidly in regard to technical feasibility, whereas the less advanced economies find themselves seeking that technical capacity. The divergence between these rates of advancement in technical feasibility is the key to the difference in the policy implications of the more developed as compared with the less developed economies" (960). "For a very long time," Foster reminds us,

> the rate of capital formation in the more developed economies far outstripped the limitations imposed by a commodity money. Fractional reserve banking with its flexibility in the creation of additional funds has brought immediacy to the proposition that whatever is technically feasible is financially possible. The system has been. . .awkwardly successful in facilitating the actual use of what is feasible, and it has at times been used for unwise allocations of resources; but as an institutional device, it has removed increments of money funds from the peradventure of good luck on the part of gold prospectors. The increasing and comparatively high rate of technical change is the foundation fact in the array of policy formation problems faced by more advanced economies (960).

Oligopolistic Pricing

Foster invites attention to the difficulties, in developed economies, of explaining why it is that there is a "tendency toward constantly rising prices." More particularly, how does one explain the fact that "oligopolistic prices increase during periods of declining effective demand and increase, (but less rapidly) during periods of increasing effective demand?" ([(1960) 1981, 960-61]. The orthodox tenet that "so long as productivity per unit of the factors increases more rapidly than price per unit of the factors, commodity prices could not increase, [a]nd the converse, the notion that price increases result from too much money being offered for too few goods" loses its explanatory significance. But these "aberrations" merit a more adequate response. The traditional orthodox view takes insufficient account of the "managerial revolution." An implication is that administered pricing has become a characteristic trait of megacorps in the developed economies. Discretion over pricing is but one form, albeit an essential one, of corporate dominion. Foster considers a roster of alternative corrective policies as "remedial adjustments."

> The most fruitful of these would be to remove the more obstructive policies of restricting entry into an enterprise. Another would be to adjust corporate policy so as to render the motives of owners more effective in corporate enterprise. Still another would be to reduce protective tariffs. Removing legal restrictions against price adjustment as a method of struggling for the market would help. Delimiting patent rights would jar loose price structures in many industries. Adjusting banking policy in conformity with the production and income cycles of the various regions would help. And in enterprises in which the size of the optimum plant is the major part of the market and in which the commodity is important, the use of effective public utility regulation would

> add greatly to stability of prices conjoined with economic progress [(1960) 1981, 961].

The point to be made here is not that these particular policy proposals necessarily continue to offer plausible instrumental solutions to oligopolistic control over pricing, although it is clear that many have continuing relevance. It is that the public's *quest for accountability* of achieved pricing power continues; that quest requires constant surveillance and remedial institutional adjustments to enhance through interventions the instrumental functions and suppress ceremonial functions in megacorps.

Autonomous Investment

Where discretion over pricing impacts upon oliogopoly investment levels, there is a related concern: maintaining aggregate expenditures (all forms) sufficient to generate enough effective demand fully to employ the labor force. Foster explains the situation as follows:

> The idea of developmental continuity envisions the uninterrupted use of the factors of production. Since the quantity of the factors constantly changes, policies must be devised for allowing adjustments in their pattern of correlation.
>
> The most notable change in the rate of provisions occurs in the case of capital, although labor can and does display surprising variations. Shifting the official central banking policy toward an inferior position to that of the demonstrated marginal efficiency of capital rather than to the demonstrated marginal efficiency of speculation not only would be a great aid to maintaining investment but also would shift inclination toward more productive employment of the factors.
>
> Labor has become the center of attention in the employment problem. So much is this the case that the word *employment* unmodified ordinarily refers to labor as such. The maintenance of effective demand for capital at a sufficient rate, in view of the existing schedule of the propensity to consume, to maintain full and effective use of the labor force has been adjusted in the more developed economies to a rising rate of autonomous investment. The magnitude of this category of investment cannot be ascertained with anything like tolerable accuracy, but it is plainly increasing. And the largest single item in the category is federal government expenditures for military purposes. This circumstance lends an air of uncertainty to our ability to maintain the size of the required autonomous investment in case disarmament becomes effective.
>
> But the economy as a whole is experiencing its greatest relative dearth of investment in the public sphere in those facilities which are extremely productive to the entire economy but which cannot maintain a positive marginal efficiency for an individual firm. The cause of stability and progress would be greatly enhanced if official policy included sufficient alternatives to offset any necessary diminution in any one of them. This popularly is known as a shelf of projects. As war becomes more clearly obsolete, the urgency of the further development of this policy becomes more patent.

> Among the autonomous investments which are in relative scarcity, highways, health facilities, recreational areas and opportunities, flood contro' devices, and educational facilities are examples. Education is insensibly but inescapably related to instrumental feasibility in general [(1960) 1981, 961-62, emphasis in original).

Foster suggests, then, that even when private investment expenditures do not make a sizable contribution to total expenditure in pursuit of full employment, a governmental policy of encouraging "a rising rate of autonomous investment" is instrumentally warranted.

Financial Feasibility of Options

As we observed above, Foster argues that if the banking system is carefully regulated so that the "correspondence between increments in money income and increments in real income" is maintained, the *capacity* to create funds for policy options need not be a constraint on economic policy making. Foster remarks on some "heady proposals" that are, in his view, wholly technically and financially feasible. These proposals were contained in a "1966 Report of the National Commission on Technology, Automation, and Economic Progress." This Commission was created by Congress and appointed by the President" [(1966b) 1981, 967]. Commission membership included major national corporate executives and labor leaders. They proposed dramatic institutional adjustments:

> Their unanimous report included recommendations to guarantee a minimum income of $3000 to every family in the United States, the provision of fourteen years of "free" education to every qualified person, and to use the U.S. Government as the residual employer of all of those unable to find employment elsewhere. The report projected the level and pattern of income and employment over the next two decades in view of projected variations in productivity, and it suggested institutional adjustments to implement its recommendations. In all of this, there is no finding of financial incapacity. The only question is, again, whether these recommendations should be adopted, since they are technically feasible (967, emphasis added).

It is our presumption, that Foster, if asked, would recommend these institutional adjustments as policy options, the absence of an explicit statement of support notwithstanding. They are consistent with his more general view of what are feasible and constructive modifications of structure. They appear to be devoid of invidious intent or substance.

Interestingly, the proposal to establish "government as the residual employer of. . .those unable to find employment" has recently again become a topic of wide national consideration.[4] The proposal for the provision of a basic minimum income for everyone has also resurfaced as a serious policy option.[5] We consider the former proposal at greater length below.

Constructs for Environmental Policy

Foster's contribution to environmental policy making consists in the main of generating and explaining some fundamental and evidentially grounded aspects of environmental conditions. He does not, in this context, make specific recommendations of policy. The inquiry and behavioral need to understand these very basic characterizations of environmental reality must, in Foster's view, precede and preempt any definition of an environmental problem, and therefore any formulation of instrumental policy. This understanding is critical in formulating an initial conception of an environmental problem.

A social problem, as explored herein, is a comprehended difference between "what is" and "what ought to be." Proposed institutional adjustments indicate "what is to be done." Foster's views presented here regarding "environmental control" and " resource management" are addressed initially to the "what is" facet of inquiry. But the "what is" is necessarily and analytically interwoven with any rational consideration of "what ought to be," of what could be identified as an environmental problem and its potential resolution, as the making of instrumental policy. Foster's conceptions of environmental realities are processual and evidentially grounded.

Environmental Control

For Foster, man is continuously and consciously engaged in an interaction with his environment. And with rational reflection, that interaction comes more and more to be grounded in observed causal sequence and emergent consequences. Man's impact on and control over the environment has increased commensurate with the acceleration of scientific understanding and its cumulative progression. Formerly, concern was expressed over specific abuses or disfigurements of parts of the environment or depletion of a resource, or loss of a species. Now the problem of environmental control has become an encompassing and continuing policy concern of global significance. Foster observes that: "Recent technological developments and their more general theoretical foundations have provided man with the capacity to modify his environment in such striking fashion that he is no longer able to regard each operation as singular; he must, in each case, consider the 'widening circle of consequences.' The problem has taken the more general form of finding the proper use of man's capacities to modify his environment" [(1963), 1981, 1011].

Foster's dramatic illustration needs little amplification: "[T]he release of atomic radiation through explosions and other operations" has been, and remains, a central and significant international concern. Fortunately, after years of contentious discussion, international agreements to ban further atmospheric testing of nuclear weapons have been reached. Those who recall the radiation release resulting from the meltdown of the nuclear energy generating plant at Chernobyl in the Ukraine, need no reminders. The negative impact on the health of the residents in the area is substantial and is still under study. Swedes in the fallout pattern will readily discuss the impact on their agriculture. For Foster, and currently, there remain international concerns regarding the "genetic incidences of various levels of radiation" and the "impact on hydrologic cycles and other meteorological phenomena" (1963, 1011).

The policy implications are awesome: Through what institutions (new or revamped) can the nations of the world exercise some minimum control over the character and extent of use of nuclear plants, reach and sustain agreements over the further development and control of nuclear weaponry, and find ways of safely disposing of radio-active waste (e.g., spent fuel rods). The compelling need is for continuing pursuit of international institutional structure through which intimidative postures based on weaponry, and status postures based on industrial use, can be constrained and instrumental mechanisms of accountability made effective and continuing.

Policy making in this area will continue indefinitely to be based on an exceedingly complex and conjoint pursuit of physical theory and socio-political theory. The former must inform increasingly of the technical options that can be made available. The latter must inform increasingly regarding international control institutions to permit the use of nuclear fission for instrumental purposes but to find effective institutional constraints on its invidious use. Foster acknowledges a continuing need for a compelling policy agenda.

Resource Management

Neoclassical economists, who have traditionally identified the scope of economics, have contended that it is "the study of the allocation of scarce means among unlimited ends"; it is "the study of the allocation of scarce resources in man's efforts to satisfy his unlimited wants," or some such. Thus, resources are allegedly given. "They are what they are; there is no labor involved; there is no cost of production." They are gifts of nature [Foster (1975b) 1981, 1]. It follows, then, that the supply side of the determination of real income, is a quantity, not just so much over a period of time, but a given resource bundle. "On the demand side, the productivity per unit of labor is increased by the accumulation of real capital which is made out of these resources by the application of human labor." The determination of income depends on the level and character of demand as reflected in market exchange. The characterization of economics as a "dismal science," then, derives from increasing demand confronting fixed supply. "The Club of Rome takes these two data, feeds them into a computer, and gets an answer: human destruction" (1975b, 2). The conventional position regarding *given* resources is deeply and irretrievably archaic.

Foster asks: "Are resources given data?" He answers, certainly not. "Resources are the portion of the nonhuman environment that we use in providing . . .real income. Such resources. . .are not given; they are not static; they are a dynamic in the equational system applicable to the economic process. . . .The materials we use are functions of. . .the state of the industrial arts. . .and that state is not a static thing. It is developmental" [(1975b), 1981, 2]. Actually, the resource base is *defined* by the levels and applications of warranted, scientific knowledge. Substances have no instrumental status or economic significance until and unless scientific inquirers are able to identify and incorporate their presence and define their role as a part of the fund of warranted knowledge in one or another functional facet of the provision of the means of life. "Natural resources are not natural. . . . [T]echnological developments. . .specify how much of what kind of material is available to man. It is a function of his intelligence as it has been successfully applied to his problems" (3).

> If the state of the industrial arts specifies the character and quantity of resources. . .what determines the state of the arts[?] [The latter is determined by] what human beings devise in response to problematic situations. . .[they] encounter good, bad and indifferent responses. When you have a problematic situation, which means that there is something wrong, incomplete, something missing, then you are coerced by circumstances—not by persons, but by the circumstances of the problem—to seek. . .resolution of the condition. And the character of the problem you encounter. . .determines the focus of your attention. The more telling the problem the more fervent your attention (1975, 4).

Accordingly, "[t]he character of our problems determines the focus of our attention, both individually and as a group. . . .[T]he focus of our attention specifies the areas of technological development. And the areas of technological development specify the character and level of economic resources. . . .[Thus] the dynamic in the economic process is human creativity—the application of intelligence to problems" [(1975b) 1981, 4]. This dynamic is the critical "natural" resource. The protection and expansion of human creativity is the essential and instrumentally warranted "resource" policy for developed and developing economies.

CONTEMPORARY INSTRUMENTAL POLICY ADVISORIES

Introduction

We now address, drawing on Foster's contribution, instrumental analyses and institutional policies for problem solving in two quite different and dramatically significant areas: First, increasing inequality of income and attendant poverty. Second, the use of ism-ideological models as guides to economic transition in developing economies. Our purpose is to demonstrate, however briefly, something of the relevance and significance of Foster's theoretical contributions to contemporary inquiry and policy making in application to these two major topical areas of political economy. Of course, no claims to definitiveness can be made.

In the following commentary are examples of the application of Foster's theory of the economic process, instrumental theory of social value, and of the theory of institutional adjustment. We will organize comments on these respective substantive areas as responses to the following queries:

What is the problematic situation? What are the instrumental functions addressed? What is the character of, and who has discretion over, existing institutional structures? What are the problematic conditions and determinants of inadequate economic provisioning (obstruction, impairment, invidiousness, ceremoniality, coercion and/or disjunction) that require revision or rejection to enhance instrumental efficiency in the economic process?

What ought to be? What specific institutional adjustments are recommended that would constitute a solution to the problems identified, i.e., to erode invidious or coercive impediments and to restore or create instrumental efficiency in the provisioning process?

What is to be done? In application of Foster's theory of institutional adjustment, do the proposed structural changes reflect recognition of and responses to the principles of technological determination, recognized interdependence and minimal dislocation? In sum, do the proposed institutional adjustments create, restore and/or enhance the instrumental efficiency of the institutional fabric and functions under scrutiny?

Income Inequality and Poverty

What is the Problematic Situation?

Instrumental Functions

In contemporary exchange economies, the production and distribution of real income (goods and services) is the inclusive instrumental function. Here we address only the *distribution* of real and money income. The distribution facet of that economic process, the provision of access to real goods and services in an exchange economy, is almost entirely determined by the continuing receipt of money income. If one is employed (including self-employed), money income as wages, salaries, and/or monetary supplements of various kinds provide the main access to the flow of goods and services. If one is not employed or is unable to be employed, income from other, including public, sources will be required to sustain rudimentary existence. Continuity in this flow of money income, given its purchasing power, determines real income. It is an encompassing, contingent and critical matter. Any significant reduction, (e.g., from inflation), or interruption (e.g., job loss) in that flow generates, for all but upper income receivers, near immediate crises of sustenance.

The problematic situation, for an institutionalist, then, consists of the fact of dramatic inequality of money income distribution and the attendant imposition of poverty on substantial segments of the population. Prevailing institutional structures are not adequately responding to residual poverty. And residual poverty, given the crippled community thesis (to cripple a part is to cripple the whole of the community), impairs not only the funding, stature and potential of lower income persons, but those of the middle and upper classes as well. When a community fails to use its accumulated and warranted social and economic knowledge to achieve more equitable distribution of income and reduction in poverty levels, the potential instrumental contribution of those adversely affected is foregone.

Some defend inequality of distribution on grounds that it provides incentives for economic endeavor and participation and that, in deference to the savings theory of capital formation, inequality is required in order that there be sufficient savings by the rich to generate needed capital formation for economic development. "The unspent incomes of the well-to-do" are claimed as the unique source of capital formation. But since the Keynesian revolution, it is widely understood that funding of capital goods is financed, if not out of retained earnings, then by debt creation mainly in banks. The incentives argument is apologia. The savings theory of capital formation has since Keynes been understood to be mistaken and inapplicable.

As Baldwin Ranson explains:

> In truth, the only aggregate activity in a modern economy to which the supposed effect of saving can apply is the spending of newly created funds on goods produced but not consumed. Funds to finance new investment are made available by new debt, not by failures to spend. The money value of new investment must always equal the rate of spending of new debt—which is the meaning of savings Keynes intended when he argued that saving is equal to investment. But the rates of this saving and investment are determined by the willingness of the banking system and the government to create new debt, not by the willingness of "savers" to refrain from consuming. (Ranson 1988, 325).

Savings by the rich, then, do not generate the investment that fuels economic growth. Accordingly, inequality of money income distribution is therefore not required for economic growth. Poverty for some is not a requisite for the economic health of others. On the contrary, evidence of prevalent poverty is indicative of a gross failure to enhance the instrumental functioning of *all* segments of the community. Reformers can not deal knowledgeably and adequately with the problem of inequitable distribution of money income so long as the cultural myth, that savings of the rich fuel the economy, remains the "common sense" of the community and stands unchallenged. Redistributive proposals are stillborn. The problem is evaded by characterizing those in poverty with invidiously rooted attributes (lazy, un-wed, non-white, et cetera.) that demean them by denying their actual or potential significance.

Derivative instrumental functions, contingent on the central process of provision and distribution of goods and services accessed through money income, are also significantly impaired by poverty status. Support for child rearing and education, adequate medical care, development of professional skills and intellectual capacities, and participatory involvement in communal responsibilities, e.g., are insufficiently accessible.

Loci of Discretion

Existing centers of decision making, through which personal income flows are determined, include the following:

In the private sector, employers in non-union enterprises have discretion over wages and salaries paid but are constrained by minimum wage laws, by wage levels that have become customary, and by their uncertainties about consequences arising from departures from existing wage structures. Employers in firms where workers are organized in unions have discretion that is constrained by co-determined contracts negotiated in collective bargaining. Employers sometimes have discretion generated in contacts and/or contracts with foreign firms and labor pools. Self-employed individuals engaged in providing products or services have some discretion over their own operations but have very limited impact on or control over the markets which they enter. But only middle and upper income individuals have some discretion over their own sources, levels, or transfers of money income from social security, pensions, interest on accounts, dividends, gifts, etc. For these particular individuals, obviously, money income will typically be derived from several of these discretionary sources.

In the public sector, obviously, governmental bodies determine the wage and salary structure for all public employees. At all levels, agents of government implement public laws governing unemployment compensation and other basic income distributions. The Federal government determines minimum wage levels for most areas of employment.

Critical, then. is the general recognition that wages, salaries, and supplements are paid as administered distributions. Unfettered markets do not determine income flows. Agents with acquired or conferred discretion determine income flows. Market reactions to distributive income decisions *may* prompt changes in distributive decision making by income dispensing agents.

Threats to both the continuity and size of these income flows arise from the exercise of discretion by owner/managers and other decision sources and agents, as noted above, from changes in the general level of income and employment, and from changes in legislation bearing on these income flows. The latter should be emphasized. Public policy addressed to spending and/or taxation are frequently fashioned substantially to alter both the aggregate level and the distribution of income. They are administered decisions. In sum, money income flows to members of the community are determined by those holding discretion stipulated by existing institutional structures, public and private. And, as affirmed in preceding Chapters, all exercises of judgment by discretionary parties inescapably reflect recourse to criteria the normative identity of which is itself a critical factor in problem identification and resolution.

Moreover, as with any area of social policy making, mechanisms through which the decision makers can be held to account for their judgments are absolutely essential in any democratically organized economy. Accountability hinges on the community's political review and assessment of pricing judgments made by dispensing agents. The presumption that accountability is an automatic and routine consequence of market involvement and functions has long since been laid to rest. Economies operate on the basis of overt discretionary judgments by participants in the exchange process, as identified above.

Problematic Distributional Conditions

These administered income decisions in the aggregate, whatever their intent individually, continue to leave significant segments of the community with insufficient money income adequately to provide the flow of goods and services to sustain themselves and their families. The encompassing instrumental function of providing comprehensively the means of life and experience is substantially impaired, and for some denied, for significant fractions of the American community.

In the United States, a sampling of data provided by governmental bodies indicates the currently prevailing income distribution patterns as established by discretionary sources noted above. The following statistical summaries of the character of income distribution and differentials indicate something of the character and extent of inequality of income distribution in the U.S. including the fact that inequality is increasing (Clark 1996b, 204-11).

Unemployment: In the United States, the percent of the civilian labor force that is involuntarily unemployed has dropped from a recent high in 1985 of 7.2

percent, to the current figure, for 1998, of 4.5 percent. Even so, over *6.2 million* people in 1998 were without jobs (*Statistical Abstract of the United States 1999*, 411).

Extent of poverty: Statistically specified "poverty thresholds" by the U.S. government establish the poverty line or poverty level in determining the extent of economic deprivation in the US. In 1997, the poverty level for one person was, in rounded numbers, $8,350, as annual income. That is, single persons with less than $8,350 income were below the poverty line. The comparable figures for a two person family unit were $10,470, for a three person unit $12,800, for a four person unit, $16,400, and similarly for larger family units (484). In 1997, *35.5 million* Americans (13.3 percent) were living below the poverty line; *47.8 million* Americans (17.8 percent) were living below 125 percent of the poverty level. (483). For blacks 23.6 percent, and for Hispanics 24.7 percent, of families were living below the poverty line (487). Predictably, 15.4 percent of white children, 36.8 percent of black children, and 36.4 percent of Hispanic children were living below the poverty line (483).

Income: The median income of families in 1997 was $44,600; in constant dollars it has not significantly increased in the last 10 years (478). In 1997, the shares of aggregate income received by families, in quintiles ranging from the lowest to the highest percentages, (and of the top 5 percent), is indicated in the following Table I for various years.

Table I. SHARE OF AGGREGATE INCOME RECEIVED BY EACH FIFTH AND TOP 5 PERCENT OF FAMILIES

Year	Lowest	Second	Third	Fourth	Fifth	Top 5%
1970	5.4	12.2	17.6	23.8.	40.9	15.6
1980	5.3	11.6	17.6	24.4	41.1	14.6
1990	4.6	10.8	16.6	23.8	44.3	17.4
1996	4.2	10.0	15.8	23.1	46.8	20.3
1997	4.2	9.9	15.7	23.0	47.2	20.7

(*Statistical Abstract of the United States*, 1999, p.479)

In 1997, the top 20 percent of family recipients received over half again as much income as the bottom 60 percent of family recipients. The income of the top 5 percent substantially exceeded that of the bottom 40 percent (479). Income distribution is increasingly and significantly unequal, as noted.

Minimum wage: In 1997, Congress increased the minimum wage to $5.15, or $5.03 in constant 1996 dollars. This is about the equivalent of the constant dollar minimum wage in 1984, but is only some 80 percent of the constant dollar figure for 1976 (447). This recent increase is hardly a recovery from a decade long slippage in the purchasing power of the minimum wage.

Health care: In 1997 some *43.7 million* persons, 16.1% of the total, in the U.S. were without health insurance coverage of any kind, public or private (127). The consumer price index of medical care services (with 1982-1984 = 100) went up from 162.7 in 1990 to 246.8 in 1998 (126).

These data, then, indicate something of the extent and character of the increasing maldistribution of income in the United States. These data also indicate that, as is widely understood, blacks and Hispanics are economically deprived relative to whites.

A most significant implication is that the inequities and deprivations indicated above dramatically and negatively impinge not only the individuals and families continuously deprived of fuller participation in the economic process, but upon the community-at-large as well. The general community experiences massive and continuing *underemployment* and the loss of substantial aggregate income resulting therefrom. Deprivations then are not confined to the poor and alienated. Whatever cripples the segment, cripples the whole community.

What ought to be?

Introduction

Institutional adjustments have, in recent years, been proposed to enhance the instrumental function of providing the means of life especially for those in the community living in poverty in a manner that also reduces invidious economic discrimination. Two of these proposed adjustments, *guaranteed employment*, and *reduced invidious discrimination* are discussed below. Corollary adjustments including the provision of basic (guaranteed) income, universal single-payer health care, further increases in the minimum wage, publicly funded access to higher education (new GI Bill not tied to military service), merit serious consideration but are not addressed herein.

A minimum goal of reducing poverty would be to bring aggregate incomes of all families (whites, blacks, Hispanics, Asians et al.) above the poverty line. A related goal would be to guarantee employment for all at, or somewhat above, the minimum wage level. A more ambitious, but achievable, goal would be to bring the earned incomes (including assistance in kind, e.g., health care, education) of families in the bottom quintile into correspondence with what is now the second-from-bottom quintile. This would mean an increase in income for the bottom 20 percent of families of about 150 percent of present levels.

In any case, the reduction of invidious discrimination in directing the flow of real and money income in the economic process is also a significant policy goal; it is essential. What is needed is a continuation and expansion of public measures to end discrimination in employment based on gender, race, ethnicity, ancestry, age, et cetera. Because the incidence of these problems of discrimination are largely economy-wide, responsibility falls on governmental structure of the community-at-large for their resolution. All such institutional adjustments require abandonment of invidious structure through the initiation, revision, expansion, and/or implementation of instrumentally warranted alternative structures .mainly by government bodies, especially but not exclusively, by federal agencies. We briefly consider two proposed adjustments.

Guaranteed Employment

If employment is guaranteed, involuntary unemployment is eliminated. The adoption of a guaranteed employment program means that everyone who wants paid employment can have a job. The federal government would hire all unemployed workers full time that are able and willing to work at a wage level perhaps at or a bit higher than, the current minimum wage. The toleration of varying levels of unemployment over recent decades has, of course, deprived the national community of many millions of person-years of productive employment. The introduction of guaranteed employment would provide an unparalleled opportunity to enhance the flow of real income and, e.g., to salvage and restore the community's environment and infrastructure. A partial list of productive and instrumental activities permitted by actually full employment, that extend Foster's suggestions above, might well include:

> (a) ecological enhancement: cleaning up hundreds of toxic waste sites, replanting clear-cut forests, developing an environmental restoration technology and industry. . .(b) improved health: providing universal access to quality health care that extends coverage to the . . .[43 million] without health insurance and therefore without adequate medical care (c) educational rehabilitation: universal access to quality learning, small classes, restored physical plant. . .(d) macro stability: increased aggregate demand from rising aggregate incomes to stimulate the appearance of increasing numbers of professional and commercial providers of goods and services and [to] generate countercyclical pressures; (e) salvage of youth: assured employment to dramatically undercut the [destructive] subculture among the young [rooted, e.g., in drug trafficking] (Tool, 1998, 291. See also Wray 1998, 142-43).

Two significant questions are routinely raised about guaranteed employment. One is that it will inevitably generate significant inflationary pressures. A second is that the governmental outlays required would be excessive and beyond the capacity of government to provide. L. Randall Wray responds to the these concerns by demonstrating that introducing "government as the employer of last resort" (ELR) would *not* necessarily generate unmanageable inflationary pressures nor place unreasonable financial demands on government.

> Many, perhaps most, economists doubt that it is even possible to achieve anything close to a 3% unemployment rate without at the same time inducing *accelerating* inflation. . . .[W]e. . .argue that stable prices and truly full employment are indeed possible. . . .[T]he proposed full employment policy *would not* generate the sort of inflationary pressures that many economists believe must result from policies that generate high employment. Thus inflation. . .could certainly co-exist with our proposed full employment policy but would not be *caused* by the policy. . . .[Indeed] the full employment policy would help reduce economic fluctuations. . .through a powerful built-in stabilizer feature. (Wray 1997, 1-2, emphasis in original).

In a later consideration of the issue, Randall Wray adds:

> Indeed, it is hard to imagine that true full employment with an ELR programme would be more inflationary than the current system. The current system relies on unemployed labour and excess capacity to try to dampen wage and price increases; however, it pays unemployed labour for not working, and allows that labour to depreciate and in some cases to develop behaviors that act as barriers to private sector employment. Social spending on the unemployed prevents aggregate demand from falling excessively, but little is done to promote aggregate supply (or growth of potential output). With ELR in place, however, labor is paid for working, which can lead to production of publicly supplied goods and services, can promote efficiency of the private sector. . .and can increase the education and skills of ELR workers. . .Thus ELR might increase aggregate supply. . .and thereby place downward pressure on prices, rather than causing inflation (Wray 1998, 133).

Increased employment through ELR would result in increased product and aggregate income. The orthodox view of inflation as "too much money chasing too few goods," is accordingly suspect. Many, including Foster, share the view that administered pricing by private megacorps has a causal, continuing and substantial inflationary impact on the price level generally. The U.S. destabilizing experience with the large and dramatic administered price increases for oil some two decades ago is a continuing reminder of the presence and use of substantial economic power over pricing and its potential inflationary impact.

As for the concern that demands of guaranteed employment on governmental revenues would constitute an unbearable burden, two responses merit exploration. First, increased expenditures on guaranteed employment by government would, in significant measure, be offset by substantial reduction of governmental spending on unemployment compensation, and perhaps on some other support programs. Second, if deficit budgets did result, the risks are quite manageable. As Wray explains,

> [T]here is *nothing* inherently wrong with big deficits; these do not necessarily cause "crowding out," they do not "burden" future generations, they cannot lead to "financial ruin" of the government. . . .[*A*]*ll* government spending is in the first instance financed by crediting a member bank's account at the central bank, that is, government spending is "financed" by money creation. Taxes are required only to generate a demand for this money; they are never required to "finance" the government spending. Bond sales are then required to "drain" reserves. . .in order to hit interest rate targets. Thus government deficits are not "financed" by bond sales, deficits do not raise interest rates and "crowd out" private investment. . .and deficits do not automatically set up a stream of interest payments. . .[and] even when they do, these are always met through crediting bank reserves; thus there is no "burden" of servicing government debt. [F]ear of deficit spending is irrational and should never be allowed to stand in the way of spending that may be required to generate full employment (1997, 3-4, emphasis in original).

There are significant and divergent "fringe" benefits from an institutional adjustment that introduces governmentally assured employment: (a) It generates an "enhanced sense of self-worth" in individuals from their productive contribution to the economic process." (b) It reduces "the extent of invidious discrimination in employment by reducing competition over jobs." (c) It provides a "larger real product and service output" for the community and reduces "social costs of lost output." (d) It enhances political participation of the bottom 40 percent of the population who see politics as a process unrelated to their basic needs and concerns. (Tool 1998, 290-92). Recently, we wrote:

> Universal assurance of employment—access to adequate earned income as a human right—connotes. . .nondiscriminatory status within the community. For an instrumentalist, universality means non-invidious access to political, social and economic processes. An individual's obligation, given access to employment and community membership, is significantly to contribute to the economic well-being of the community. Employment as an enforceable human right, then, is an affirmation of the right to be in, to belong to and to help reconstruct a human community (Tool 1998, 286).

What is to be Done to Guarantee Employment?

Institutional adjustments to bring some four to five million persons into the labor force to add their instrumental contributions to the total economic effort of the economy, are comparatively speaking, simple and uncomplicated. No dramatic institutional upheavals, that might pose threats to existing employee or employer contributions to the generation and distribution of real income, are required or anticipated. Consider the following:

Technological Determination

This principle, recall, affirms that social problems can be resolved only by "bringing the institutional structures involved into instrumentally efficient correlation with the technological aspects of the problem." That is "the instrumental functions of the institution must be carried on at a level of efficiency tolerable to the members of the institution" given their knowledge of the actually known possibilities [Foster (1948) 1981, 932].

The warranted knowledge underlying the proposal to guarantee employment is simple and accessible. We know from our experience during World War II, that the economy can operate at full employment. We can knowingly presume that two thirds, at least, of the involuntary unemployed want jobs and are employable. We know that that labor pool is in the main educable, that is, that its members can acquire the skills needed to perform adequately, if given the opportunity. We know that the desire to participate and contribute to the economy is an acquired and probable trait. We know that employment contributes to a sense of self worth and significance. We know that institutional structure already exists through which the recruitment and training (if necessary) of this labor pool can be arranged. We know that the statistical procedures and staff to help locate, recruit and track movement of large numbers of persons into the working labor force is available. There appear to be no technical or institutional barriers that preclude the institutional adjustment contemplated.

Recognized Interdependence

The principle of recognized interdependence, recall, "is simply that the immediate pattern of any institutional adjustment is specified by the pattern of interdependencies recognized by members of the institution. . . .[A]n adjustment . . .requires that a deliberate choice be made among the possible alternatives recognized by those who must alter their behavior [Foster (1948) 1981, 933.].

This principle reaffirms that structural changes obviously do not occur except in consequence of deliberate choices being made by all of those who, with discretionary options, can affect outcomes. The federal government obviously must choose to establish the option. Employers (that may include governmental bodies in various jurisdictions) must choose to hire workers from the idle pool. Those hired must be willing to make significant choices as necessary—accept training, move family to vicinity of job site, agree to initial wage proposed, and modify work habits and schedules. Choices made are linked and interdependent.

Minimal Dislocation

The principle of minimal dislocation affirms that all institutional adjustments must be capable of being incorporated into the remainder of the institutional structure without significantly disrupting instrumental functions of nonproblematic structure. It "discloses the limits of adjustment in terms of rate and in terms of degree and area" [Foster (1948) 1981, 934].

We see no problem here with guaranteed employment being dislocative. What is proposed is the introduction of a singular program. It displaces, presumably, the current program of unemployment compensation that may require some bureaucratic restructuring and reassignment, but one would expect it to be minimal. The program conforms with the culture's deference to the work ethic. One can imagine some competition among persons seeking jobs, but the overriding concern for job access should prevent this from becoming a threat to the introduction of the program.

What is to be Done to Reduce Invidious Discrimination?

Policy proposals to reduce invidious discrimination in social, political and economic contexts are fairly elemental. Governments, at all levels, need to refurbish, apply and enforce legislative prohibitions against using race, gender, ancestry, etc. as criteria in determining who can participate generally in the social order; and, more particularly, who can enter the work force, in which occupations, and with what income and benefits. Legislative gains in reducing discrimination over the last several decades have been substantial, but are not sufficient.

Evidently it is still the case that "glass ceilings" limit the economic advancement of women in discretionary responsibility and income; these ceilings must be removed. Racial discrimination, that assigns persons of color and/or ethnic ancestry to particular categories of work, especially those that "dead end", that is, provide no or few opportunities to advance in income and responsibility, need to be ended. Affirmative action was introduced as an institutional adjustment to enhance access to higher education, especially for persons of color (Livingston 1979). Evidently the policy did reduce racial discrimination in educational access and employment. But now it is under successful attack at the state level (i.e. repealed in California). The disabling conceptual conflict that persists is the difficulty of having to generate quotas to enhance minority access which therewith appear as race-based preferences suppressing the options of someone else. The instrumental solution is to move from the "*either* black *or* white" formulations to "*both* black *and* white" concepts and structures; from "*either* male *or* female" to "*both* male *and* female constructs and rules in establishing instrumental connections to the economic process..

Technological Determination

The invidious use of distinctions among persons tends *not* to be based on warranted knowledge, although claims to such do still appear. Evidential inquiries repeatedly indicate that the behavioral characteristics of persons of divergent races, different genders, diverse ethnic backgrounds are mainly a product of widely differing acculturation processes. Capacities for learning warranted knowledge appear not to be based on genetic differences; they are minuscule and insignificant in comparison to cultural conditioning. Every culture does indeed develop an impressive legacy of warranted knowledge. Even folk knowledge often has an evidential, i.e. causal, significance. Accordingly, there is no basis in warranted knowledge supporting the invidious characterizations of discernible differences in appearance and ancestry.

The import of the foregoing for present purposes is that it undergirds our perception that public policy to reduce the normative use of invidious distinctions, that appear as differentials in income distribution and in access to employment, is not compromised by reference to *alleged* warranted knowledge supporting the invidious use of distinctions among persons.

Recognized Interdependence

Institutional adjustments, as noted, require that habitual patterns of thought and conduct continue until and unless deliberate choices are made to shift from prior patterns and conduct to altered modes and practice. Any new pattern of behavior requires that the behavior be "directed" in its initiation, It becomes habitual through repetition" [Foster (1948) 1981,933]. Legal measures can assist in the redirection of institutional change to remove or reduce invidious discrimination in many areas of public choice. Historically, efforts in this direction have been introduced with reference to educational access (as noted), access to employment, location of housing, use of public facilities, et cetera. Recall the struggle over racially identified drinking fountains in some cities in the American South.

But that recognized interdependence can be impaired, if not destroyed, by the very human quest for purposiveness, for significance, "to make a difference," to enhance one's own sense of self-worth, to seek esteem in recognition by others. The quest for self-identity and significance can easily turn *invidious* if our personal quest is thought to be blocked, compromised, impaired or destroyed by others identified invidiously. Any such becomes an exceedingly emotional concern.

Minimal Dislocation

Given the extent of that concern, the community must seek ways to minimize the negative reactions of those who perceive themselves to be threatened by the proposed institutional adjustments. Concern should be expected over the extent to which legal measures to reduce invidious discrimination, e.g., in employment and in income distribution, would prompt those who perceive themselves to be significantly hurt by invidiously defined others, to agitate politically and vigorously seeking to repeal some or all such public anti-discrimination measures. The problem must be recognized and responded to constructively. No one shoul(underestimate the need for careful planning, full communication, and accommodating adjustments. The answers must be found in analyses of individual cases. But anything more than minimal dislocation aborts constructive institutional adjustments.

Economic Transitions and Ideologies

What is the Problematic Situation?

As we observed above (in concluding Chapter 7): "People formulate isms; they attempt to apply isms, but always non-ism-generated changes in institutional structure are required to sustain the social process and the production of the means of life and experience" at some level of competence, however limited. Foster reminds us that "[w]e have *never* seen the [consistent] application of an ism. There has always been institutional change. New institutions coming, old institutions changing, and completely new additional institutions arising. None of them ever constituted an ism or structure" [Foster 1950, (LN) CompEconSyst, 46]. But the insistence on applying an ism as the vehicle of transition from an unproductive and maldistributive economy to something more acceptable, generates near economic chaos. Such has been the case in the last decade or so in employing ism models to guide the economic transition of socialist economies to something more productive and efficient.

Instrumental Functions

Instrumental functions, as alluded to above, are those that are basic to the operation of any modern economy: generation and distribution of warranted knowledge, creation and operation of productive organizations, production and distribution of real income, democratic control over economic policy, noninvidious participation of citizens, et cetera.

In Chapter 7 above, Foster characterizes an ism-ideology "as a systematized body of theory which validates a particular institutional structure" [1950 (LN) CompEconSyst, 24]. Can capitalist ideology, specifying a capitalist institutional structure, displace Marxian socialist or communist institutional structure and serve as a guide and vehicle for the transition of a *developing* economy to the status of a *developed* economy? Does the application of a capitalist model to the rehabilitation of a post-communist Russia reflect instrumental policy making or does it represent a mistaken ideological effort that degenerated into invidious control over policy making by a self-protective political cadre; a "Mafia" minority?

Loci of Discretion

Predictably, discretionary political agents in positions of power, whether selected by pro forma democratic procedures or by appointment as subordinate department heads by those holding de facto centralized discretion over public policy, have the responsibility to formulate and implement economic policies. Accountability to the political leadership is required. Accountability to the larger community will be claimed but it may well be a proforma rather than substantive responsibility. Since central political leaders are not often competent economists, responsibility for specific formulation of policies will be delegated to a subordinate few whose claims to competency are accepted. But the consequences of economic policy falls on the rich and the poor, the schooled and the illiterate, the party line followers and dissidents; the incidence cannot be avoided or concealed. De facto accountability is present, whatever the intent of those harboring discretion. Failed, because mistaken, policy is out there for all to see; only the elites, however identified, can sometimes escape its differential impact.

In the quest for transition from a developing economy to a developed economy, the route followed is often, if not typically, plotted by one or more Western advisor. Advisors have de facto discretion, their claims to the contrary notwithstanding! The latter are generally professional economists, trained at the most prestigious universities in developed economies. And since for half a century and more the dominant model of economic inquiry and policy making has been that of the neoclassical school, "validating" allegedly capitalist models for the transition, the advisors are, at bottom, peddlers of the ism called capitalism. In their view, scholarly dominion equates with economic truth. The actual experience of transitioning economies, if it is to be successful, requires an alternate perspective, as the following exploration suggests.

Existing Structure

The shift from communism to capitalism was vigorously urged beforehand: "Only the wholesale, complete replacement of the [Soviet command economy's] defining characteristics opens room for an alternative, market-based system. . . .An entire world must be discarded, including all of its economic and most of its social and political institutions. . . .Radical reformers are correct to seek the total replacement of the traditional system" (Ericson 1991, 25). Two years later, the following dissent, among others, is voiced: "Russia has had a plethora of big bang crash programmes of impossibilist technical reform, none of which has survived—and whose failure is beginning to discredit the whole idea of a market economy." (Hutton 1993).

The major capitalist institutional adjustments introduced in Russia can be summarized as follows: Economic liberalization (freeing prices, open trading, establishing legal structure of economy). Macroeconomic stabilization (cuts in subsidies, devaluation, positive interest rates, constraints on credit expansion). Privatization: (transfer of state firms to private ownership). The public government's role is reduced and will shrink further. In Jeffrey Sachs's view this triad constituted the "three pillars of economic transition to a market economy" (Sachs, 1991a, 43-48). After devastating consequences of market shock appeared, he added two more pillars: "creation of a social safety net," and "economic support from the West," neither of which is ideologically specified. There is a lesson there.

Problems of Impairment

Critics in the AGENDA-Group suggest that "the *main error* lies in the belief in the spontaneous appearance of a capitalist market economy once private property is established, prices are set free, currency is stabilized and unregulated competitive markets are introduced" (Kregel, Matzner, Grabher, 1992, 112, emphasis in original). Although this observation is correct in the sense that all institutions have to be specifically created and introduced to become effective in coordinating behavior, the more inclusive institutionalist's critique suggests that all three of Foster's principles of institutional adjustment were violated by the Sachs's model for the "big bang," market shock economic transition.

Technological determination was ignored; there seems to have been no recognition of the need for continuity in the conduct of instrumental functions using available technology. Insufficient effort was made to adjust structure so as to get efficient correlation with available technologies.

Recognized interdependence was ignored: There appears to have been insufficient recognition of the need for people whose behavior was being modified to have an understanding of the accompanying disruption in familiar interdependencies and the need therefore to establish new and instrumental linkages with others.

Minimal dislocation, evidently was nowhere considered. Maximal dislocation was characteristic of changes introduced. Institutional changes, to be successful, must be capable of being incorporated into the remainder of the institutional structure. With maximal dislocation, the rate of change exceeds the capacity of people to accommodate to it and to continue to function instrumentally.

What Ought to Be?

Suggested Institutional Adjustments

A more recent assessment of approaches to economic transition from a socialist economy is suggested by a Polish economist, Jerzy Hausner (1998, 42). In his view, two rival interpretations of a decade of change in Eastern Europe compete for adherents and guidance. The first is the imperative approach, pursued by Sachs and other orthodox neo-liberals; the second is the interactive approach recommended as an alternative by Hausner and others. Here we suggest that Foster, and institutionalists generally, would support the interactive approach and reject the imperative approach.

The *imperative* approach to transition, in a somewhat updated neo-liberal [capitalist] "Washington consensus," has been introduced in "the majority of post-socialist countries" (Hausner, 1998, 42). It is "a package of economic measures aiming to ensure macro-economic stability and market reform"; it is a cook-book manual. Its tenets instruct as follows: maintain fiscal discipline, cut government subsidies, broaden the tax base, determine interest rates by markets, determine exchange rates by markets, liberalize export trade, abolish restrictions on direct foreign investment, privatize state enterprises, deregulate economic activity, guarantee property rights, et cetera. (42). Implicit throughout is the concept of the minimal state. Its tax base diminishes; devolution of ownership shifts discretion into private hands for private purposes. Whether one characterizes this ideological shift as "wild capitalism," "copycat capitalism" or "Zerox capitalism", the consequences are insidious and invidious. As a Russian reformer observed:

> the main problem of present-day capitalism that has formed in Russia is. . .the complete intertwining of property and power. . . .If we look at the operation of Russian enterprises, [and] the work of government agencies. . .time and again we see the closest intertwining of business and bureaucracy. . .the success of an enterprise depends not on the ability of the director or owner to organize normal production, but on his ability to give appropriate bribes, or whether his patrons are sufficiently high up, or his ability. . .to secure for himself a set of individual benefits and exceptions from the rule, etc. (Gaidar 1995, quoted by Hausner 1999, 46).

The comparative diminution of *public* authority, to require or to generate accountability, leaves basic economic discretion in the hands of those who, by virtue of opportunity and circumstance, serve their private interests of power acquisition and income enhancement. Elections matter only where choices made permit or direct the relocation of political authority to individuals or groups that have some credible concept of a public interest, of instrumental adjustments that might moderate or constrain, the insidious linkage between private "business and bureaucracy."

The *interactive* approach to transition may be characterized as "restructuring with the participation of the state." Hausner lays out the following agenda for a participatory role for the national government: (a) generate a "comprehensive long term programme of economic development;" (b) "carry out macroeconomic policy that maintains the current economic equilibrium;" (c) "forge an infrastructure (technical, institutional, legal, social). . .to increase economic efficiency;" (d) "possess the means and instruments. . to become involved in restructuring;" (e) "participate in negotiations between various types of partners. . .over specific programmes and restructuring measures;" (f) provide " resources by the state for specific programmes and restructuring measures" (Hausner 1998, 47-48). He concludes as follows: "the cornerstone of the 'restructuring with the participation of the state' approach is the creation of institutions that complement market and administrative co-ordination mechanisms, and at the same time ensure social control over these mechanisms" (48).

Foster, we think, would concur with and recommend the following caveat: The success of the participatory state depends upon its unwavering constitution of, and commitment to, democratic processes and procedures. In no other way can the confidence of a community in its governance be established and sustained. This is the most critical condition of all. If the "social control" alluded to is indeed democratic, the prospects of judgments made in and through the "participatory government" of being instrumental, in the Fosterian sense, rather than invidious or ceremonial, will be appreciably enhanced. Power held must be accountable to the general community. Otherwise, private interests override public interests. Foster's recommendation for all transition economies, and for others as well, then, is to avoid ism models and pursue instrumental functions of the economy through responsive and responsible democratic institutions, indigenously acceptable and accountable.

What is to be Done?

Technological Determination

Consider the significance of warranted economic knowledge for any political economy. No economy, developed or developing, can successfully serve its citizens unless the application of warranted knowledge to the technological and institutional problems of organizing and operating a productive economy becomes dominantly characteristic, virtually a routine operation. In the present case, technological determination of institutional adjustments implies the comprehensive displacement of capitalist ideologists and their archaic institutional truisms with pragmatic and pluralistic approaches to the generation of economic knowledge that builds on a number of heterodox traditions reflected in the contributions not only of Veblen and Dewey in the U.S. but also, e.g., in the contributions, among others, of Gunnar Myrdal and K., William Kapp, leading European institutionalists. Indeed, over the last decade and more, pertinent and warranted knowledge is being developed in myriad centers of inquiry and policy development around the globe. Institutional economists, social economists, post-Keynesian economists, evolutionary economists, regulation economists, et al. address the real world of warranted knowledge, institutional adjustment, and democratic accountability. As a group they are diverse heterodox thinkers, but they share a commitment to the development of causal accounts for observed phenomena, the need for continuing institutional adjustment, the irrelevance of pre-packaged isms, and implicitly the recognition that instrumental efficiency as developed herein is in fact the only criterion of judgment that identifies the *kinds* of non-invidious institutional adjustments that will permit the respective economies to continue to grow, develop, and enhance the real income status of all of their respective citizens.

Recognized Interdependence

Successful economic transitions are not to be expected where a *comprehensive* recasting of structure is imposed on a substantially different economic system in a comparatively short time period. As was earlier observed, all persons are necessarily creatures of habit, on the job no less than in other areas of activity. Changing habits obviously requires recognition of its extent and character and an initiating judgment to *alter* that habitual behavior. If recognized interdependence is ignored, if demands for change are institutionally comprehensive, the intended redirection and enhancement of performance will not appear. As Foster observes, "persons cannot perform in any correlated manner unless they know at least the immediate point of correlation between their own behavior and that of others with whom they are brought into immediate contact. The caption of the principle bespeaks its content" [(1972) 1981, 941]. All productive activity encompasses human interaction and human interdependence. Unless that interdependence is understood, coordination of productive activity is stillborn.

Minimal Dislocation

Ism-ideologists, seemingly without exception, violate this principle of minimal dislocation. Foster argues that social and economic change, if it is to be successful, must be gradual, processual, and selective. To move from one ism model to another ism model is in fact impossible, if the continuity of the economic process is to be sustained. The Communistic revolution in Russia should serve for another century as an example of this inability. Leaders cannot abandon one comprehensive system and impose another comprehensive system as its replacement without invoking comprehensive chaos. Even peaceful transitions, if comprehensive, must also fail because the changes invoked exceed the capacity of a people promptly to recast their behaviors in accord with the unilateral and unexceptional demand. If the proposed structural change is comprehensive; its introduction is necessarily more than minimally dislocative. It cannot succeed, if success is judged by Foster's criterion of "the continuity and instrumental efficiency of the economic process."

* * * * * * * *

A closing comment: It is the argument of this volume that Fagg Foster's contribution to economic inquiry provides fundamental and significant theoretical analyses for comprehension of the economic process and for identification and resolution of pervasive economic problems. Contemporary conditions of underdevelopment, instability, invidious discrimination, ineffectual performance, inequitable distribution and megacorp dominion, among others, merit instrumental inquiry and remedial institutional adjustments. Foster's extension, refinement and application of the institutionalists' approach to inquiry provides pertinent and potent analytical tools with which to address these problems. As is now evident, instrumental *value theory* provides the meaning of, *and* an intellectual strategy for, *economic progress.*

EPILOGUE

In 1985, a few months after Fagg Foster's death, his widow, Gladys, wrote a short paper commenting on "Fagg's Thinking" in the last several years of his life. It is appropriate to conclude this volume by presenting some selected observations from that paper:

> Fagg never deviated from his basic principles about human nature, the theory of logic, the theory of progress, the theory of esthetics, the theory of knowledge, value theory, the nature of [the] scientific process, the nature of economic inquiry, democracy, income analysis, and the integration of all disciplines or areas of inquiry. . . .
>
> He continued to consider the principles of institutional adjustment he had formulated and wondered about the possibility of a fourth principle or the expansion of the third principle. . .[addressed to] energy, capacity and utilization.
>
> He gave considerable attention to the concept of time and thought it both important and difficult. In economics. . .we have to use some concept of time because we are dealing not with simple quantities per se but with quantities over time; but time-period analysis gets us into trouble. The long run is made up of short runs, but each is differently comprised, so how could short runs add up to the long run?. . .Mathematically time can be expressed in differential equations. . .[rather than] difference equations. He regarded the Keynesian model as a system of instantaneous equations using the differential calculus rather than lagged variables and difference equations, and thus [it was] dynamic rather than static. This contrasts with the Marshallian notion of time-period analysis. . . .
>
> He also thought. . .about the concept of entropy. . .[and regarded] its application to economics as generally misconceived. He discounted the notion [that] we are running out of "natural" resources because [they] are determined by the state of technology and thus by the ingenuity of man. . . .
>
> He read biographies of Jefferson [and] thought about Jefferson's theory of capital formation. . .as coming out of the American experience on the frontier and thus at odds with the orthodox idea of investment as dependent on prior saving.
>
> He looked at the environment movement and viewed environmental goals as compatible with economic growth and the advancement of technology. . . .[T]he issue [for] Fagg was. . .[one] of mutual support and integration, rather than tradeoff or "balance."
>
> He. . .thought of inflation as determined not by demand pull or cost push but by a complex of institutional factors, one of the most notable being monopoly power. He saw price in an oligopolistic market structure as more nearly an independent variable, thus agreeing with Gardiner Means's concept of "administered prices."
>
> He thought about employment and income. He looked at productive versus unproductive employment in terms of his theory of value. . .instrumental efficiency. He thought. . .about [and accepted] the Keynesian relationships between consumption and investment but wondered about the

development of concepts other than consumption and investment as alternative ways of analyzing income.

He continued to be optimistic about mankind and civilization.

ENDNOTES

[1] Interestingly, his "letter to the editor" of the *Dallas News* (with Wendell Gordon and Nelson Peach) in 1942, protesting a one-sided public forum attacking the Fair Labor Standards Act, led the Regents of the University of Texas in Austin to refuse to renew his teaching contract.

[2]In 1944, at age 37, Foster volunteered for service in the United States Army and served in the infantry in the Pacific theater until Japan surrendered. He continuously refused battlefield appointments to commissioned rank.

[3]In addition, he was nominated to be a Member of the President's Council of Economic Advisors in the Truman Administration, but was not accepted for that position.

[4]On guaranteed employment, see: Wray, L. Randall. *Government as Employer of Last Resort: Full Employment Without Inflation*. The Jerome Levy Economics Institute, Working Paper No. 213. November 1997. See also, Harvey, Philip. *Securing the Right to Employment.* Princeton: Princeton University Press; Tool, Marc R. "Employment as a Human Right," in Michie, Jonathan and Reati, Angelo, eds. *Employment, Technology and Economic Needs.* Cheltenham UK: Edward Elgar; and publications of the National Jobs for All Coalition , 475 Riverside Dr. Suite 832, New York, NY 10115.

[5]On guaranteed basic income, see Clark, Charles M.A. and Catherine Kavanagh. 1996a. "Basic Income, Inequality, and Unemployment: Rethinking the Linkages between Work and Welfare." *Journal of Economic Issues*. 30:399-406.

REFERENCES

Bush, Paul D. 1986. On the concept of ceremonial encapsulation. *The Review of Institutional Though;* 3: 25-45.

Clark, Charles M.A. and Catherine Kavanagh. 1996a. Basic income, inequality, and unemployment: rethinking the linkages between work and welfare. *Journal of Economic Issues;* 30:399-406.

———. "Inequality in the 1980s: An Institutionalist View." In *Inequality: Radical Institutionalist Views on Race, Gender, Class, and Nation.* William M. Dugger, ed. Westport CT: Greenwood Press.

Ericson, Richard E. 1991. The classical soviet-type economy: nature of the system and implications for reform. *Journal of Economic Perspectives;* 5: Fall.

Foster, J. Fagg. 1950. Lecture Notes. (LN). Comparative Economic Systems.

———. (1960) 1981. Policy implications of increasing growth rates in the more developed countries. *Journal of Economic Issues;* 15: 959-962.

———. (1963) 1981. Environmental control. *Journal of Economic Issues;* 15:1009-12.

———. (1966b) 1981. The reality of the present and the challenge of the future. *Journal of Economic Issues*; 5:963-968.

———. (1975a) . The current structure and future prospects of institutional economics. *Journal of Economic Issues;* 15:943-47.

———. 1975b. The economics of natural resources. 1-5.

———. (n.d.) The lecture method. 1-2.

Hausner, Jerzy. 1998. The state and the post-socialist economic transformation. *Journal of Transforming Economies and Societies(EMERGO);* 5: Autumn, 40-52.

Hutton, Will. 1993. Free marketeers ignore Russia's real needs. *Manchester Guardian Weekly; 4 April.*

Keynes, John Maynard. 1926. *The End of Laissez-Faire.* London: Hogarth Press.

Kregel, J. Matzner, E. & Grabher, G. 1992. *The Market Shock: An AGENDA for the Economic and Social Reconstruction of Central and Eastern Europe.* Vienna: Austrian Academy of Sciences.

Livingston, John C. 1979. *Fair Game? Inequality and Affirmative Action.* San Francisco: W. H. Freeman

Ranson, T. Baldwin. 1986. Planning education for economic progress. *Journal of Economic Issues*; 20:1053-1065.

Sachs, Jeffrey. 1991. Crossing the valley of tears in East European reform. *Challenge Magazine;* 34: September/October.

Tool, Marc R. 1998. "Employment as a Human Right." In Michie, Jonathan and Reati, Angelo, eds. *Employment, Technology and Economic Needs.* Cheltenham UK: Edward Elgar.

U.S. Department of Commerce, Bureau of the Census. *Statistical Abstract of the United States 1999.* Washington, DC: U.S. Government Printing Office.

Wray, L. Randall. 1997. Government as Employer of Last Resort: Full Employment Without Inflation. The Jerome Levy Economics Institute. Working Paper No. 213.

———. 1998. *Understanding Modern Money.* Cheltenham: Edward Elgar.

SOURCES

The Papers of J. Fagg Foster, 1937-1976

Selected Graduate Papers: University of Texas, 1937-1946

1937a. Fred Henderson's economic theory. Mimeographed, 1-28.
1937b. Some socialistic aspects of medieval social economics. Mimeographed, 1-13.
1939a. Institutional aspects of Adam Smith's economic considerations. Mimeographed, 1-25.
1939b. Agriculture as a factor in the economic history of Europe. Mimeographed, 1-42.
1941a. Wage movements as institutional adjustments. Mimeographed, 1-88.
(1941b) 1981. The theory of institutional adjustment: introduction. *Journal of Economic Issues;* 15:923-28.
(1942a) 1981. John Dewey and economic value. *Journal of Economic Issues;* 15:871-97.
(1942b) 1981. The approach to land-use planning in a changing technology. *Journal of Economic Issues;* 15:985-1007.
1942c Effect of the frontier on the American labor movement. Manuscript, 1-54; typescript 1996, 1-35.
1943. Uncertain objectivity, magic and logic. Mimeographed, 1-6.
1944. Public housing and the level of employment. Mimeographed, 1-6.
1946. Theoretical Foundations of Government Ownership in a Capitalist Economy. Ph.D. diss., University of Texas, Typescript, 1-188. (In Archives of the University of Texas, Austin)

University of Denver 1946-1976

(1946) 1981. The institutionalist theory of government ownership. *Journal of Economic Issues;* 15:915-22.
(1947) 1981. Syllabus for problems of modern society: the theory of institutional adjustment. *Journal of Economic Issues;* 15:929-35.
1948a. Value and its determinants. Course lectures. (Taped by Harry Brown; transcribed by Gladys Foster. Computer printout; bound. 1-382).
1948b. The character of the process and the specific identification of the theory of value. Typescript, 1-4.
1948c. Prospectus of the doctoral program in social science at University of Denver. Mimeographed, 1-5.
1948d Official policy of the University of Denver concerning academic freedom. Mimeographed, 1-2.
(1949a) 1981. The relation between the theory of value and economic analysis. *Journal of Economic Issues;* 15:899-905.
(1949b) 1981. The United States, Russia, and democracy. A paper presented at the Great Issues Seminar, University of Denver. *Journal of Economic Issues;* 15:975-80.

1951b. Loyalty oaths in higher education. A paper presented at meetings of the Colorado-Wyoming Academy of Science. Typescript, 1-5.

(1951c, 1966) 1981. Freedom and license in higher education. *Alumna*, Mercy College of Detroit 4 (1): 8-9. Republished in *Journal of Economic Issues;* 15:969-73.

(1960) 1981. Policy implications of increasing growth rates in the more developed economies. A paper presented at meetings of the Rocky Mountain Social Science Association. *Journal of Economic Issues;* 15:959-62.

1962b. Review of *Wealth and Power in America* by Gabriel Kolko. New York: Frederick A. Praeger. 1962. *Monthly Labor Review*; Oct.

(1963a) 1981. Environment control. A paper presented at a faculty seminar, University of Denver. *Journal of Economic Issues;* 15:1009-12.

(1966a, 1968) 1981. Understandings and misunderstandings of Keynesian economics. A paper presented at meetings of the Association for Evolutionary Economics. *Revista Internazionale di Scienze e Commerciali;* anno XV, (Diciembre) N.12:1234-44. Republished in *Journal of Economic Issues;* 15:949-57.

(1966b) 1981. The reality of the present and the challenge of the future. *Journal of Economic Issues;* 15:963-68.

(1969) 1981. Economics. (Written for *Experience in Being* by Bernice Marshall, but not used.) *Journal of Economic Issue;* 15:857-69.

(1972) 1981. The fundamental principles of economics. A paper presented at meetings of the Rocky Mountain Social Science Association. *Journal of Economic Issues;* 15:937-42.

(1975a) 1981. The current structure and future prospects of institutional economics. A paper presented at meetings of the Rocky Mountain Social Science Association. *Journal of Economic Issues;* 15:943-47.

1975b. The economics of natural resources. A paper presented at Western State College of Colorado, Gunnison. Mimeographed, 1-5.

[n.d.] 1981. The American economy. *Journal of Economic Issues;* 15:981- 84.

[n.d.] 1981. The effect of technology on institutions. *Journal of Economic Issues;* 15:907-13.

1991. Gladys Foster, ed. J. Fagg Foster on the equational theory of justice. *Journal of Economic Issues;* 25:1155-60.

[n.d.] Adult education. Mimeographed, 1-2.

[n.d.] Fatalism.Mimeographed, 1-3.

[n.d.] Free will. Mimeographed, 1-4

[n.d.] Industrialization and the stabilization of population. Mimeographed, 1-4.

[n.d.] The lecture method. Typescript, 1-2.

[n.d.] Monopoly, employment and inflation. Mimeographed, 1-5.

[n.d.] Philosophy and science. Mimeographed, 1-2.

[n.d.] Problem solving within the community and between communities. Mimeographed, 1-5.

[n.d.] Robinson Crusoe example. Mimeographed, 1-2

Lecture Notes

from Courses Taught at University of Denver

by J. Fagg Foster

Note Takers :	Date	Course Title	Form/Length
Burmeister, Daniel	1950?	Neoclassical EconomicTheory,	Typescript, 1-21.
Foster, Gladys	1947.	Transportation.	Typescript: 1-17.
Foster, J. Fagg	1948.	Value and Its Determinants.	Computer print: 1-382 (Audio tapes of Harry Brown; transcribed by Gladys Foster)
Foster, Gladys	1948.	History of Econ. Thought.	Typescript: 1-48.
Foster, Gladys	1949.	Comparative Econ. Systems.	Typescript: 1-49; Computer print: 1-158
Foster, Gladys	1969.	Comparative Econ. Theories.	Comp. print: 1-14.
Powers, Kenneth (& JFF notes)	1974.	American Contributions to EconomicThought	Typescript: 1-10.
Snyder, Kristin	1968.	History of Economic Thought.;	Typescript:1- 19.
Snyder, Kristin	1968.	Business Cycles.	Manuscript: 1-44.
Tool, Marc R.	1949.	Business Cycles.	Typescript: 1-39.
Tool, Marc R.	1950.	Value and Its Determinants.	Typescript: 1-17.
Tool, Marc R.	1951.	Contemporary Economic Theory.	Typescript:1-42.

SOURCES

Contributions of J.Fagg Foster's Students

Paul D. Bush

Bush, Paul D. 1957. The Concept of Balance in the Theory of Collective Bargaining. Master's thesis. University of Denver. Supervised by J. Fagg Foster.

———. 1964. Marginalism and Institutionalism in Labor Economics. Doctoral dissertation, Claremont Graduate School.

———. 1968. The normative implications of positive analysis. A paper presented at meetings of the Western Economics Association, Corvallis, Oregon.

———. 1969. The variety of marginalist methodologies: a critical approach. A paper presented at meetings of the Western Economics Association. Long Beach, California.

———. 1977. A Veblen-Ayres model of institutional change. A paper presented at meetings of the Western Economics Association. Anaheim, California.

———. 1980. Analyzing the energy problem: pecuniary logic versus institutional analysis. A paper presented at meetings of the Western Social Science Association/Association for Institutional Thought, Albuquerque, New Mexico.

———. 1981a. Radical individualism vs. institutionalism I. *The American Journal of Economics and Sociology;* 40:139-48.

———. 1981b. Radical individualism vs. institutionalism II. *The American Journal of Economics and Sociology;* 40:287-98.

———. 1981-2. The normative implications of institutional analysis. *Economic Forum;* 12:9-29.

———. 1983. An exploration of the structural characteristics of a Veblen-Ayres-Foster defined institutional domain. *Journal of Economic Issues;* 17:35-66.

———. 1986. On the concept of ceremonial encapsulation. *Review of Institutional Thought;* 3:25-45.

———.1987. The theory of institutional change. *Journal of Economic Issues;* 21:1075-116. Republished in Marc R. Tool., ed. 1988. *Evolutionary Economics I: Foundations of Institutional Thought.* Armonk, N.Y.: M.E. Sharpe. Republished in Geoffrey M. Hodgson, ed. 1993. *The Economics of Institutions*. Aldershot: Edward Elgar.

———. 1989. The concept of "progressive" institutional change and its implications for economic policy formation. *Journal of Economic Issues;* 23:455-64.

———. 1991a. Reflections on the 25th Anniversary of AFEE: current philosophical and methodological issues in institutional economics. *Journal of Economic Issues*; 25:321-46.

———. 1991b. The contemporary American institutionalist contribution to the theory of social change. A paper presented at the Fourth Colloquium of the Charles Gide Association for the Study of Economic Thought, University of Aix-Marseilles. September.

———. 1993. "The Methodology of Institutional Economics: a Pragmatic Instrumentalist Perspective." In Marc R. Tool, ed. 1993. *Institutional Economics: Theory, Method, Policy.* Boston: Kluwer Academic Publishers.
———. 1994a. The pragmatic instrumentalist perspective on the theory of institutional change. *Journal of Economic Issues;* 27:647-57.
———. 1994b. "The Theory of Social Change." In Geoffrey M. Hodgson, Warren J. Samuels, and Marc R. Tool eds. *The Elgar Companion to Institutional and Evolutionary Economics, L-Z.* Aldershot: Edward Elgar.
———. 1995. "Marc R. Tool's Contributions to Institutional Economics." In Charles M.A. Clark, ed. *Institutional Economics and the Theory of Social Value: Essays in Honor of Marc R. Tool.* Boston: Kluwer Academic Publishers.
———. 1996. First and second order complexity in American institutional economics: an elaboration on Delorme's thesis. A paper presented at meetings of the European Association for Evolutionary Political Economy, Antwerp.
———. 1999. "Ceremonial Encapsulation," "Institutional Change and Adjustment," "Minimal Dislocation," Neoinstitutionalism," "Pragmatism," "Recognized Interdependence." In Phillip Anthony O'Hara, ed. *Encyclopedia of Political Economy,* I A-K & II L-Z. London: Routledge.
———. with Marc R. Tool. (forthcoming). "The Evolutionary Principles of American Neoinstitutional Economics." In Kurt Dopfer, ed. *The Evolutionary Principles of Economics.* Boston: Kluwer Academic Publishers.
———. (forthcoming). Veblen's "Olympian Detachment" reconsidered. *History of Economic Ideas.*

Gladys Foster

Foster, Gladys. 1949a. An inquiry into the principle of the multiplier and the principle of acceleration.
———. 1949b. The M-point and the Theory of Real Income. Masters thesis; University of Denver. Supervised by J. Fagg Foster.
———. 1950. Some institutional aspects of Keynesian economics. Typescript:1-57.
———. 1981a. Keynes and some other macro theorists: a comparison. Typescript 1-20.
———. 1981b. On Leijonhufvud's interpretation of Keynes. Typescript 1-13.
———. 1983. The "new" Keynesians and the "post" Keynesians compared with Friedman and the synsthesis. Typescript 1-13.
———. 1986. The Endogeneity of Money and Keynes' General Theory. Doctoral dissertation, University of Colorado, Boulder.
———. 1986. The endogeneity of money and Keynes's General Theory. *Journal of Economic Issues;* 20:953-68.
———. 1987a. Financing investment. *Journal of Economic Issues;* 21:101-12.
———. 1987b. Keynes and Institutionalism. Typescript 1-3.
———. and T. Baldwin Ranson. 1987c. Thorstein Veblen on money and production. *Economies et Societes;* Serie MP, 4:221-28.
———.1990. Keynes and Kalecki on saving and profit *Journal of Economic Issues;* 24:415-22.

———. 1991a. The compatibility of Keynes's ideas with institutional philosophy. *Journal of Economic Issues;* 25:561-68.

———. 1991b. Cultural relativism and the theory of value. *The American Journal of Economics and Sociology;* 50:257-68.

———. 1991c. Administered price inflation. *Economies et Societes;* Serie MP, 8:155-70.

———. ed.1991d. J. Fagg Foster on the equational theory of justice. *Journal of Economic Issues;* 25:1155-60.

———. 1994a. The obsession with deficits in the U.S. in the 1990s. *Economies et Societes;* Serie MP, 9:189-206.

———. 1994b. "Equality and the Women's Movement." In Janice Peterson and Doug Brown, eds. *The Economic Status of Women under Capitalism.* Aldershot: Edward Elgar.

———. 1995. "Institutionalism and Value Theory: an Identity Crisis?" In Charles M. A. Clark, ed. *Institutional Economics and the Theory of Social Value: Essays in Honor of Marc R. Tool.* Boston: Kluwer Academic Publishers.

———. 1996. Institutional economics, Keynes's theories, and finance. *Economies et Societes*; Serie MP, 10:211-28.

———. 1998. "Veblen and the "Woman Question" in the Twenty-First Century." In Doug Brown, ed. *Thorstein Veblen in the Twenty-First Century.* Cheltenham: Edward Elgar.

Louis J. Junker

Junker, Louis J. 1967a. Capital accumulation, savings centered theory and economic development. *Journal of Economic Issues;* 1:25-43.

———. 1967b. The meaning of the twentieth century: Boulding versus the reviewers. *Journal of Economic Issues;* 1:349-54.

———. 1968. Theorectical foundations of neo-institutionalism. *The American Journal of Economics and Sociology;* 27:197-213.

———. 1979. Genuine or spurious institutionalism? Veblen and Ayres seen from neo-classical perspective raises the question. *The American Journal of Economics and Sociology;* 38:207-223.

———. 1981. Instrumentalism, the principle of continuity and the life process. *The American Journal of Economics and Sociology;* 40: 381-400.

———. 1982. The ceremonial-instrumental dichotomy in institutional analysis: the nature, scope and radical implications of the conflicting systems. *The American Journal of Economics and Sociology;* 41: 141-50.

———. 1983. Institutionalism and the criteria of development. *The Economic Forum;* 14 (Summer):27-56.

———. 1983. The conflict between the scientific-technological process and malignant ceremonialism. *The American Journal of Economics and Sociology;* 42:341-52.

Hamilton, David, F. Gregory Hayden, James I. Sturgeon, William T. Waller, Jr., Marc R. Tool. 1986. Louis J. Junker Memorial Session: The contributions of Louis Junker to theoretical institutional economics. *Review of Institutional Thought;* 3:49-68.

Edythe S. Miller

Miller, Edythe S. 1972. Veblen and women's lib: a parallel. *Journal of Economic Issues;* 6:75-86.

———. 1975a. On the economics of poverty and the poverty of economics. *Rocky Mountain Social Science Journal;* 12:11-19.

———. and Lewis E. Hill. 1975b. The political economy of women's liberation: an institutional interpretation. *Business and Economic Dimensions;* 11:1-7; 11:21-22.

———. 1978. Institutional economics: philosophy, methodology and theory. *The Social Science Journal;* 15:13-25. Republished in Warren J. Samuels, ed. 1989. *Institutional Economics, II.,* Aldershot: Edward Elgar.

———. 1978. Rate structure reform: A review of the current debate. *Journal of Economic Issues;* 12:609-26.

———. 1981. A perspective on load forcasting. *Problems of Electric Utility Load Forecasting: Proceedings* (March).

———. 1982. The advance of deregulation in the utility industry. *Proceedings,* Conference on Public Utility Valuation and the Rate-making Process. Ames: Iowa State University, 14-22.

———. 1983. "Is there a Meaningful Role for Economic Regulation in a Supply-side World?" In Harry M. Trebing, ed. *Adjusting to Regulatory Pricing, and Marketing Realities.* East Lansing: Michigan State University, Institute of Public Utilities, 3-12.

———. 1985. Controlling power in the social economy: the regulatory approach. *Review of Social Economy;* 43:129-39.

———. 1986. Ideology, jurisdiction, and deregulation of the telephone network. *Public Utilities Fortnightly;* 118, No.7:14-18.

———. 1987. "FCC Preemption, State Telecommuications Deregulation and the Public Interest." In Patrick C. Mann and Harry M. Trebing, eds. *Public Utility Regulation in an Environment of Change.* East Lansing: Michigan State University, Institute of Public Utilities.

———. 1988. "Potential Abuses in the Application of Social Contract and Incentive Regulation." In Harry M. Trebing, ed. *Alternatives to Traditional Regulation: Options for Reform,* East Lansing: Michigan State University, Institute of Public Utilities, 29-44.

———. 1989. Economics for what?: economic folklore and social realities. *Journal of Economic Issues;* 23:339-56.

———. *1990a.* On public and private control in a "reasonable society." *Journal of Economic Issues; 24:239-48.*

———. 1990b. Economic efficiency, the economics profession and the "affected-with-a-public-interest" concept. *Journal of Economic Issues;* 24:719-32.

———. 1991. Of economic paradigms, puzzles, problems and policies. *Journal of Economic Issues;* 25:993-1004.

———. 1992. The economics of progress. *Journal of Economic Issues;* 26:115-24.

———. 1993a. Some market structure and regulatory implications of the brave new world of telecommunications. *Journal of Economic Issues;* 27:19-39.

———. 1993b. "A Consideration of Contracting and Competitive Bidding as Alternatives to Direct Economic Regulation in Imperfect Markets." In Harry M. Trebing and Michelle F. Wilsey, eds. *Utilities Policy;* (October):323-32.

———. 1993c. The economic imagination and public policy: orthodoxy discovers the corporation. *Journal of Economic Issues;* 27:1041-58.
———. 1994a. "Foster, J. Fagg," "Regulation, Theory of Economic," "Harry M. Trebing." In Geoffrey M. Hodgson, Warren J. Samuels and Marc R. Tool, eds. *The Elgar Companion to Institutional and Evolutionary Economics, A-K & L-Z.* Aldershot: Edward Elgar.
———. 1994b. Economic regulation and the social contract: an appraisal of recent developments in the social control of telecommunications. *Journal of Economic Issues;* 28:799-818.
———. 1995a. Is the public utility concept obsolete? *Land Economics;* 71:273-85.
———. 1995b. "The Instrumental Efficiency of Social Value Theory." In Charles M.A. Clark, ed. *Institutional Economics and the Theory of Social Value: Essays in Honor of Marc R. Tool.* Boston: Kluwer Academic Publishers.
———. and Philip A. Klein. 1996. Concepts of value, efficiency, and democracy in institutional economics. *Journal of Economic Issues;* 30:267-77.
———. 1996a. "Seen Through a Glass Darkly: Competing Views of Equality and Inequality in Economic Thought." In William M. Dugger, ed. *Inequality: Radical Institutionalist Views on Race, Gender,Class, and Nation..* Westport: Greenwood Press.
———. 1996b. Economic regulation and new technology in the telecommunications industry. *Journal of Economic Issues;* 30:719-35.
———. 1997. "The Interdependence of Theory and Practice." Presidential Address, Association for Institutional Thought, Albuquerque, April. In Sasan Fayazmanesh and Marc R. Tool eds. 1998. *Institutional Theory and Applications: Essays in Honor of Paul Dale Bush.* Cheltenham: Edward Elgar.
———. 1998a. "Institutional Economics and Eternal Verities." In Sasan Fayazmanesh and Marc R. Tool, eds. *Institutionalist Method and Value: Essays in Honor of Paul Dale Bush.* Cheltenham: Edward Elgar.
———. 1998b. "Veblen and Commons and the Concept of Community." In Warren J. Samuels, ed., *The Founding of Institutional Economics: The Leisure Class and Sovereignty.* London and New York: Routledge.
———. and Warren J. Samuels, eds. (forthcoming). *The Institutionalist Approach to Public Utility Regulation: Essays in Honor of Harry S.Trebing.* East Lansing: Michigan State University Press.
———. (forthcoming). "Introduction" and "Implications for the Social Control of Business of Competing Economic Visions." In Edyth Miller and Warren Samuels. eds. *The Institutionalist Approach to Public Utility Regulation.* East Lansing : Michigan State University Press.

T. Baldwin Ranson

Ranson, T., Baldwin. 1977. The alternative paths to theory of Clark and Ayres. *Journal of Economic Issues;* 11:461-67.
———. The limits to growth: is Ayres's position unwarranted? *Journal of Economic Issues;* 13:655-67.

———. 1980. Rival economic epistemologies: the logics of Marx, Marshall, and Keynes. *Journal of Economic Issues;* 14:77-98.
———. 1981a. AFEE or AFIT: which represents institutional economics? *Journal of Economic Issues;* 15: 521-29.
———. ed. 1981b. The papers of J. Fagg Foster. *Journal of Economic Issues;* 15:853-1012.
———. 1983a. The unrecognized revolution in the theory of capital formation. *Journal of Economic Issues;* 17:901-13.
———. 1983b. The contribution of J. Fagg Foster to institutional economics. A paper presented at meetings of Southwestern Economics Association, March, Houston, Texas.
———. and Stuart James, Kristin Paulson, Larry Senesh, & Marc R. Tool. 1985a. Memorial to John Fagg Foster, 1907-1985, by former students and colleagues. Evans Chapel, University of Denver. 18 July.1985. Typescripts.
———. 1985b. Government deficits and economic stability: evaluating alternative theories. *Economies et Societies;* Serie MP 2, 197-207.
———. 1986. Planning education for economic development. *Journal of Economic Issue;* 20:1053-65.
———. 1987. The institutionalist theory of capital formation. *Journal of Economic Issues;* 21:1265-78. Republished in Marc R. Tool, ed. 1988. *Evolutionary Economics: Foundations of Institutional Thought I.* Armonk, N.Y.: M.E. Sharpe.
———. 1988a. The contribution of rural education to economic development in China, Mexico, Japan, and the United States. *Comparative Education Review;* 32:213-225.
———. 1988b. Education for modernization: meritocratic myths in China, Mexico, the United States and Japan. *Journal of Economi Issues;* 22:747-62.

Marc R. Tool

Tool, Marc R. 1953. The Philosophy of Neoinstitutionalism: Veblen, Dewey, Ayres. Ph.D. diss., University of Colorado, Boulder.
———. 1978. Constructs of value, freedom, and equality in institutional economics. *Social Science Journal;* 15:27-38.
———. [1979, 1985] 2000. *The Discretionary Economy: A Normative Theory of Political Economy.* Piscataway NJ: Transactions Press
———. 1981. The compulsive shift to institutional analysis. *Journal of Economic Issue*; 15:569-92.
———. ed. 1984. *An Institutional Guide to Economics and Public Policy. Armonk,* N.Y.: M.E. Sharpe.
———. 1986. *Essays in Social Value Theory.* Armonk, N.Y.: M.E. Sharpe.
———. ed. 1988. *Evolutionary Economics I: Foundations of Institutional Thought.* Armonk, N.Y.: M.E. Sharpe.
———. ed. 1988. *Evolutionary Economics II: Institutional Theory and Policy.* Armonk, N.Y.: M.E. Sharpe.
——— and Warren J. Samuels, eds. 1989a. *The Methodology of Economic Thought.* Second edition. New Brunswick: Transaction Publishers.

——— and Warren J. Samuels, eds. 1989b. *The Economy as a System of Power.* Second edition. New Brunswick: Transaction Publishers.

——— and Warren J. Samuels, eds. 1989c. *State, Society and Corporate Power.* Second edition. New Brunswick: Transaction Publishers.

———. 1989. An institutionalist legacy. Remarks upon the receipt of the AFEE Veblen-Commons Award. *Journal of Economic Issues;* 23:327-38.

———. (1992).(2nd ed. forthcoming)."Marc R. Tool (born 1921)." In Philip Arestis and Malcolm Sawyer, eds. *A Biographical Dictionary of Dissenting Economists.* Aldershot: Edward Elgar.

———. ed. 1993a. *Institutional Economics: Theory, Method, Policy.* Dordrecht: Kluwer Academic Publishers.

———. 1993b. "The Theory of Instrumental Value: Extensions, Clarifications." In Marc R. Tool, ed. *Institutional Economics: Theory, Method, Policy.* Dordrecht: Kluwer Academic Publishers.

———. with Geoffrey M. Hodgson and Warren J. Samuels, eds. 1994. *The Elgar Companion to Institutional and Evolutionary Economics, Vols. A-K & L-Z.* Aldershot: Edward Elgar.

———. 1994. "Clarence E. Ayres." "John Dewey." "Instrumental value theory." In Geoffrey M. Hodgson, Warren J. Samuels, and Marc R. Tool, eds. *The Elgar Companion to Institutional and Evolutionary Economics. A-K.* Aldershot: Edward Elgar.

———. 1995. *Pricing, Valuation and Systems.* Aldershot: Edward Elgar.

———. 1996a. "Choose Equality." In William M. Dugger, ed. *Inequality: Radical Institutionalist Views on Race, Gender, Class, and Nation.* New York: Greenwood Press.

———. 1997. "Employment as a Human Right." In Jonathan Mitchie and Angelo Reati, eds. *Employment, Unemployment and Public Policy.* Cheltenham: Edward Elgar.

———. 1998a. "A Neoinstitutional Theory of Social Change in Veblen's Theory of the Leisure Class." In Warren J. Samuels, ed. *The Founding of Institutional Economics: The Leisure Class and Sovereignty.* London: Routledge.

———. 1998b. with Philip Anthony O'Hara. "The Contribution of Paul D. Bush to Academic Freedom and Institutional Economics." In Sasan Fayazmanesh and Marc R. Tool eds. *Institutionalist Method and Value: Essays in Honor of Paul Dale Bush..* Cheltenham: Edward Elgar.

———. 1998c. "Instrumental Inquiry and Democratic Governance." In Sasan Fayazmanesh and Marc R. Tool, eds. *Institutionalist Theory and Applications: Essays in Honor of Paul D. Bush..* Cheltenham: Edward Elgar.

———. 1998d. with Sasan Fayazmanesh, eds. *Institutionalist Method and Value: Essays in Honor of Paul Dale Bush..* Cheltenham: Edward Elgar.

———. 1998e. with Sasan Fayazmanesh, eds. *Institutionalist Theory and Applications: Essays in Honor of Paul Dale Bush..* Cheltenham: Edward Elgar.

———. 1999a. "Instrumental Value Theory." In Phillip Anthony O'Hara, ed. *Encyclopedia of Political Economy.* I, A-K. London: Routledge.

———. 1999b. "TOOL Marc R." In Mark Blaug, ed. *Who's Who in Economics: A Biographical Dictionary of Major Economists,* 1776-1999. 3rd Ed. Cheltenham: Edward Elgar.

William D. William

Williams, William D. 1972. The Mathematics of Veblenian Economics. Ph.D. diss. Supervised by J. Fagg Foster. The Union Graduate School.

INDEX

A

absolutism, 39
adjustments, institutional. *see* institutional adjustments
aggregate growth rates, 187–188
agreed compromise, principle of (Commons), 122–123
Alexander, Sidney, 45
American experience, 105–127
  attributes of, 106–115
  contributors to institutional thought, 116–127
  frontier in, 107–111
  institutional inventions and innovations in, 112–115
  problem solving in, 111–112
  stimuli for change in, 106–107
Antonino, Saint, 41
Aquinas, St. Thomas, 41, 132
Aristotle, 41
authority, power compared, 102
Axiomatic-Choice theorists, 45
Ayres, Clarence E., 72–75, 120–122, 163, 169
  determinants of economic progress, 120–121
  impediments to economic progress, 120–121
  theory of economic development, 121–122

B

Bush, Paul Dale, 12, 29, 115

C

Canonists, 41
capitalism, 146–152
  fundamental inadequacies of, 150–152
  institutional structure of, 148–149
  invidious criteria employed by, 149–150
  theoretical underpinnings of, 147
choices, 25, 83
Clark, John Maurice, 125–126
Classicists, 42–44
coherence theory of truth, 30
Commons, John R., 122–124
correspondence theory of truth, 30

D

deductive processes of inquiry, 23–24
democracies
  institutional adjustments and, 100–103
  ism-ideology and, 156–157
  noninvidious participation in, 102–103
  rule making in, 100–101
democratic implementation, principle of, 100–103
determinants of economic progress, 120–121
Dewey, John, 75–77, 118–120
  characterizations of instrumental logic by, 20–21
  on data in social inquiry, 17–18
  on equational justice, 58
  on hypotheses, 23
  on processes of inquiry, 23–24
Dillard, Dudley, 171
discrimination, reduction in, 202–204
dislocation, principle of minimal. *see* minimal dislocation, principle of

E

economic development, theory of (Ayres), 121–122
economic growth and macro-management, 187–190
economic inquiry, 66
economic problems, 66–67, 83–84
economic transitions, 204–209
  existing structure, 205–206
  institutional adjustments for, 206–208
  instrumental functions of, 204–205
  loci of discretion, 205
  problems of impairment, 206
Emerson, Ralph Waldo, 117
employment, guaranteed, 199–202
environmental control, 191–192
equational justice, utility value and, 57–59
Equilibrium theorists, 46

F

Fabian socialism, 141–146
  fundamental inadequacies of, 145–146
  institutional structure of, 143–144
  theoretical underpinnings of, 142–143
fascism, 152–155
  fundamental inadequacies of, 155
  institutional structure of, 154
  invidious criteria employed by, 155
  theoretical underpinnings of, 153–154
feudalism, 131–134
  fundamental inadequacies of, 133–134
  institutional structure of, 132–133
  invidious criteria employed by, 133
  theoretical underpinnings of, 132
financial feasibility of options, 190
Foster, Gladys, 210–211
Foster, J. Fagg
  American Contribution to Economic Thought course, 52, 70
  contributions of, 2–3
  employment history of, 185
  institutional adjustment theory of, 87–103
  1966 Report of the National Commission on Technology, Automation, and Economic Progress, 190
  Syllabus on "Institutional Adjustment," 92
  Theoretical Foundations of Government Ownership in a Capitalism Economy, 98, 152, 162
  value theory of, 63–84
  on Veblen's critique of orthodoxy, 52–55
  works by, 4
Fourier, Charles, 134, 135, 136
Franklin, Benjamin, 117
freedom, license compared, 101
frontier, American, 107–111

G

Galbraith, John Kenneth, 114
The General Theory of Employment, Interest and Money, 161, 165, 167, 172
George, Henry, 141, 142
G.I. Bill, 115
government ownership, 98–100
Greeks scholars, 41
growth rates, aggregate, 187–188
guaranteed employment, 199–202

H

habits, 25, 82–83
Hausner, Jerzy, 206–207
health care, 198
hedonism, 49, 117
Homan, P. T., 35
hypotheses, role of, 22–23

I

ideologies. *see* ism-ideologies
impediments to economic progress, 120–121
income inequality. *see* poverty
Indifference Demand theorists, 45
inductive processes of inquiry, 23–24
inquiry. *see* scientific inquiry, theory of; social inquiry
institutional adjustment, theory of, 87–103
  applications for, 95–100
  ism-ideology and, 130
  principles of (*see* principles of institutional adjustment)
  setting for, 88–90
  value theory and, 87–88
institutional adjustments, 26, 67
  dynamic factors prompting, 168–170
  economic solutions as, 178
  for economic transitions, 206–208
institutional economics, 111
  dynamic factors in, 168–170
  interconnectedness in, 12, 14
  philosophic foundations of, 166–168
  philosophy and, 13
  questions asked in, 165–166
  valuation theory and, 79–80
institutionalists
  American, 116–127
  Keynes as, 162, 174
institutional structures, 68
  in America, 106, 107, 112–115
  capitalism, 148–149
  Fabian socialism, 143–144
  fascism, 154
  feudalism, 132–133
  Marxism, 139–140
  in transitions, 205–206
  utopian socialism, 136–137
instrumental efficiency, 77–80
  condition *versus* direction, 78–79
  measurement, 79–80
  value in process, 77–78
instrumental logic, 19–21
instrumental policy. *see* public policy
instrumental value theory, 58, 63–84
  attributes of, 80–82

economic analysis and, 66–68
implications, 82–84
institutional adjustment and, 87–88
Keynes and, 171–174
locus, 68–69
sources, 69–77
substance, 77–82
interdependence, principle of recognized. *see* recognized interdependence, principle of
investment, autonomous, 189–190
ism-ideologies, 129–158
capitalism, 146–152
and democracy, 156–157
economic transitions and, 204–209
Fabian socialism, 141–146
fascism, 152–155
feudalism, 131–134
Marxism, 58, 138–141
utopian socialism, 134–138

J
Jefferson, Thomas, 116

K
Kaplan, Abraham, 65
Keynes, John Maynard, 3, 161, 186. *see also* Keynesian theory
contributions by, 161–164
The General Theory of Employment, Interest and Money, 161, 165, 166, 167, 172
as instrumentalist, 174
Keynesian theory
aggregate income transfers, 179–180
dynamic factors in, 168–170
economic activity level in, 179
financial possibility and technical feasibility, 180–181
general applicability of, 177
hoarding in, 176
institutional adjustments and, 168–170, 178
institutionalism and, 165–170
investment in, 175, 176–177
non-invidiousness of, 173–174
normativism of, 171–173
philosophic foundations for, 166–168
questions asked by, 165–166
saving in, 175, 176–177
value theory, 171–174
knowledge
character of, 27–28
private (Knowledge 2), 26, 28
warranted (Knowledge 1), 26, 27–28, 168–169

L
labor-cost theory, 43
land frontier, 107–111
land use planning, 95–98
license, freedom compared, 101
logic of scientific inquiry, 19–23
foundations of, 19
hypotheses role in, 22–23
instrumental logic, 19–21
pure logic, 21–22

M
macro-management and economic growth, 187–190
Malinowski, Bronislaw, 9
Malthus, Thomas Robert, 43
Marx, Karl, 138
Marxism, 58, 138–141
fundamental inadequacies of, 140–141
institutional structure of, 139–140
invidious criteria employed by, 140
theoretical underpinnings of, 138–139
Melton, Rosser B., 48
Mercantilists, 42
minimal dislocation, principle of, 94–95
for economic transitions, 209
for guaranteed employment, 202
for invidious discrimination, 204
for land use planning, 97–98
minimum wage, 197–198
Mitchell, Broadus, 114
Mitchell, Wesley Clair, 124–125
mores principle, utility value and, 55–57

N
neoclassical economics, 2, 12–13
deductivistic a priorism of, 19
equational justice theory, 57–59
principles of economics, 91
saving in, 169–170
scope of economics in, 192
utility value in, 44–46
value analysis and, 37–38
Veblen critique of, 48–52, 117

New Deal, 113–114
New Lanark, 135, 136
nihilism, 38–39
normativism, 13
  of Keynes, 171–173
  of Veblen, 71

O

oligopolistic pricing, 188–189
Owen, Robert, 134, 135–137
ownership, government, 98–100

P

Paretian Optimum theorists, 45
participation in government, 102–103
Phalanstère, 135
philosophy and science, 12–16
physical science and science, 16–19
Physiocrats, 42
policy, public. *see* public policy
positivism, 13, 39, 59
poverty, 194–204
  extent of, 197
  guaranteed employment to reduce, 199–202
  instrumental functions in, 194–195
  invidious discrimination reduced for, 202–204
  loci of discretion, 195–196
  problematic distributional conditions, 196–198
power, authority compared, 102
price, 35, 91
price control, World War II, 114
pricing, oligopolistic, 188–189
principle of agreed compromise (Commons), 122–123
principles of institutional adjustment
  character of, 90–92
  democratic implementation, 100–103
  minimal dislocation, 94–95, 97–98, 202, 204, 209
  recognized interdependence, 93–94, 97, 98, 202, 203–204, 208–209
  technological determination, 92–93, 96, 98, 201–202, 203, 208
private knowledge, 26, 28
Public Choice theorists, 45–46
public policy, 185–211
  for economic transitions and ideologies, 204–209
  environmental policy constructs, 191–193
  for income inequality and poverty, 194–204
  macro-management and economic growth, 187–190
public utilities, 112–113
pure logic, 21–22
purposiveness, 65, 115, 163

R

Ranson, T. Baldwin, 4, 75, 153, 168, 170, 195
rational expectations theory, 2
recognized interdependence, principle of, 93–94
  for economic transitions, 208–209
  for guaranteed employment, 202
  for invidious discrimination, 203–204
  for land use planning, 97, 98
relativism, 40
resource management, 192–193
Ricardo, David, 43
Rice, Philip Blair, 60
Robbins, Lord Lionel, 60
Robinson, Joan, 52

S

Sachs, Jeffrey, 206
Say, Jean Baptiste, 43
science
  emergence of, 9–11
  nature of scientific truth, 26–31
  non-science and, 11–12
  philosophy and, 12–16
  physical science and, 16–19
scientific inquiry, theory of, 7–31
  logic of, 19–23
  nonscientific thought and, 11–12
  object of social inquiry, 24–26
  processes of, 23–24
  truth in, 26–31
  value analysis and, 64
Smith, Adam, 42–43, 116
social functions, 25, 68–69
social inquiry
  object of, 24–26
  physical science compared, 17
  purpose of, 65
  valuation in, 80
  value theory and, 36
social institutions, 25, 68

socialism
  Fabian, 141–146
  utopian, 134–138
social policy. *see* public policy
social process, 68–69
social value, theory of, 76
Sumner, William Graham, 55

T
tautology, 51–52, 117
taxonomy, 50–51, 117
technological determination, principle of, 92–93
  for economic transitions, 208
  for guaranteed employment, 201–202
  for invidious discrimination, 203
  for land use planning, 96, 98
teleology, 50, 117
Theoretical Foundations of Government Ownership in a Capitalism Economy, 98, 152, 162
theory of. *see* specific theory
The Place of Science in Modern Civilization, 48, 49, 53, 69
Thoreau, Henry David, 117
Tool, Marc R., 70–71, 171, 174, 201
transactions (Commons), 123
transitions, economic, 204–209
Trebing, Harry, 112–113
truth, scientific, 26–31
  character of knowledge, 27–28
  claims about, 29
  theories of, 30–31

U
unemployment, 196–197
utilities, public, 112–113
utility, 79
  as criterion of value, 40–46
  definition of, 35
  measurement of, 168
utility value theory, 35–60
  avoidance of value analysis, 36–38
  character of, 40
  critique of, 46–60
  in economic analysis, 36
  equational justice and, 57–59
  evasion of value analysis, 38–40
  historical development of, 41–44
  inadequacies of, 46–48
  mores principle and, 55–57
  neoclassical view of, 44–46
  normative-positive distinction and, 59–60
utopian socialism, 134–138
  contributions of, 137–138
  institutional structure of, 136–137
  shortcomings of, 137
  theoretical underpinnings of, 135–136

V
value theory. *see* instrumental value theory; utility value theory
Veblen, Thorstein Bunde, 55, 69–72, 117–118
  critique of neoclassical theory by, 48–52, 117
  dichotomy of, 70–72
  Foster's views of, 52–55, 72
  The Place of Science in Modern Civilization, 48, 49, 53, 69

W
warranted knowledge, 26, 27–28, 168–169
The Wealth of Nations, 42, 116
Webb, Walter Prescott, 109
Wray, L. Randall, 199–200

Printed in the United States
82126LV00002B/175

9 780792 378303